Rewired

Also by Larry D. Rosen and
available from Palgrave Macmillan

Me, MySpace, and I: Parenting the Net Generation

Rewired

*Understanding the iGeneration
and the Way They Learn*

Larry D. Rosen, Ph.D.
with
L. Mark Carrier, Ph.D.
and
Nancy A. Cheever, M.A.

palgrave
macmillan

REWIRED
Copyright © Larry D. Rosen, 2010.
All rights reserved.

First published in 2010 by PALGRAVE MACMILLAN® in the United
States—a division of St. Martin's Press LLC, 175 Fifth Avenue, New York, NY
10010.

Where this book is distributed in the UK, Europe and the rest of the world,
this is by Palgrave Macmillan, a division of Macmillan Publishers Limited, registered in England, company number 785998, of Houndmills, Basingstoke,
Hampshire RG21 6XS.

Palgrave Macmillan is the global academic imprint of the above companies and
has companies and representatives throughout the world.

Palgrave® and Macmillan® are registered trademarks in the United States, the
United Kingdom, Europe and other countries.

ISBN: 978-0-230-61478-9

Library of Congress Cataloging-in-Publication Data

Rosen, Larry D.
   Rewired : understanding the igeneration and the way they learn / Larry D.
Rosen.
      p.   cm.
   Includes index.
   ISBN 978-0-230-61478-9 (pbk.)
   1. Computer-assisted instruction.   2. Computers and children.
3. Computer literacy.   4. Educational technology.   5. Learning strategies.
6. Cognitive styles in children.   I. Title.
LB1028.5.R575   2010
371.33'4—dc22

                                                                    2009036678

A catalogue record of the book is available from the British Library.

Design by Letra Libre, Inc.

First edition: April 2010
10 9 8 7 6 5 4 3 2 1
Printed in the United States of America.

Contents

To Vicki, who always amazes me by how she truly encourages me to be me. I love our life together, including our NYT crosswords, zillions of movies, concerts, vacations, sunsets from bed, and our mutual love of anything that Jon, Stephen, and Rachel have to say.

Chapter 1

Why Tweens and Teens Hate School

Despite the revolutions wrought by technology in medicine, engineering, communication, and many other fields, the classrooms, textbooks, and lectures of today are little different than those of our parents. Yet today's students use computers, mobile telephones, and other portable technical devices regularly for almost every form of communication except learning.

—National Science Foundation Task Force on Cyberlearning[1]

I absolutely hate school. They make me sit and listen as some old, stuffy teacher drones on and on about stuff from a book written like in the dark ages. We have to read pages of facts and then barf them up on tests that will make or break whether we get into a good college or not. Oh sure, they have pretty pictures on all the pages, but the book is so one-dimensional. Geez, pictures? Don't they know anything about video and what kids like to do? We get to go to the computer lab once a week for like an hour—if that—and even then most of what I want to do is blocked. I can't wait until I am out of this place and I can go to college where they let us bring computers to class and know how to treat wired kids like me.

—Vanessa, age twelve, New York City

I was visiting my daughter's high school and decided to peek in on her Spanish class. From what was written on the blackboard, the class was working on an assignment translating a passage from English to Spanish—at least that's what they were *supposed* to be doing. I counted nearly half the students clearly doing something else. They appeared distracted. When I looked more carefully I discovered that many had their cell phones in their laps and were rapidly moving their fingers. After class, my daughter and her friends told me they were bored with the lesson and were texting each other across the room. Two of her friends bragged that they could text blindfolded.

Fast forward to the same day, after dinner: I see my daughter, sitting on her bed with the television on, iPod earbuds firmly implanted, her laptop showing one window with a school report beside a browser window open to Facebook, several instant messaging alerts flashing at the bottom of the screen, and her phone vibrating, signaling a text message. Can she really study with all these distractions? How can she possibly get good grades while she is chatting the night away?

Welcome to the iGeneration. While the previous generation, referred to as the Net (as in Internet) Generation, was born in the 1980s and 1990s, the iGeneration children and teens are in elementary school, middle school, and high school.[2] They spend their days immersed in a "media diet,"[3] devouring entertainment, communication, and, well, any form of electronic media.[4] They are master multitaskers, social networkers, electronic communicators and the first to rush to any new technology. They were born surrounded by technology, and with every passing year they add more tools to their electronic repertoire. They live in social networks such as Facebook, MySpace, and Second Life gathering friends; they text more than they talk on the phone;[5] and they Twitter (or tweet) the night away, often sleeping with their cell phones vibrating by their sides.[6]

On the one hand it may seem like they are just using too much technology. In the research my associates and I have conducted with thousands of parents, children, tweens, and teens,[7] parents tell us that they are very worried that their children don't seem to want to go outside and play anymore.[8] They would rather chat online than visit with their friends at the mall. They are happiest when their cell phone is vibrating and their computer is beeping. It troubles their parents who grew up playing in the street, hanging out with friends, and having a life outside of the cyberspace cocoon their children have created in their rooms. On the other hand, their children achieve higher grades in school,[9] create tech businesses before they even graduate from high school, and apply to and enter college at unprecedented rates.[10]

So, what is the problem? *They hate school.* Why? Education has not caught up with this new generation of tech-savvy children and teens. It is not that they don't want to learn. They just learn differently. Gone are the days when students would sit quietly in class, reading a book or doing a math worksheet. Literally, their minds have changed—they have been "rewired." With all the technology that they consume, they *need more* from education. The educational content is not the problem. It is the delivery method and the setting. Today's youth thrive on multimedia, multitasking, social environments for every aspect of their lives *except* education. As aptly put by Professor Paul Gee, a member of the National Academy of Education, "Given that the digital age is enveloping our world, and its influence is not likely to decrease, educators need to meet the emerging challenges on two fronts. Educators must determine the new learning styles of students and develop educational methodology and teaching strategies to meet the learning needs."[11]

In the United States 56 million K–12 students are being taught by nearly 4 million teachers.[12] A whopping 25 percent of the U.S. population is currently under seventeen years old.[13] More than 8 in 10 schools have computers with Internet access, with an average of four students per computer.[14] Sounds great, doesn't it? The problem lies not in the number of computers, but rather in how they are being used. Schools have the tools to provide a good, motivating education for our children. The problem is that schools are using educational strategies that worked fine for their students' parents and teachers. They are forgetting that this is a whole new generation of learners, with a host of qualities that are drastically different from those of previous generations. They are simply not happy learning the way we are teaching them. They want—and need— something different to spark their imaginations. That is our challenge as parents and educators: to create a match between students' technological interests and skills, their sociological—often virtual—environments, and the educational system that propels their performance to higher levels and is, at the same time, engaging enough to rekindle a love of school and learning.

Parents are well aware that technology needs to play a larger role in their children's education. In my recent interviews, more than half of the 1,200 parents of children and preteens who I interviewed felt that it was *very important* that schools provide technology for classroom teaching, have both teachers and administrators who embrace technology, and invest *significant money* in classroom technology.[15] Parents of preteens felt the strongest about this critical need, with 6 in 10 telling us that they felt it was *very important* that their children's schools become more invested in technology that could be used both in the classroom and at home. Mitchell, the father of twelve-year-old Danny, told me, *"I just don't get what his school must be thinking. He comes home, turns on his laptop, pulls out his homework and starts doing paper-and-pencil worksheets. He keeps peeking at Facebook or whatever is on the screen and checking his text messages. He's a good student and I may be naïve, but why can't the school figure out how to combine his paper-and-pencil homework (which bores him literally to tears some nights) with his love of everything he does on the computer? I try to help him by finding websites that present interesting ways to understand his homework but it really isn't my job, is it? The school has lots of computers in his class-*

rooms but mostly they are used for playing educational games that my son (and I), quite frankly, find boring and tedious."

The purpose of education is to provide knowledge and critical-thinking skills. Book learning, classroom teaching, paper-and-pencil homework, research reports, and creative writing activities have always been fine ways to accomplish these tasks. However, as noted earlier, and as I will detail later, we are teaching a whole new generation of students. This book will help you understand how and why they have developed superior multitasking skills, a virtual lifestyle, a penchant for creating media content, and a brand new communication repertoire—none of which are being exploited by our current educational systems. These kids are not like those of previous generations, and they learn through technologies that didn't exist just a decade ago. As educators, we must find new tools to engage our students and help them learn in ways that work for them and for teachers. I am not advocating a wholesale revamping of our educational system. I am not suggesting that we change the curriculum we teach our children. What I am saying is that we need to capitalize on our children's amazing high-tech knowledge and skills when we present that curriculum. This book is designed to help parents and teachers understand that children rely on technology for many aspects of their lives—except education—and we need to find ways to match our teaching methods to their virtual lifestyles. The following example shows just one way that we might meld technology and education into an engaging, exciting learning vehicle for our young iGeneration students.

A Future Homework Assignment

Imagine the following scene. Your daughter is working intently on the computer, and when you look at the screen you see a strange-looking cartoonish character (called an avatar, a sort of three-dimensional "alter ego" or persona for the computer user) gliding down a walkway past a series of attractive, multicolored buildings. Her avatar turns and reads a bright glowing green sign that says "Welcome to the Fractions Building." She pops open the Multiplying Fractions door—since that is her homework assignment for the night—and sees avatars of two other students writing on their own whiteboards. She finds a blank board and immediately a voice welcomes her by name and starts by asking her what ½ times ¼ equals. If she gets the question right, she moves on to others, increasing in difficulty. If she misses a question the virtual teacher is equipped to instantaneously determine what the likely problem might be and provide examples or go back and offer additional questions to build the necessary skills. Performance is continually monitored and evaluated in milliseconds. If the student feels the need for "personal" help, all she needs to do is "ask" the teacher by typing a question, or, if this virtual campus is wired for sound, simply voicing the question aloud. If she feels like taking a break, her avatar walks to the virtual break room to chat with other students for a few minutes. When she returns to the Multiplying Fractions room, the homework/lesson starts right back up where it left off. As she works, your daughter garners rewards in the form of "classroom cash" for completing assignments and learning how to multiply fractions. Later, she exchanges the "cash" for objects in a virtual store or for special access to a part of the virtual world that enables her to add accessories to her avatar. If you allow it, she uses the "classroom cash" at home to buy privileges such as extra time playing video games or a special dessert.

This is, of course, just an example of how educators might make homework more attractive—and even fun—by taking the assignments from a flat, two-dimensional piece of paper into a simulated three-dimensional world. The benefits of such a teaching tool are endless. The teacher would receive instant, continuous feedback on how the student performed on the assignment, including which portions were more difficult and required additional work, and which teaching strategies worked best for that student. This would be difficult, if not impossible, using a math textbook. Parents would also get feedback, obviously streamlined to their busy lives, telling them how their daughter is doing on multiplying fractions. In essence, what you have is a virtual classroom that is continually learning how best to teach each student the same material. The opportunities are boundless. The success of the virtual classroom would simply depend on tapping into the media and technology that this generation uses daily in their personal lives. It can be easily customizable, not only to the material, but to the specific student.

According to one mother of an eight-year-old, *"My son started using a program this year called Study Island. His motivation for studying was that for every correct answer he earned points to play a video game—so the more correct answers, the more points, the longer he got to play—and he was playing against fellow classmates—so everyone in the class could compete against each other—my normally homework-resistant child could not wait to come home to 'play.'"*

The Rapid Pace of Technology

I am a Baby Boomer, and like most of my generation and our parents' generation, I have always regarded technology with wonder and awe. My parents and grandparents used to talk about the arrival of radio and then television, and I remember that for most of my childhood, Sunday nights were devoted to gathering around the television for *The Ed Sullivan Show.*

Technological progress did indeed move slowly. But then in the last two decades of the twentieth century, the pace of technology started to accelerate, and new gadgets started showing up with increasing regularity. Take a look at Figure 1.1 on page 9. At the left of the page are some technologies—including both physical products and Internet websites—that have become routine parts of our lives. Each bar reflects how long it took that technology to reach the benchmark, or what marketing researchers call the "penetration rate," of being purchased or used by 50 million consumers. While radio, telephone, and television took many years to penetrate society, notice how rapidly some of the new devices are making their way into our lives. MySpace and Facebook were complete unknowns in 2003, and as of this writing more than 100 million people visit each site monthly, the largest portion of whom are preteens and teens, with our research showing that 15 percent are even under the "required" age of 14.[16]

Now look at some of the newer technologies and websites and you will see that it is not unusual for them to "penetrate" society *within a single year.* YouTube, for example, went from inception to 50 million consumers within a single year. More than half of adult American Internet users have now visited YouTube, and one in six do so daily. In April 2008, 73 million children and adults watched YouTube videos more than 4 billion times. *Four million of those viewers were under eleven years old.* Teens watched an average of 74 YouTube videos that month alone.[17] Look around and count all of the technologies and websites that did not exist five years ago—iPhone, Wii, Second Life, Twitter—and the list goes on and on. It is mind-boggling to say the least, and look at who are the first to rush out and buy the gadgets or use the websites: the iGeneration.

These new technologies have not just invaded our stores and our computers, but they have marched right into our language. In 2008, Merriam-Webster added the nouns "malware," "webinar," and "fanboy," which joined the verbs "Google," "text," "blog," and thousands of other

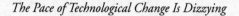

Figure 1.1   The "Psychology of Technology"

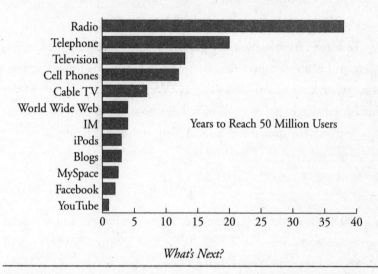

The Pace of Technological Change Is Dizzying

Years to Reach 50 Million Users

What's Next?

Number of years between introduction and purchase or use by 50 million consumers. (This is the number consumer psychologists say indicates that a product has penetrated society.)[18]

newly minted, technology-related words, most of which were heralded and developed by the younger generation. When a teenager gets into his car to drive somewhere, he has either MapQuested or Google-mapped the directions or GPS'd them. Teens don't email much anymore; instead, they IM, text, Facebook, and Twitter, and their communication is full of shortcuts, acronyms, and other abbreviations to help them squeeze the most out of their cyberspace language with the fewest keystrokes. Many of us know that LOL is short for "laughing out loud," but this term just scratches the surface of teen communication. Here's a brief text message conversation I had with my daughter recently. Can you figure it out?

Hw r u 2day?
gd & u?
nd to tlk 2 u. txt me whn i cn cl.

To some this may look like gibberish, but to teens, it is *their* language and it is one aspect that is rapidly defining this unique generation. Some have questioned whether it represents the demise of the English language, but we will talk about how to integrate their communication style into an educational plan later in this book.[19]

Crashing Waves

In 1980 Alvin Toffler, a well-respected American futurist and author of *Future Shock,* published *The Third Wave,* which chronicled his view of how technology has changed society.[20] He depicted change as coming in waves, with each succeeding wave marking the introduction of a technological change that transforms the world. Toffler's first wave was the agricultural society, in which tools such as the plow changed our ancestors from hunters and gatherers to farmers. This first wave spanned some three thousand years. The second wave began in the late 1600s and encompassed the transition from an agricultural society to an industrial society, which began with the invention of the steam engine. According to Toffler, this industrial wave lasted three hundred years. The third wave, dubbed by Toffler variously as the computer era, global village, or computer revolution, had its roots in the late 1950s and was active when *The Third Wave* was written. This third wave was expected to last roughly thirty years and lead to the next stage of technological change.

Note that each wave was shorter than the previous wave by a factor of ten, lasting from 3,000 years to 300 years to 30 years. Extrapolating, this means that the fourth wave should be 3 years, and the fifth wave one-tenth of that, or about four months, and so on. Presumably, Toffler did not intend to imply that we were going to be inundated by rapid, monthly waves of new technology, but Figure 1.1 certainly depicts rapidly accelerating waves of change. Note, by the way, that Toffler wrote his book in 1980, when personal computers were just entering the market, and more than a decade before the World Wide Web was developed and became a standard for the business world and our personal lives. When *The Third Wave* was published, email, cell phones, text messaging, and biotechnology either did not exist or had little impact on society.

Who will drive the ups and downs of these waves? Categorically, that will be the iGeneration and their younger brothers and sisters in succeeding generations. According to consumer researchers, teens account for a substantial portion of all family purchase decisions, of which many, if not all, are driven by either advertising or Internet research.[21] In a recent study, we asked parents of children between 6 months and 12 years old how much they felt that media influenced their children's purchase decisions.[22] The results were fairly astounding. Twenty-three percent of the 6-month to 4-year-old children were strongly influenced by television. By the time they reached 5 to 8 years old, that count rose to 50 percent and was the same for the 9- to 12-year-olds. In addition, more than one-fourth of the 9- to 12-year-olds were also strongly influenced by what they saw on the Internet. Coupling how much influence adolescents have on their parents' decision making, we are looking at a new generation that promises to be even more influential given the strong pull that both television and the Internet have on their desire to buy products and services. Before we take a look at the iGeneration—the elementary and secondary school students of the year 2010—let's first set the stage by capturing the world they inherited from their older brothers and sisters who were the first to be raised in an Internet environment.

Who Are the Net Generation?

Born in the 1980s, these older teens and young adults differed dramatically from their parents' generation primarily in their access to technology. Net-Geners were raised with electronic devices from infancy. Parents kept tabs on them with baby monitors near their cribs. As the children got older, some parents watched their daily activities at home or preschool through video camera feeds. Their first toys were talking, flashing, and technological. No more simple stuffed bears for these children. Their games buzzed and beeped and kept digital score. They watched DVDs of Disney movies from birth, and television often substituted as their babysitter when Mom and Dad were busy. Their younger siblings, born after the World Wide Web became popular in the 1990s, were pressing keys and clicking the mouse as soon as they could sit up in a chair, and sent their first emails before they went off to preschool. These youngsters form the iGeneration, our first generation of truly cyber-savvy children.

As Net-Geners grew up they continued to add technology to their repertoires. Television, music, the Internet, cell phones, text messaging, instant messaging, videos, social networks, and blogs all became an integral part of their lives. Our studies of preteens, teens, and young adults find that they consistently consume media *upwards of 20 hours per day!*[23] This is no simple task, given that they spend six to seven hours a day at school, eat meals, and sleep. How do they do it? Multitasking. Although everyone multitasks, the Net Generation and the iGeneration perfected it to a science, a way of life. Whether they are just hanging out or studying for an important exam, they are always multitasking. Just peek into the bedroom of any preteen or teen and you will see at least six forms of media engaging their attention at the same time. Our research shows that they are likely to have the TV on; have music coming from an iPod,

CD player, or computer; have the Internet running with multiple windows showing one or two social networks; be IMing at least three or more friends; and either be talking on the phone or, more likely, having a rapid string of back-and-forth text messages. Add to that a dash of YouTube, Twitter, and a plate of food and you have the typical teenager consuming a hefty daily diet of media.

The oldest Net-Geners are now in their mid to late twenties and are entering the workforce. Needless to say, their multitasking, media-heavy lives often do not match with the typical work environment. With bosses who may be technologically adept but not nearly as immersed in media as their new employees, there is an inherent friction underlying many workplaces. This is not to say that they are not good workers. All indications are that they may be the smartest, most well rounded generation. According to a study by the Downtown Women's Club, Net-Geners spend substantial time each day gathering news and information from online newspapers, TV newscasts, CNN.com (as well as CNN on television), and blogs.[24] They are politically astute and were a major force in the 2008 presidential election.

Meet the iGeneration

Those children born in the 1990s and the new millennium are turning out to be even more enmeshed with technology than their older brothers and sisters. Our most recent research with more than 1,500 parents of these children shows they are consuming media, multitasking, and using all the tools that their older siblings have popularized. Social networks for these children are popping up daily and are becoming mainstream overnight.[25] Many children have their media right at hand in the bedroom. Strikingly, 38 percent of parents of 6-month-olds to 4-year-olds admitted that their child has a television in the bedroom; two-thirds to three-fourths of the 5- to 12-year-olds do too. When is it too young to have a cell phone? Well, while only 2 percent of the youngest children have one, but half of the 9- to 12-year-olds have their very own cell phone and many have a texting plan. Two-thirds of these children have an iPod or MP3 player, and more than half of the 5- to 12-year-olds have a video game console in their bedroom in addition to one or more handheld games. These kids are clearly "technologized" to the max and promise to be exposed to even more media than the Net-Geners. If teachers and parents today feel at a loss to understand their technologically immersed students and children, how will they be able to begin to comprehend the iGeneration who are already taking technology into new directions?

The iGeners have redefined communication. They own cell phones, but use them more for sending text messages than talking. They blog, vlog (using videos to transmit information), Twitter, Facebook, My-Space, video chat, share photos, and latch on to and embrace any new communication tool and give it their own personal spin. And they are forcing the older generations to follow suit. One father of an iGener I interviewed told me, *"If I want to talk to my high school senior daughter I have to text or Twitter her. She doesn't answer her phone, nor does she even listen to her voice mail. The only way to get her attention is to text her. I had to learn how to push those buttons to make words and it was (and is) very frustrating. But it is her world and I have to go there if I want to get to her."*

I have seen the same thing in my family. I have four children, ranging in age from nineteen to thirty-three—two Net-Geners and two Gen-Xers.[26] They have their own preferred communication modalities. When my university was locked down not long ago because someone spotted a person carrying a gun on campus, I was forced to lock my office door and remain there. It was all over the news and I didn't want my children to worry, so I texted my 19-year-old daughter, IMed my 22-year-old son, and phoned my 31- and 34-year-olds. It is a challenge, but I am learning that we have to adapt to their world, and that world is constantly changing and a continual challenge for us old folks.

This new iGeneration is also highly social—at least with others their age. They live immersed in at least one social network, if not two or more. MySpace and Facebook are a must to build and maintain friendships. They have redefined the concept of "friend." How is it possible to have 300 MySpace friends, an additional 250 Facebook friends, an online gaming group that may include 50 or more people spread worldwide, an IM buddy list that spans well beyond the screen size, and dozens of texting friends? They are social animals and it is not unusual to hear teenagers say in all seriousness that they truly, absolutely have 300 best friends. They may not be best friends in the sense that I understood the term at that age, but they confide in them, trust their advice, and share their lives with each and every one of them. Their cyberworld is a place for them to explore their identity, figure out who and what they want to be when they grow up, and connect, connect, connect. Net- and iGeners have also adapted technology to "represent" themselves in myriad ways. They blog to let the world know what they feel about politics, school, and their life in general. They "tweet" everyone about what they are feeling at the moment and then ten minutes later tweet again to update those feelings. Despite the fact that a large portion of their communication is not face to face, they are engaging in meaningful connections with their friends. To augment these relationships, they post photos of what they do on a daily basis, customize profiles to declare their interests, dating status, sexual orientation, music and movie tastes, and more. They present themselves to the world with an ever-changing, always wired cyber identity. The older generations who are their teachers, parents, and grandparents are often appalled at how "out there" they appear, but this is their world and we have to learn to understand it or we won't be able to connect with them. As you will see in later chapters, it is the iGeneration student's love of all things technological that needs to be incorporated in the way we teach them in and out of the classroom. If we continue to try to reach them on our terms, using traditional teaching tools, we will fail them. As the quotations that opened this chapter so aptly point out, education is one of the last institutions to adapt to their different world. The longer educators wait to appreciate and integrate iGeners' cyberworlds, the more students will be bored with traditional classroom learning, and the more we will miss out on opportunities to reach them within environments where they have already shown us that they are happy to reside and learn. It is not simply a matter, however, of keeping our students less bored. Educators need to find ways to take easily available technologies and use them to reinvigorate learning.

Why Do These Kids Hate School?

Although many schools have tried to integrate technology into the curriculum, I feel that they have gone about it the wrong way. These kids are so technologically advanced that simple adaptations to technology and media in the classroom and in school is *borrrrrring*. Add to that the fact that any curriculum changes take time, often years, to be approved and implemented, and then look at how fast the kids jump at newer and newer technology. By the time the teachers put PowerPoint presentations into their lectures to make the material more visual, the kids had moved on. One twelve-year-old told me, *"My teacher thinks she is so cool and with it because she makes these PowerPoints for each lecture with text and graphics that fly in, twist and turn, and display the same information that is in the book and that she lectures about. Maybe when I was 8 that might have been fun and interesting, but it is so yesterday."*

So what can we, as teachers and parents, do to make sure that our children are engaged and even stimulated in their daily school experiences? This is the theme of this book. Over the next eight chapters I will introduce and discuss the special characteristics of the iGeneration and provide strategies for educators and parents to take advantage of the new and evolving cyberworlds that are replete with media, the Internet, social networking, and more. Chapters will highlight how iGeners are both similar to and different from previous generations and why teachers and parents, who are members of Generation X or the Baby Boomer generation, need to understand and embrace them and their techno view of the world. I will explore how to integrate into their educational experience their love of social networking, omnipresent use of communication tools, electronic creativity, enhanced writing production, and media literacy. In addition, chapters will explore topics of concern to parents and teachers including privacy, video games, and confusion between the teen's real life (RL) and screen life (SL). The concluding chapter will peer into a crystal ball and try to help the educational system learn to adapt to the ever-changing landscape that forms school students' cyberworld.

It is important to note that I am not going to tell teachers how they must teach and which lessons to use in the classroom, nor am I going to tell parents how to make their children do homework. I will, however, highlight educational *approaches* that tap into this younger generation's remarkable technological strengths and passions so that no matter what technology children adopt, educators and parents will be able to use approaches to learning that make use of those technologies and help children shed their current aversion to schooling.

Chapter 2

Welcome to the iGeneration

Chances are you know a young person aged 11–31. You may be a parent, aunt, teacher, or manager. You've seen these young people multitasking five activities at once. You see the way they interact with various media. They use their mobile phones differently. To them e-mail is old-school. They use the phone to text incessantly, surf the Web, find directions, take pictures and make videos, and collaborate. The bottom line is this: if you understand the Net Generation, you will understand the future. You will also understand how our institutions and society need to change today.

—Don Tapscott, *Grown Up Digital*[1]

My younger brother, Aiden, is only 7 and already he is doing techie stuff that I haven't even tried. And he picks it up so fast. He was on the web when he was 3 and already has a cell phone and knows how to text me. I can't imagine what he will be doing when he is my age.

—Adrian, age thirteen

Now that we have seen how young people consume an enormous variety of media, and do it more hours a day than any generation before them, it is important to understand how they use it so educators can begin thinking about alternative ways to stimulate their students. As I explained in Chapter 1, the point of this book is not to prescribe specific educational models. The data we have collected in our studies of thousands of school students and their parents, however, should make educators and school systems aware of how much media is already used by students and should suggest myriad options for new, technologically based educational models. The students already use these tools at home, so why not take advantage of something they choose to do for fun to make learning part of that experience?

In my previous book *Me, MySpace, and I*, I chronicled the similarities and differences between three generations—grandparents, parents, and children.[2] Among the adults, Baby Boomers (born between 1946 and 1964) were vastly different from Generation Xers (1965–1979) in both personal values and work ethic. But the Net Generation, the oldest of whom are now turning thirty, comprises the largest and most unique of the three. Born in the 1980s and early 1990s, Net-Geners—also known as Millennials, Generation Y, the MySpace Generation, and Generation M (for media)—arrived amid the height of the technological revolution. Most Net-Geners have never experienced a world without the Internet, cell phones, video games, and more media (including countless cable TV channels) than they can possibly consume. Yet they do gobble it up, spending more hours a day using media than they do either sleeping or attending school.

Right behind the Net Generation is the "iGeneration," named after all the available devices and websites with an "i"—iPod, iTunes, Wii, iChat, iHome, iPhone, iEverything. Little research has been done on these preschool, elementary, and secondary school–age children born in the 1990s and the new millennium, but our interviews with parents of more than two thousand of them show that they are embracing technology and media much earlier than their older brothers and sisters.[3] In fact, as Adrian pointed out in the quote above, these children are getting their first taste of personal technology very early, often before they can even sit up without assistance. A parent I interviewed told me, *"I have taught my son, Carlton, who just turned 5, how to use the Internet but only when I am sitting with him. We visit Disney.com, Club Penguin, and a few other toymaker websites. I even showed him how to put a toy that he likes on an Amazon wish list. The other day I was on Amazon and took a look at his wish list. It was packed with things that I had never seen during our time online. When I asked him about this he told me that he did not need me anymore and he could do it on his own and had been online many times when I was at work and he was home from kindergarten. Heck, he can barely write his ABC's and his name, but he can click the mouse and navigate multiple websites! Unbelievable!"*

In the previous chapter I discussed Alvin Toffler's Wave Theory, which says that crashing waves of technology are coming more and more rapidly. This theory could explain why the Baby Boomer generation lasted nineteen years, Gen X fifteen years, and the Net Generation only ten. As the pace of technology accelerates, new generations arise based on their use of new technologies. Teachers in today's schools range from the oldest Baby Boomers, now nearing retirement age, to the older members of the Net Generation, who are just starting their careers. Regardless of their technological sophistication—and there is no denying that many teachers, old and young, are quite tech-savvy—they approach, master, and use technology differently than their iGen students. Recently, two former students emailed me that they were now teaching and wrote about how their experiences mirrored the ideas that we discussed in our class on the impact of media and technology on children and adolescents. Their emails were fascinating and pointed out the dilemmas teachers face with today's primary and secondary school students.

Joan, a forty-three-year-old fourth-grade teacher, wrote that she was teaching in a "smart" classroom with access to the Internet through a laptop connected to a whiteboard and four desktop computers in a corner of the room. She felt proud, and rather high-tech, that over the summer before her first year she was able to turn some of her lessons into Power-Point presentations, and she even included video clips she downloaded from YouTube. She brought in some math learning software and installed it on the desktops and built her in-class lessons and remedial work with these technologies. She went on to say that she was totally surprised when her students were bored during her flashy PowerPoints and stayed away from the remedial software. She was shocked when she caught three students accessing MySpace and sending email from the desktop computers. She confronted them and they all said that they were bored with technologies that they learned to use ages ago and PowerPoint was something their parents used for work. They told her that they did like some of the YouTube videos but found most of them too boring.

Shawn, a twenty-six-year-old middle school English teacher, painted a picture of how out of touch he was with technology. Shawn graduated with a dual major in English and computer information systems, so he went into his classes with some great ideas for making the reading assignments more fun for his eleven- to thirteen-year-old students. In his eighth-grade honors literature class, the first reading was Ayn Rand's *The Fountainhead,* and each day's assignment was to read a chapter to be discussed in class the following day. From the outset he was concerned and confused. This was, after all, an honors class and all of the students were very bright, yet only a few seemed to be willing to talk in class and their comments were superficial at best. When he tried to prompt the students to address some of the themes in the book their answers were similar and lacked any depth. The students were supposed to bring their books to school but he noticed that quite a few of them either did not have the book or it appeared to be unread. In Shawn's words, *"They clearly had not read the chapter, but they did seem to know what it was about. Finally I noticed that one student in the back row had Cliff Notes open inside his book. When I asked the class about this, much to my sur-*

prise, I found out that only a handful had read the chapter while the others had either read the Cliff Notes or found a summary online. I had never done this as an English major and I just figured these kids, who all were bound for top-notch universities, would do the reading and be ready to discuss it as I had assigned."

Shawn started all over again and told the students that they had to bring in their books with relevant passages from Chapter 1 highlighted, and they would be spending the entire period discussing it. *"Only five of the 30 students had anything to say but nearly all of them had highlighted parts of the chapter. We spent the entire hour talking about why most of them wouldn't talk. They all had their reasons, but I think that one of the kids summed up what was going on. She said, 'Talking in class is difficult cuz I am shy and not really all that comfortable saying things that might sound stupid.' At lunch I talked to another new teacher and he told me that as a prelude to class discussions in his trigonometry class he set up an online discussion group on Facebook and told the students that they had to at least make one comment. He lurked in the background and was amazed at how much discussion happened. Students went back and forth about the topic and many of the comments were time-stamped after midnight. What blew him away were the intense discussions continued in class and, for the most part, even the shyest students seemed to open up more once they had started their comments online."*

Now, I am not suggesting that we simply halt all face-to-face in-class discussions. However, we do know from our research with children and teens that they feel more comfortable speaking "behind the screen," and that comfort then translates into real life. In one study of more than 1,200 MySpace users, 78 percent felt that they were able to be more honest online and that their online honesty translated into offline comfort. Those who spent more time communicating online—behind that screen of anonymity—had higher self-esteem than those who were online less.[4]

While face-to-face communication must still be part of any classroom experience, as the trigonometry teacher discovered, allowing students to communicate online engaged them and somehow liberated them to be more comfortable communicating in class.

Joan and Shawn both discovered that even though they thought they knew a lot about technology, they were far behind the kids in their classes. Certainly they had mastered some educational technologies in college, but the "digital natives" in their classrooms were bored by those approaches.[5] Both their emails to me reflected back to our class discussions about how different their students would be when they started teaching, but they just hadn't quite been able to anticipate the magnitude of those differences. *This is the crux of our educational dilemma.* Technology is advancing at a rapid pace and today's students are the ones who are on the cutting edge. They are consumed with (or immersed in) technology outside the classroom and want the same in school. Unfortunately, even the youngest teachers are trained to teach using a set of tools, some of which include computers, but many of which are not technology based. Many classes require only reading books and doing paper-and-pencil assignments, which are not technological at all and which, quite honestly, pale in comparison to the fast-paced multimedia world of today's youth.

The question is how are these highly motivated teachers going to succeed if they can't get even the brightest kids to read or participate in class? The key is in understanding how their students are very different in the ways they value and approach media and technology. It is not only that they are using more up-to-date technologies, but also that they approach technology differently than their teachers and even their older college-age brothers and sisters. If educators can better understand how their students process multimedia technology then they can more creatively imagine how to teach them and how to select or develop curricula that will engage these tech-savvy learners.

The remainder of this chapter presents an overview of thirteen distinct traits of iGen students that directly or indirectly involve their passion for technology. It is important to note that not every student possesses every one of these qualities. Each student is unique. However, based on our research with more than five thousand preteens, teens, and their parents, we have a good sense that the typical student can be described if we first understand what is distinctive about their generation. I will expand on these thirteen traits and present potential educational ramifications in later chapters, where we'll include more detail on iGeners' ubiquitous electronic communication, wireless mobile devices, and, of course, social networks.

When I speak to educators and parents, among other groups, I often present a blank chart with generational values and preferences listed on the left side and the four generations—Baby Boomers, Gen-Xers, Net-Geners, and iGeners—listed on the top. Small groups of audience members are then given the generational qualities scrambled and asked to place them under the proper generation in each row. For example, under the heading "Preferred Communication Style" the choices are: (1) face-to-face or telephone; (2) email or cell phone; (3) text message, IM, Facebook; or (4) text message, Twitter, Skype, MySpace, Facebook, iPhone. Although that last one should be pretty obvious, I have yet to have a group, be it educators, psychologists, or parents, who get half of the items on the chart correct. Following a speech I gave recently to a combination of teachers and parents, one fifth-grade teacher wrote on her evaluation, *"The chart exercise was incredibly eye opening. My group, which included one Baby Boomer (me), two Gen Xers, and one Net Gener, critically discussed and agreed on each one and were sure that we got them all right. Turns out we got only 7 out of 15. After your talk we sat with the chart and realized how little we knew about the other's generation. I took our chart with me and made our teaching staff do the exercise."*

The rest of this chapter presents the thirteen distinct traits of iGeneration students: their (1) introduction to technology, literally at birth; (2) constant media diet; (3) adeptness at multitasking; (4) fervor for communication technologies; (5) love of virtual social worlds and anything Internet-related; (6) ability to use technology to create a vast array of "content"; (7) unique learning style; (8) need for constant motivation; (9) closeness to family; (10) confidence; (11) openness to change; (12) need for collective reflection; and (13) desire for immediacy.

Raised by Technology

To put it simply, today's children have grown up in an environment in which technology is everywhere and much of it is invisible. Most children and adolescents have grown up with the largest storehouse of information in history—the Internet. From an early age they have learned to play online games, send email to Grandma and Grandpa, and watch videos. As they got older, they learned to Google anything they wanted to know, consult MapQuest for directions, use Wikipedia for school reports, and go to dictionary.com for definitions. Many have never used a card catalog, a "real" encyclopedia, or Webster's dictionary. Some have never set foot in a library other than as a place to study after school. To children and teenagers, the Internet has always been just a click away and, as you will see from the data we have collected over the years, they use it for a variety of purposes that are beyond the scope of anything imagined just a decade ago.

Older Net-Geners played video games on Nintendo 64 and the younger iGeners often have three or four game systems. Each year, new, more exciting gaming systems are unveiled with an instant appeal to the iGeneration. In 2006, just in time for Christmas, Nintendo released the Wii (pronounced "we"), which created a buying frenzy. Steven, a seventeen-year-old high school senior, desperately wanted a Wii for Christmas and slept in front of his local Target store for two days in order to be first in line. His father, Bob, talked to me about that experience. *"Steven really wanted the Wii so badly that he had to make sure he got one. Target wouldn't say how many units they were getting, so he had to be first to guarantee that he would get one. For two nights, he slept in front of the store. During the day, I took off work and took over so that he could go to his classes. What a spectacle! There were literally hundreds of kids with sleeping bags, lawn chairs, coolers, and fast food wrappers. It was pretty orderly but I was amazed at how many parents took over during the day. We all talked about how crazy it was but we all admitted that we didn't want to disappoint our kids."*

I have interviewed thousands of children in both formal research studies and informal settings. I will never forget an interview with Ashley, the ten-year-old daughter of a friend of mine. I asked her why she liked technology so much. Ashley looked at me blankly and said, *"What do you mean why do I like technology? Isn't everything technology? I guess I don't even think about it. It's sorta like the sky, ya know. I don't think about the sky. I just know that when I look up it's there. Same with technology. It's just everywhere."* To Ashley, technology is not a tool to use, as it is for many adults. It is the center of her life and as we shall see next, she most certainly is consumed with it and by it.

Gorging on a Constant Media Diet

Preteens and teens are "wired." ("Wired," a Generation X term in use since at least the early 1990s—*Wired* magazine began in 1993—means essentially what "i" means now: connected, especially to the Internet.) Most preteens and teens are literally tied to technology from the moment they awaken to the moment they go to sleep. Many are hooked in and logged on throughout the night when they sleep, with their cell phones set on vibrate, and they wake and respond to nighttime text messages.[6] According to a recent study by the national Consumer Electronics Association, 8 out of 10 teens "can't imagine a day without technology."[7]

My colleagues and I have studied the use of media and technology by children, preteens, teens, young adults, Gen-Xers, and Baby Boomers through thousands of online interviews. Table 2.1 on page 29 shows the number of hours elementary and secondary school students spend using a variety of media; the data are combined from several of our studies.[8] In each of our studies we ask about the use of a variety of technologies. The twelve- to seventeen-year-olds supplied their own estimates, while parents of the younger children provided the information. The table includes the core technologies examined in all of our research studies (some of which explore the use of other technologies and media as they become part of the youth culture).

The data in this table, which are very consistent across other major research studies, are striking as you see technology and media consumption rise from roughly 5½ hours a day for the youngest children to more than 21 hours a day for the older teens.[9] Clearly, teenagers are not spending more than 18 hours a day using each technology one at a time. They have mastered the art of *multitasking,* allowing them to watch television, text message friends, listen to music, surf the web, chat on MySpace and Facebook, watch YouTube videos, and more, all at the same time. For now, however, it is important to understand that the data in this table reflect the staggering amount of media that our children are consuming on a daily basis.

Before looking at specific media activities of the younger generation, it is instructive to look at what "older" generations are doing technologically. According to our research studies, Baby Boomers spend about 9½ hours daily with media, Generation Xers are immersed in media 15 hours per day, and Net-Geners (18 or 19 to 29 years old) nearly 20 hours per day. So, all generations are using media and technology, with the iGeneration leading the way.

Returning to our four groups of students, several things stand out in Table 2.1. For one, there is a major jump in online activity between the preteen and teen years. While 9- to 12-year-olds are online an hour a day, their older siblings spend more than double that amount visiting websites. What is on their computer screens while they are surfing through cyberspace? Most of high schoolers' online time is spent for entertainment and socializing with friends, instant messaging, chatting, and one to two hours a day communicating on social networks such as MySpace and Facebook.[10]

Table 2.1   Time Children and Teens Spend Using
Technology and Media Each Day (Hours:Minutes)

	6 Months– 3 Years	4–8 Years	9-12 Years	13-15 Years	16–18 Years
Internet	0:04	0:27	0:59	1:58	2:24
Computer (not online)	0:02	0:23	0:57	1:44	1:59
Email	0:01	0:06	0:26	1:08	1:19
IM/Chat	0:01	0:05	0:28	1:24	2:16
Telephone	0:08	0:17	0:43	1:07	1:50
Texting	0:01	0:07	0:46	2:19	3:32
Video Games	0:18	1:32	2:07	1:20	1:17
Music	0:30	0:42	1:24	2:49	3:33
Television	1:30	1:56	1:56	1:58	2:10
TOTAL	**2:35**	**5:35**	**9:46**	**15:47**	**20:20**

Another interesting trend is the increasing use of all communication tools, including email, instant messages, chats, telephone calls, and text messages. All told, 4- to 8-year-olds communicate "electronically" a half hour a day, which increases to nearly two and a half hours for 9- to 12-year-olds, more than six hours for 13- to 15-year-olds, and a whopping eight and a half hours a day for 16- to 18-year-olds. As I will show in more detail below, this is an extremely important issue in understanding how best to educate our youth. Communication is a key element in their daily lives and must be factored in to any successful educational program.

Several other trends are obvious and noteworthy. Music becomes increasingly important as children move into adolescence, as does text messaging. Interestingly, watching television appears to be more popular among the younger teens than any other group, as is video game playing.

Another issue concerning the proliferation of media in our children's lives concerns where they actually use their media. Universally, psychologists and educators caution against allowing young children to ensconce themselves in bedroom "TechnoCocoons" for a variety of reasons including parental monitoring and safety.[11] However, my most recent studies of more than 1,300 parents of children and teens between the ages of six months and eighteen years indicates that many younger children are indeed owning and using technology behind closed bedroom doors.[12] Table 2.2 shows the percentages of children's private technology ownership according to their parents.[13] Educationally speaking, since many school-age children, particularly those in high school, spend their after-school studying time in their bedrooms this is an issue that may be important in linking school-based learning with after-school learning. Antonio, a typical seventh-grader, told us, *"I come home from school, boot up my laptop, grab a snack, and get online. I stay there studying and talk-*

ing to friends until mom calls me for dinner and then head back there right after dinner. Unless my mom or dad needs me I stay in my room until I go to sleep. Usually I have the TV on, but if I am trying to study for a test or something I mute it."

Several statistics leap out of this table. First, more than one-third of children under the age of five have a television in their bedrooms, as do two-thirds of four- to eight-year-old children, preteens, and teenagers. Second, more than half the school-age children—up to the early teens—have a video game console and a handheld video game player. Half the preteen students have their own cell phone and iPod; nearly all of the

Table 2.2   Technology Owned by Children and Teenagers

	Child's Age				
	6 Months– *3 Years*	*4–8* *Years*	*9-12* *Years*	*13-15* *Years*	*16–18* *Years*
Television in the bedroom	35%	62%	67%	68%	73%
Computer in the bedroom	0%	10%	24%	34%	43%
Have their own cell phone	0%	10%	51%	81%	92%
Have their own iPod or MP3 player	7%	26%	66%	85%	87%
Have a video game console (e.g., Wii, PlayStation) in the bedroom	6%	54%	74%	70%	56%
Have their own handheld video game players (e.g., Nintendo)	10%	53%	68%	54%	31%

teenagers own these devices. Third, although only one in four nine-to twelve-year-olds has a computer in their bedroom, nearly half of all high school students do. Combining the bedroom technologies with the extensive media use by these students creates a variety of vehicles that educators might choose to use for delivering content, having virtual classroom discussions, and completing homework assignments. Although the point of this book is not to prescribe specific educational models, the data that we have collected nonetheless should make educators and school systems aware of how much media is already used by students both at home and in their bedrooms, suggesting myriad options for new, technologically based educational models. The students already use all these tools at home, so why not take advantage of something they choose to do for fun to make learning part of that experience?

Multitasking the Night Away

Human beings are multitaskers. Gen-Xers and Net-Geners feel that they are good multitaskers. iGeners reign supreme in their belief that they can juggle more tasks than once thought humanly possible. They believe that they literally cannot perform only a single task at a time without being bored to death. Mariela, a thirteen-year-old middle-school student, told us that her math teacher is really strict and gets angry when students talk or do anything other than pay attention to his lectures or complete the required worksheets in class. *"I don't want to get sent to detention but it is really hard for me to just sit still and work on my math problems. I find myself fidgeting around and my friend Helen even pointed out that while I was working on the math with one hand my other one was twitching like I was sending a text message. Teachers just don't understand that we don't do very well when we have to just do a worksheet or look at a problem on the board or read the chapter. When I'm at home I never do any-thing that way. Even when I study for a test I have the TV on and text my friends and watch to see who is on Facebook. I think it helps me study when I get to do all those things. Otherwise I just get into my head about who might be texting me or what's going on with my friends."* In her lifestyle, Mariela, like most teens, simply can't unitask. It is too slow and too quiet and too restricting.

In two of our studies we asked people from the age of eleven to sixty to imagine that they had free time and tell us which of a list of things they would be doing. The list included all of the forms of media in Table 2.1 plus other nontechnological activities such as eating, talking to some-one, or reading a book or magazine for pleasure. The generational dif-ferences were astounding. The Net Generation and iGeneration preteens, teens, and young adults imagined doing more than six things simultaneously during their free time compared to Gen-Xers at around five and Baby Boomers doing four things at the same time. More telling was the activities they imagined doing. Looking at the top five activities, all three generations would be eating, listening to music, and being on-line, although in a different order of preference for each. Net- and iGen-ers, however, would be texting, while Gen-Xers would be sending email and watching TV, and Baby Boomers would be talking on the telephone and watching TV. Net- and iGeners multitask more and they multitask with different media and technologies, and this is important to recog-nize in understanding the vast difference between the choices our chil-dren make when they have free time.[14]

In order to see if students would decrease their multitasking when faced with a task that required them to really think something through, we also asked them what they imagined doing while studying for a final exam and while writing an important report that was due the next day. iGen students did reduce their multitasking, *but* they still imagined doing more than three activities while studying or writing, including listening to music, texting, and being online. They just can't—or won't—unitask.[15]

Remember Shawn, the teacher that I interviewed earlier in the chapter who discovered that instead of reading *The Fountainhead,* his students opted for the Cliff Notes and online summaries? In order to read a book and really gain the kind of deep understanding that Shawn was looking for, the students would have to unitask for a long time. They opted to go the easy route and were able to multitask and get a more cursory experience of the book. A recent report entitled *To Read or Not to Read* by the National Endowment for the Arts combined the results of multiple national research studies and noted severe declines in reading time and ability in recent years.[16] According to the report, "The story the data tell is simple, consistent, and alarming. Although there has been measurable progress in recent years in reading ability at the elementary school level, all progress appears to halt as children enter their teenage years."[17] One of the reasons the report proffers for this decline is multitasking. Quoting data from a Kaiser Family Foundation national study, 58 percent of middle and high school students use other media while they are reading, including watching TV, playing video or computer games, IMing, emailing, or surfing the web.[18] However, there is a bright light in this dismal report. The study did show that for the first time since data were initially collected by the National Endowment for the Arts, 18- to 24-year-olds—the same young adults who grew up with technology—demonstrated the biggest and most rapid rate of increase in literary reading. So, perhaps this bodes well for the iGen students and their future interest in reading.

Our students are consuming media in massive doses and multitasking all the time, even when the multitasking is detrimental to their performance. In a later chapter I will talk more about what happens when people multitask extensively and how doing so might affect their brain. Next, let's explore another area where our iGen students differ dramatically from other generations—their communication styles and preferences.

Communication: Always Wired, Always On

No doubt the most unique aspect of the younger generation is how they have embraced new tools that foster communication. Telephones have changed from a means to "talk" to instruments for text messaging, IMing, accessing MySpace and other social networks, video conferencing, and more. New cell phone uses seem to show up monthly and nearly all lead to alternative means of communicating. Jonathan Spira, CEO of Basex, an educational consulting firm, has dubbed Net-Geners the "Thumb Generation" saying, "Generation Y is wired with all 10 fingers."[19] Among school students, email is now a forgotten tool except to keep up with those few older folks who haven't mastered more immediate tools. Children as young as four or five learn how to Skype (using a video camera) with their grandparents who live in other cities, and teens Twitter or Facebook each other quick notes about what they are doing at the moment. The bottom line is that these are all just tools to connect, and connection is important to this generation.

But are two people really connecting when they send a quick sequence of ten text messages back and forth? Is the communication hindered by the use of shortened words and acronyms? Can you have a real conversation without looking someone in the eye? The funny thing about this is most of the students I interviewed simply laughed at the questions. Augustine, a fourteen-year-old, high school freshman, told me, *"I almost never talk to my friends on the phone anymore. Everyone is so busy that you end up leaving messages and it's way easier to send a text. No matter what I am doing I always read my texts when they vibrate my cell phone and then it is really no big deal to text back and forth while I am doing whatever else I need to do. Now that I think of it, I probably only use about 500 minutes a month but do at least 3,000 texts."*

Augustine is most certainly not unique in his communication style. In two recent studies we found that younger teens—13 to 15 years old—talked 441 minutes per month and sent and received 228 texts per month. Our older teens—16 to 18 years old—however, used 495 minutes and 486 texts. More strikingly, an earlier study in late 2007 revealed 476 minutes and 391 texts for this older teen group, while a second identical study only six months later showed a reversal, with 15- to 17-year-olds talking 590 minutes per month but sending and receiving 978 texts during the same time period.[20] Why talk to one person when you can talk to many at the same time?

The Net Generation college students and their younger iGen counterparts feel compelled to communicate and to do so with as many people as possible simultaneously. They text during class, between classes, after school, in their cars (even though it is now illegal in many states to do so), anywhere they can quickly tap their fingers over the keys. Two-thirds of teens say their cell phone is their most essential technology and half view it as "key to their social life." In fact, they place their cell phone as second only to their clothing in representing their social status.[21] They personalize their phones with fancy covers and download ringtones for each of their friends. I was talking with a fourteen-year-old when her phone trilled a few seconds of a song. Without missing a beat, she reached into her purse and stopped the ringing. When I asked why she chose not to answer the call, or even see who it was from, she said, "That's just my mom. I can call her back later." That took our conversation into a totally different direction as she explained to me that she worked really hard to assign songs to peoples' personalities to make it easier for her to know who was calling and whether to answer the call or let it go to voicemail. I didn't recognize her mom's ringtone song but it smacked of the 1970s. Our fifteen-minute chat turned into thirty minutes of variations on, "Wait, I have to take this call or Janet will think I am mad at her." Should I mention that during the same time she was nearly always getting a text message or texting someone, and she did this without breaking stride or losing track of our conversation? I was impressed and awed by the number of people she communicated with in just a half hour, but as a Baby Boomer I also found myself overwhelmed at the constant electronic interruptions and was somewhat taken aback by her rudeness and disrespect. When I asked about whether she felt that it was rude for someone else to take a call or send a text *when talking to her* she said, *"All my friends do it all the time and I know it bugs my mom and she tells us that we are being rude, but I don't know anyone who doesn't check their texts the second they come in no matter what they are doing. You think it is rude but I guess we are just different that way."*

When they are online, communication is still key as iGeners IM simultaneously with between three and four friends and use their social networks to broadcast their life updates, thoughts, feelings, and social plans to dozens of "friends" at the same time.[22] These social networks are another key aspect that makes today's students drastically different from those just a generation older.

Virtual Social Worlds and the Internet

Every teacher, administrator, and parent knows about MySpace. MySpace has been vilified in the press as a haven for sexual predators, pornography, and cyberbullying. Our own studies of major media outlets showed that between 2005 (two years after MySpace became a teen hangout) and 2008 the number of negative articles about MySpace in-creased 1,700 percent.[23] However, solid research has shown that the media vastly overstates the negative aspects of what happens online.[24] In fact, according to Mizuki Ito, one of the lead researchers for a recent three-year MacArthur Foundation Digital Youth Project,[25] "What is dif-ferent is that so much of what kids are learning about is how to use media, manipulating information, and finding things online are taking place in an informal social context, rather than things they are learning in school." Ito went on to say, "I think it has been challenging for teach-ers and educational institutions in the formal school space to incorpo-rate all of these communities. Part of what we're seeing is a generational gap between parents and teachers, on one hand, who tend to perceive the online spaces as threatening, and young people, on the other, who view them as full of positive potential." The comprehensive MacArthur report recommended that rather than ban students from using online social networks, teachers and school administrators should instead consider incorporating them into a new model of education.

The Digital Youth Project confirmed what our own research has shown. Social networks provide two critical outlets for preteens and teens: a source of friends and a forum for social interaction with peo-ple who share common interests. As you are undoubtedly aware, the teen years are difficult ones. Bodies are changing daily as are friend-ships. School presents constantly new and dynamic challenges as pre-teens move from comfortable, small neighborhood primary schools to larger middle schools, and then into even larger high schools. The num-ber of after-school programs has skyrocketed, with each student en-couraged to join a sports team, club, or participate in some other activity. School has also become more competitive, with college ad-mission rates declining, leaving the student with more homework and less time for socialization during school or after school. With no time to hang out at the mall or visit friends, the only vehicle that kids have to be with friends is online.

MySpace is not the only social network. In fact, Facebook, originally developed for college students, but now open to anyone, has mushroomed over the past few years and passed MySpace as the major teen hangout. Not to miss out on anything social, many students maintain both a MySpace and Facebook account. A variety of social networks have also appeared, including those for younger students such as Club Penguin and Webkinz. All social networks share two things in common: they are social in nature and nearly every school student is a member of at least one. Recent research indicated that 80 percent of 12- to 17-year-olds use MySpace weekly and half of those visit daily.[26] Our research on MySpace users reported an average of nearly 200 friends.[27] When we studied more than 1,200 MySpace users we discovered that pretty much everyone took advantage of all the social network had to offer. They posted photographs, wrote bulletins, talked with people, joined groups, played music, displayed videos, and anything and everything they could manage. Most noteworthy was that they interacted with other people. This feature makes social networks a prime candidate for educational use. Students spend hours there each day doing their version of "work" and communicating with their classmates, which is a perfect setup for developing lessons embedded within their already favorite virtual worlds.

The MacArthur study summary trumpets the enormous educational value and potential of social networks:[28]

> To stay relevant in the 21st century, education institutions need to keep pace with the rapid changes introduced by digital media. Youths' participation in this networked world suggests new ways of thinking about the role of education. What would it mean to really exploit the potential of the learning opportunities available through online resources and networks?

What makes these social networks so attractive? First and foremost, they open the world to hundreds of millions of people, all available to interact socially. For many shy and awkward preteens and teens, being online allows them to be more outgoing. In our research on the impact of MySpace, we discovered that preteens and teens feel less shy online than in the real world and more capable of socializing.[29] This is a concept that I referred to in *Me, MySpace, and I* as being "behind the screen." Somehow, having the computer screen—or any screen for that matter, including a cell phone—between the teens and the world, makes them feel less inhibited and more willing to disclose personal information. It also encourages them to be more direct and more communicative. I see this with my college students, too. There are those who are happy to talk in class and others who are meek, shy, and unwilling to contribute. When I allow them to make their comments online on a discussion board everyone contributes. Even though the shy students know that everyone will read what they write, they feel safe doing it from behind their personal screen.

Second, social networks afford students a way to gain help with school material. They form study groups, swap notes, share homework answers, and collaborate on projects. Each of these social network features can be a source for a new educational approach. The students are already communicating about school online, which makes this behavior ripe for use in classrooms. A third important feature of how students use social networks is in creating written, audio, and visual content. Content development is a major part of the school curriculum, and social networks are a great way to encourage preteens and teens to do this in an environment that they visit often and enjoy.

Although there have been many detractors of MySpace, Mizuki Ito of the MacArthur Foundation's project on social networking said, "It may look as though kids are wasting a lot of time hanging out with new media, whether it's on MySpace or sending instant messages. But their participation is giving them the technological skills and literacy they need to succeed in the contemporary world. They're learning how to get along with others, how to manage a public identity, how to create a home page."[30] Smart educational models must consider social networks as a valuable source for enhancing student interest and participation in the classroom. The kids are there in droves. The trick is to leverage their love of social networks to create educational tools built around them.

Social networks are just one aspect of the Internet that dominates the lives of today's students. As is evident in Table 2.1, the Internet gradually becomes a focal point in the media lives of school students. Younger elementary students spend a half hour a day online, rising to an hour for older elementary students, two and a half hours for middle school students, and three hours for senior high schoolers. These latter numbers may underestimate online time because other recent studies have found that middle school and high school students are on the web upwards of four hours per day. The *State of Our Nation's Youth 2008–2009* report, a national study by the Horatio Alger Association, documented that thirteen- to nineteen-year-olds spend 4.5 hours per week online for help with their homework, 6.2 more hours on social networks, and 7.1 hours for entertainment, noting that this means that online time for non-school-related issues was three times the amount of time spent for schoolwork.[31]

So, what do they do online other than social networking? Well, pretty much everything. They create, chat, IM, play games, surf websites, listen to and download music, watch television, write, and even stay informed on world events. An August 2008 study[32] found that for thirteen- to seventeen-year-old boys the top websites were (in order): YouTube, Facebook, Google, Yahoo, and ESPN, whereas the girls' top five were Facebook, Google, YouTube, MySpace, and Yahoo. This clearly presents a mixture of social, informational, and entertainment websites visited by both sexes.

One important educational use of the Internet is information seeking. Although Wikipedia was not among the top five teen websites, it is used extensively by students and is always among the top ten most popular websites. Evaluations of Wikipedia's accuracy vary from its being just as accurate as the printed *Encyclopædia Britannica* or containing more mistakes than a printed compendium.[33] Regardless of its accuracy, it is nearly always one of the top hits on a Google search, which means that students will click on it to gather information for projects or reports.

Wikipedia's ease and popularity presents an issue that is paramount in using the Internet as a student research tool—media literacy. As part of a larger topic, Wikipedia stands as the foremost example of why we need to teach students how to evaluate the information that they gather online. Prior to the Internet's rise in popularity, student research was done in the library using printed reference material. The World Wide Web changed the thinking and actions of students. Why drive to the library when you have multiple libraries at the click of a button? What we need to do is simply accept that the information students are going to use is electronic rather than printed and teach them how to analyze its accuracy through effective critical thinking. This issue became clear when in an earlier study one of our college student subjects told us, *"The web is just a library multiplied by a billion. Everything I need is right there and I don't have to sit in a quiet, musty room reading books and journals."*

Students also gain a lot of their information from other media, including television. The "*Daily Show* Effect" is a prime example of how students derive a substantial portion of their political information from a television show that repeatedly represents itself as "fake news."[34] Regardless of the source, the Internet and other forms of media represent a vast reservoir of opportunities for misinterpretation or misinformation. Along with the use of media in education, students will need to be taught how to analyze, evaluate, and synthesize information and recognize when a source is credible or not. Volumes have been written on media literacy, and this important subject will be explored in more detail in Chapter 7.[35]

A Generation of Content Creators

Take a look at a Facebook page or MySpace page and you will see that preteens and teens are all about developing and sharing content. They design web pages, blog, make videos for YouTube, create art, share photos on Flickr, create their own T-shirts, podcast their thoughts, record and distribute personal cell phone ringtones, and send their musings to everyone on a vast friends list. Make a Facebook entry and all your friends are alerted. Add a comment on someone's photo and the person gets an email or text telling them to view what was written. According to a national study by the Pew Internet & American Life Project,[36] the vast majority of twelve- to seventeen-year-olds are content creators whom they refer to as "multichannel teens." Students are not just using the Internet, but they are contributing to it, too.

What a boon this has been to writing. Students may not be reading original sources or reading deeply as much as teachers would like, but they are writing in all new modalities. This is a golden opportunity for educators who have long complained that they can't get their students to write essays. Perhaps it is not the writing that they are reticent about, but the vehicle for that writing. Replace a paper and pencil with a laptop and online discussion board and you may find that even the most reserved students are strong writing contributors. It is not the student. It is the tool.

Find the right tool—that is, the right technological tool—and writing now becomes fun, rather than a chore. An important criterion for selecting technological tools is matching the mode of delivery to the student's preferences. Each person has a unique learning style that is tied directly to the type of content they create and their preference for how they can best access and digest information.

Learning Styles

Psychologists and educators have been studying how people learn for decades. Essentially there are two major schools of thought on "learning styles."[37] The most popular conceptualization is that there are three basic learning styles—visual, auditory, and tactile/kinesthetic. Visual learners thrive when the material is presented through pictures, diagrams, charts, and other modalities (or formats) that can be seen. They like Power-Point presentations, particularly when they can review them later. Video games have a special appeal to these students, as they are developing knowledge and skills through playing a game that requires hypervigilant visual attention. Steven Johnson, in his book *Everything Bad Is Good for You,* argues that video games provide an excellent environment for learning through a combination of visual decision making emanating from the visual brain centers plus continual rewards inherent in winning the game.[38] Visual learners also learn by watching the person who is talking (auditory) and paying close attention to their demeanor and body language. Facial expressions and body language are very important to visual learners, as they help the student understand more than just the message.

Auditory learners prefer listening. Lectures and discussion work well for them, giving them a chance to take in the information plus any intonations and speech cues. These learners are more apt to like lectures, audiotapes, and the voice portion of videos. *Hooked on Phonics,* which uses songs to help children learn how to read, was created to appeal to auditory learners.[39] Among preteens and teens, you will likely find these students listening to music and even listening to the television without having to glance up at the screen.

Tactile/kinesthetic learners require a hands-on approach so that they can touch and move the material. The Montessori approach[40] uses "manipulables," which allow children to learn math, reading, and other subjects by arranging and moving objects. Interestingly, tactile/kinesthetic learners often get labeled as having attention problems in school since they find it difficult to sit and listen or watch a teacher for extended periods of time. They work best when given the opportunity to do hands-on activities.

Howard Gardner, a Harvard psychologist, views learning styles more broadly as representing seven different types of intelligences: visual/spatial (pictures), verbal/linguistic (words), logical/mathematical (logical reasoning), bodily/kinesthetic (hands-on), musical/rhythmic (sounds), interpersonal (working with people in groups), and intrapersonal (preferring to work alone).[41] Gardner's argument is that each person has varying levels of these multiple intelligences, which then lead to different learning styles. If you want to learn more about your own personal learning preferences, there are online tests that will gauge both your style and your dominant intelligences.[42]

It is important to note that whether you believe in the three learning styles model or the multiple intelligences approach, nobody has a single preferred learning system. Most of us use all modalities to gain information, but there appear to be consistent differences between generations in the "dominant" style of taking in information. While Baby Boomers and older Gen-Xers prefer either visual or auditory modes, Net-Geners and iGeners learn best by touching, moving, and enjoying hands-on experiences. Certainly, the computer environment, with its graphic icons, pictures, and sounds is both visual and auditory, but its major feature is in being able to manipulate and move objects. The Internet is all about clicking and exploring via hand motions, which is, of course, tactile/kinesthetic. Research has shown that students retain only 10 percent of what they read, but 20 to 30 percent of what they see.[43] How much do they retain when they have hands-on experience? Research in this area is difficult, since the three learning styles are, by the nature of the materials, intertwined. When you watch young children grab the mouse, click here and there, and maneuver through the web as soon as they can sit up in a chair, and then do the same motions even faster the next day, there is no doubt that tactile learning is highly effective. When you see a teen ignore the manual for his new video game console and simply start pressing buttons, there is no doubt that there is a decided preference for tactile/kinesthetic learning. Clearly educational models must consider the delivery style in order to help iGen children learn in environments that capitalize on their strong tactile/kinesthetic abilities and preferences.

Unique Personalities

Young learners differ from their older brothers and sisters, their parents, and their teachers in many other ways that are relevant to education. Here is a short summary of those differences and how I see their role in designing both educational content and developing educational delivery systems.

1. **Motivation**: iGeners are strongly motivated by positive reinforcement . . . and lots of it. They are not satisfied, like members of earlier generations, with getting their rewards at the end of a

project. They want to be appreciated and told what a great job they are doing (reinforced) often. That is why video games are such powerful, engaging instruments. They provide constant reinforcement for maneuvering in the game as well as punishment when the player fails to win the game or loses and has to start over. As I mentioned earlier, although educators are well aware of the need for constant reinforcement, it is difficult for a teacher to do so with a class of thirty or more students. Technology, however, doesn't care how many learners it needs to reinforce.

2. **Family**: The younger generations are all about family. While their older brothers moved away from their parents, they stay close. In a 2007 MTV and AP Youth Happiness Study, the number one thing in life that teens said made them happy was spending time with family.[44] An astounding 72 percent said that the connection with their parents made them happy. In the *State of Our Nation's Youth 2008–2009* survey mentioned above, 57 percent of teens said that a family member (mostly a parent) is their number one role model.[45] Another study found that even after graduating from college, younger Gen-Xers are more likely than not to move back home for both financial and familial reasons.[46] Any educational strategy needs to involve parents in the process; their children will be happier because of their participation.

3. **Confidence**: Youngsters exude a confident air that surpasses that of any prior generation. The *State of Our Nation's Youth* survey reported that 88 percent of them described themselves as confident and, in terms of reaching their career goals, 62 percent were very confident, while another 31 percent were fairly confident.[47] Confidence makes for eager learners, as long as the learning environment is stimulating and interesting.

4. **Openness to change:** Recent research has shown that younger people are more open to change and self-enhancement than earlier generations.[48] The younger generation values change, as evidenced by how they flock to any new innovation at lightning speed. Remember, this is the generation that took YouTube from zero to 50 million in a single year. Although teachers may not be as ready for a changing educational environment, their students *are* ready and excited and crave newness. We have to figure out how to feed this appetite so as to ignite their interest in learning rather than extinguish it with lectures and boring materials.

5. **Collective reflection:** Not surprisingly, given the rise of social networks, blogs, wikis, and podcasts, the younger generation enjoys the social aspects of learning. There are many tools to accomplish this, and we will discuss some possible strategies in later chapters. Suffice it to say for now that we must figure out how to let children work together online in a way that fosters education. Online discussion groups are old hat to these kids. They need new and more hip ways of connecting with their fellow learners, and those connections do not have to be confined to students at their school. Innovative programs will discover ways to use these tools globally to enhance long-distance collaboration and learning. Preteens and teens love the fact that they can have "friends" all over the world. Letting our students discuss school topics with people from different cultures can only make learning more fun, interesting, and valuable in today's global economy.

6. **Immediacy:** I want it all and I want it now! That may well be the mantra of the iGeneration. Their tools push information and communication at them rapidly, and teens expect those technologies to be there and to function that way. Someone writes a

note on their Facebook wall and they are immediately notified and encouraged—no, compelled—to click on the link and comment back ASAP. All the new technologies scream at them to respond *now*. Text messages rarely sit for more than a few minutes before a quick note is jotted back. And they are moving so quickly that words are shortened, apostrophes left out, and acronyms are used to enable a swift response. They are connected to a rapid-fire world and they move through it at warp speed. If a website takes more than a few seconds to load, they are off clicking on another link. If a friend takes too long to respond to a text or IM, they are incensed. This need for speed is certainly something that can be a boon to educators. After all, don't we want our students to want to learn something *right now?*

It is precisely these unique qualities of the iGeneration that portend a new, invigorated attitude toward education. As long as educators understand how to reach these students through all of their technologies and media, they will devour new material as fast as it can be dished out. They *want* to learn, but our current teaching models simply bore them to sleep. Education should excite and stimulate them and it will if we make radical changes in our conceptualization of teaching and learning. This is a generation that learns differently, and unless we recognize and accept those differences, we will turn them off to education. They are ready and willing to be the future, but we have to engage them in ways that we have never imagined could be part of school.

Chapter 3

An Explosion of WMDs: Wireless Mobile Devices

Teens have created a new form of communication. We call it texting, but in essence it is a reflection of how teens want to communicate to match their lifestyles. It is all about multitasking, speed, privacy and control.

—Joseph Porus, vice president and chief architect, Technology Group, Harris Interactive[1]

The children of the mobile internet generation are getting used to being connected—to their music, their videos, their social networking sites— wherever they go. And that means we are all going to have to think hard about how we rewrite the rules.

—Rory Cellan-Jones, BBC[2]

While educators and parents might be a bit nervous to embrace this trend, the reality is that Gen Y have already embraced the mobile web and now it's up to us to figure out how to use this technology in an educational setting to keep them interested and engaged in the learning process.

—Derek Baird, Media/Educational Technologist, Designer of Yahoo! For Teachers[3]

The iGeneration is all about connecting and communicating. Just look at the communication devices and media that are now immensely popular—iPhones, Blackberries, MySpace, Facebook, Twitter, text messaging, instant messaging, Skype—and the list goes on and on. Each shares four characteristics:

1. They all afford communication between people
2. They are mobile
3. They allow 24/7, on-demand access to family, friends, information, and entertainment
4. Their popularity has been driven by young people.

Each communication device has the capability to do many tasks beyond simple communication. However, it has been up to the youth to stamp their special imprint on these devices. To Baby Boomers and many people over forty, a cellular phone is a tool to talk to another person. To an iGener, it is a device for sending text messages, surfing the Internet, sharing photos, watching videos, customizing ringtones, displaying musical tastes, playing games, and holding video chats with friends. Literally daily more applications (or "apps") are being built into cellular phones that have nothing to do with our traditional view of what constitutes a telephone. According to a 2008 Harris Interactive national study of more than two thousand teens, 57 percent reported that their cell phone is the key to their social life and *nearly half admitted that their social life would end or be much worse without their phone.*[4] Strikingly, the survey showed that to teenagers, their cell phone portrays more about their popularity than jewelry, watches, and shoes. As Neal, a sixteen-year-old high school student told me, *"I stood in line for 16 hours to get my first iPhone which I paid for with my own money. For weeks I was the most popular kid on campus. Now, two years later, it is the center of my life. I am constantly downloading exciting, clever new apps that make my iPhone even better. I have my own radio station programmed to find and play my music tastes, I can record voice message re-*

minders, read books, get directions which I can then view from a satellite, translate from any language to English, and even silly ones like turning the iPhone into a flashlight or a level that I used when I put up bookshelves in my room. Once I left my iPhone at home and I literally walked three miles each way during lunch to get it."

The cell phone has become what social scientists anticipated for the future of television. In the mid-1990s, WebTV attached a box to the television and provided the ability to email and use the Internet. TiVo and other digital video recorders perform some of the functions of a cell phone, as do video game consoles, but the problem is that you can't lug your television around in your pocket or purse. Most certainly a laptop computer has more computing power than a cell phone, but again, it is unwieldy and difficult to transport. The cell phone is small, compact, mobile, and can do pretty much anything that a teen might want. If it can't do it now, you can bet that it will in a very short time. iTunes took only two months to sell 25 million songs and two years to sell one billion. Within a single month in 2008 more than 60 million iPhone apps were downloaded, increasing to half a billion in only nine months.[5] Who is driving the proliferation of iPhones and their apps? According to a recent study, 31 percent of iPhone owners are between the ages of 15 and 24, with another 32 percent between 25 and 34.[6] Another national survey found that 46 percent of iTouch users are under 18 and, strikingly, 40 percent of these wireless mobile device owners reported accessing the Internet *more often* from their mobile device than from their computer.[7] (The iTouch offers all the musical features of an iPod plus a web browser, chat, and email, plays television shows and videos, and can handle innumerable new apps.) iGeners love their WMDs, and their uses are exploding at an unprecedented rate.

In response to the iPhone's miraculous success, similar wireless mobile devices—although they are cellular phones, the phone function is much less important than everything else they can (and will) do—have hit the market, including Research in Motion's BlackBerry Storm, Palm's Treo Pro, and other similar multifunction phones. We witnessed first-hand the popularity and draw of these devices as President Obama refused to give up his BlackBerry when he took office, and then members of Congress were seen tweeting during his inauguration.

With a single, handheld device that is enormously popular with the iGeneration and is capable of connecting students to information and communication, it seems obvious that these devices hold great promise for education. However, as yet, they have not been used as educational tools, except in isolated research studies. A special issue of the *Journal of Computer-Assisted Education* summed up this perplexing lack of attention to the educational applications of iPhones and the like by saying,

> One hundred years ago people travelled to music halls or concerts to be entertained. Then broadcasting and the gramophone brought mass entertainment into every home. Now a second revolution is underway as millions of people download music from the Internet to personal players, and create and share media on sites such as Flickr and YouTube. One hundred years ago children travelled to schools to sit in rows and be instructed by a teacher. Today, they still do the same. Why is education so resistant to change?[8]

In this chapter I will explore the critical question of how students see these wireless devices as much more than *telephones,* and how, once they are reconceptualized as mobile computers, they can be used as powerful teaching tools. First, I will provide some background on how iGeneration teens are using their communication tools, including cell phones, social networks, video cams, and myriad other devices, in novel and educationally sound ways. Next, I will present a model for communication that provides a strong rationale for educational viability, followed by an examination of how the social landscape of our current educational models fit with these mobile tools. Finally, I will explore the way educators currently see traditional education, and then present some sample applications that make clever and effective use of these tools and present opportunities for students to be educated anywhere and by anyone in the world.

Wired 24/7

The iGeneration has been referred to as a "connected class"[9] because their cell phone handset is always turned on and they are always connected to at least one screen for most of their day. In Chapter 2, Table 2.1 displayed the time spent daily using various technologies and media and Table 2.2 tallied the percentage of children and teens who owned many technological devices. From all of my group's research and other national studies of teens' communication, there is no doubt that this is truly a "wired" generation.[10]

Certainly a major part of childhood and the teen years involves connecting with friends when direct face-to-face communication is not possible. Baby Boomers hung out with friends on the streets and playgrounds and used telephones to talk to friends when they were home. Gen-Xers practically invaded malls in massive groups of friends, and when they couldn't physically be together they embraced email. The iGeneration is being raised in a world where technology affords more opportunities for effortless, instant communication. According to all the research, it is the cell phone they reach for when they want to get in touch, but they are more apt to use the phone to text than to speak. This is an important communication transition and has implications for both understanding this generation and implementing new learning strategies.

Watch Their Flying Fingers

From my research with parents of children, preteens, and teens, I have seen a striking trend about the way cell phones are being used. The children and preteens in my study, half of whom already have a cell phone,[11] spend nearly an equal amount of time using it to talk and to text (with a slight edge to texting even at this young age). Young teens show a decided preference, spending twice as much time texting as actually talking on their phones. For older teens, that jumps to more than three and a half hours a day using the phone as a texting tool.[12] A 2008 study by the Nielsen polling group used billing data for a panel of 50,000 cell phone owners and found that preteens sent and received 428 texts a month while only placing and getting 137 phone calls. For thirteen- to seventeen-year-olds, however, the number of monthly texts jumped to 1,742, compared with only 231 monthly phone calls.[13] Another Nielsen study just nine months later found that teens were making and receiving only 191 cell phone calls per month, but exchanging 2,899 text messages.[14] Our studies confirm these staggering statistics.[15] Remember, the Harris Interactive national study mentioned previously also told us that more than 4 in 10 teens can text blindfolded, and recent research tells us that 62 percent of teens use their phone after "lights out."[16] With the introduction of other quick messaging options such as Twitter, we have even more opportunities for students to embrace their seeming need for speed and brevity.

What is it about text messaging that is so attractive to teens? Juan, a thirteen-year-old eighth-grader, told me, *"It's not a phone. It's way more than that. And text messaging is so easy and I can do all my other stuff while I wait for a response. I usually have about 5 or 6 text conversations going at the same time. My mom's always yelling at me to just pick up the phone and call the person but she doesn't get it. Talking on the phone is way too intense and takes too much time. I like being able to just flip back a quick one and*

*keep the talking rolling but not have to be sitting with the phone in my ear.
Now I got Twitter where I can send tweets to all my buds at once and they
can let me know what they're up to. It is so cool and so easy and everyone gets
my tweets at the same time."* Twitter has garnered national attention and
is now just another part of the teen lifestyle. It has been poked fun at by
The Daily Show and the comic strip *Doonesbury,* which ironically only
furthers its elevation among the youth, with research showing that it is
now the third most popular social networking site after Facebook (in
first place) and MySpace.[17]

Although educators have often vilified the cell phone as a disruptive
influence in the classroom, it is important to recognize a golden opportunity. Because nearly all students own and carry their cell phones, and
since education involves communication, why not choose to use their favorite communication tools as ways to reach them? According to the
Harris study, "The education community should also take note that
66% of those surveyed said they hoped that mobile devices would *present opportunities to be educated anywhere in the world.* This data should
serve as a call to educators to start investigating ways to provide students
with mobile virtual learning environments to facilitate self-directed
learning opportunities."[18] The cell is there, it is used by all teens; it is mobile, and it is a sure way to reach them. Before looking at specific ideas
of how to capitalize on teens' love affair with wireless devices, it is important to consider the role of traditional education and how technology might expand the view of students and teachers and enhance
classroom lessons.

Traditional Education

Traditional schooling is composed of six different components. First,
there is content, which is the material that students are required, by state

mandate, to learn at each different grade level and in each course. Second, you have resources, which traditionally include books, workbooks or worksheets, encyclopedias, and, of course, teachers, to present the content. Third, there is the curriculum, which includes the way in which the content is presented to the students through those available resources. Traditionally, this means reading material in books and listening to the teacher explain that material. Fourth, education requires support from teachers, tutors, fellow students, and parents who help the student in understanding the content. Fifth, you have communication, which has always been between teachers and students during class to clarify whether the students are learning the content and perhaps between teachers and parents when the student is not performing well. Finally, education is all tied together through evaluation, which involves testing whether the student has grasped the content.[19] It is important to note that there is nothing in this description of education that mentions technology or media. It is implied, however, that the content, curriculum, and all else that comprises education and learning take place in the classroom and after school in the home. Technology has presented opportunities to change the "location" of education from the classroom to . . . anywhere. This generation, with its pervasive use of cell phones and other portable communication technologies, is ready to have their education extended from the classroom to any room.

Mobile Learning

Using technology to instruct students is certainly not a new idea. In fact, I see it as just another link in a chain of educational models that has now stretched from classroom learning to individualized learning to online distance learning to electronic classroom learning, and to what we now refer to as "mobile learning," or *mLearning* for short. As technology moved into our educational system, educators have tried to apply the traditional models of learning by using the new technological tools. Online education simply took the same content and repackaged it so that it could be delivered without a teacher physically present. Electronic classroom tools such as PowerPoint presentations, online videos, and high-tech presentation equipment were still tied to the same material in the same school environment. Certainly these tools made education more interesting and allowed for opportunities to present content in new and different ways, but they were still tied to static material presented in a static learning environment. Today's learners need something more attuned to their daily lifestyles—connected, and often virtual. That's where mobile learning comes into play.

There is nothing special about mLearning that requires fancy technologies, high-tech whiteboards, or any other expensive hardware and software. Each student carries his or her own mLearning environment— a wireless mobile device. The sale of smartphones with Internet access plus other cutting-edge features has skyrocketed, led by the Blackberry and the iPhone. At the end of 2008 smartphones accounted for 13 percent of all cell phone sales, with projections—in spite of a depressed economy—that eventually all phones will include Internet access as a standard feature.[20] The 2008 introduction of the iTouch—essentially an iPhone without the phone—signaled the arrival of high-powered, handheld Internet devices and another opportunity for an educational tool. Because a large proportion of smartphones and iTouch purchasers are students, it is pretty safe to predict that by 2015, instead of lugging a laptop computer to school, students will simply pop open their mobile Internet device and have access to all their communication tools. This presents enumerable opportunities for educators to engage students through a modality and tool that they use nearly 24/7. Educators have a golden opportunity to reach students if they recognize that communication is the first step toward a new model of education—mLearning.

Before I describe mLearning in detail, one obvious question is whether students will be capable of using their wireless devices to perform required schoolwork. There are several legitimate concerns about these devices, including their small screen size, difficulties with inputting information, printing capabilities, and battery life. Despite the small screen size, Nielsen's *Three Screen Report* indicates that consumer demand for video on wireless devices is strong and increasing rapidly, with teens watching an average of more than six and a half hours of video per month on their devices, nearly twice as much as any other age group.[21] Johan, a high school senior, summed it up this way: *"I download my favorite TV shows to my iTouch and watch them when I have time. Is the screen too small? I have never had a problem watching a show or a movie. Once I wanted to see a particular show on a larger screen so I downloaded it to my laptop and watched it there. I love watching videos on my iTouch and I even look at YouTube videos without a problem. It's small, but you get used to it really quickly."*

Educators have also expressed concern about how easy it will be for their students to type on the wireless device. Judging from how quickly they type text messages, IMs, and emails, and how full keyboards are now standard either as pull-out from a regular cell phone or as a touch screen on iPhones, BlackBerries, and similar devices, it is clear that students are ready and willing to use them as input devices. Battery life, however, continues to be an issue because using a wireless device for some functions, such as video, does use up a significant amount of battery power. However, at this writing, companies have developed fast chargers, mobile rapid chargers, and battery extenders that increase battery life up to eight or more hours a day under maximum usage. Finally, educators have expressed concern over the ability to print papers from wireless devices. This is something that is going to change with mLearning. Papers will most likely be turned in virtually, graded virtually, and returned to the student without resorting to paper copies. Since the introduction of desktop computers into the workplace in the 1970s and 1980s, we have seen the rise of "paperless offices," with files kept on computers and servers rather than in metal cabinets. With mLearning, we are moving toward a paperless school.

mLearning relies on a device with anywhere, anytime wireless access. Although we have not quite arrived at a completely wireless world, most schools, libraries, public buildings, and even whole cities[22] now feature free wireless access. Most futurists accept the prospect that by the middle of this decade, free or inexpensive wireless access will be omnipresent. At a minimum, we can expect to have our mobile devices accessible in the two most important educational environments—school and home. According to an expert in mobile learning:

> . . . (the) mobile phone is evolving towards the dominant medium. It is becoming the natural interface through which people conduct their shopping, banking, booking of flights, etc. Moreover, it is turning into the single unique instrument of mediating communication not just between people, but also between people and institutions or more generally between people and the world of inanimate objects.[23]

mLearning is based on five important concepts:

1. Information is available anywhere there is Internet access.
2. Information is available anytime.
3. Information is available through devices that are becoming commonplace and will soon be affordable to most people.
4. Information can be "pushed" from the environment to the student and "pulled" by the student from the environment.

5. The learning environment is fluid and adapts as the learner learns.

Note that these issues are very general and can actually apply to a wide variety of teaching strategies. More important, however, these five mLearning concepts are, as I have discussed, precisely the strengths and desires of the iGeneration. They want to learn whenever they want and wherever they are located. There are a variety of tools that fit nicely into an mLearning environment, which I will discuss in later chapters. For example, lectures can be delivered through podcasts, video, or audio recordings of someone speaking that can be downloaded from a website onto a mobile device. Given the iGeners' appetite for multitasking and short bursts of information, teachers can easily prepare lectures that they record in small, manageable bites that students can listen to or view. In addition, the student can pause, rewind, and listen to the material again (or watch it again if it is a video), something that is missing in the traditional classroom. Couple a podcast with the ability to ask questions and make comments through wireless communication tools such as email, text messaging, Twitter, and other services, and you now have a true mobile learning device with interactivity that mimics the traditional classroom model in which the teacher lectures and the students ask questions and make comments.

Mobile learning is actually part of a larger concept known as a "social landscape." We all exist in many social landscapes, each of which represents how we interact with people and what rules or norms govern those interactions. For example, one of our social landscapes involves our behavior in public, or what Dr. John Gottman, an expert on relationships, called our "public spaces."[24] When cell phones first started to be used, people were appalled when someone would be having a conversation—often a rather loud one—in a public place. I can remember when someone answered their phone in a long line waiting to return Christmas gifts and everyone, including myself, glared at the person, who appeared oblivious and went on prattling about what he wanted for dinner and where he was going that weekend. Nowadays, we don't even bat an eyelash when we hear someone talking on their cell phone in *any* public social landscape (unless they're particularly loud).

Our children exist in a variety of social landscapes, each of which they continually alter by their mere presence and the way they interact with people. School, for example, presents one such landscape, and home another. Each offers different interactions with the people in the environment. School traditionally affords very limited social interaction in class with brief periods of chatting and gossiping during lunch and recess breaks. Home, on the other hand, provides several distinct social landscapes, one through interactions with parents and family and another through interactions with friends. That was all before the Internet and cell phones, MySpace, Facebook, and every other "virtual" social landscape. Given the staggering figures of how much time children and teenagers spend using media and technology, their predominant social landscape is definitely social, but perhaps it should be called a "cyberscape," in that it is composed of technologies connecting people together in cyberspace.

This new social landscape has been referred to as the "social web,"[25] which is really just a combination of content and social interaction. Each of these parts of the social web is made up of whatever tools are available at the moment. For example, we could say that (as of this writing) the content available on the social web consists of websites, videos, blogs, photos, and any other form of information, while the social interaction component includes cell phones, social networks, instant messaging, online discussions, and whatever else has emerged as a vehicle to connect one person to others. The importance of the social web is not the tools that are being used, nor is it the content that is available. Rather, it is a whole new social landscape that has no fixed position in time and space. You can gather content anytime and from anywhere in the world. You can communicate with people anywhere and anytime. It is precisely this social web that provides untold new opportunities for mobile learning.

According to Table 2.2, the vast majority of iGeners already own an iPod or other MP3 player. With the 2008 introduction of the iTouch—which combines an iPod with access to the Internet without having to pay for telephone service—any student who can access a wireless network can access the Internet, text message, tweet, and send and receive email. These functions fulfill a second critical aspect of mLearning—interactivity.

Putting these five mLearning concepts together allows educators to create special learning environments that use tools that nearly every student has or can afford, appeal to their complete immersion in technology and media, and allow them to multitask and be engaged at any time. The following section presents one such environment. I am not advocating that this is the only mLearning model. Projects such as the MobiLearn[26] and M-Learning[27] in Europe are just two examples of the application of mLearning strategies and design, but they will give you an idea of what is possible. The International Association for Mobile Learning organizes an annual mLearn conference that attracts educators from around the world and highlights new mLearning projects. Dozens of mLearning projects are listed at the IAMLearn website.[28] In addition, at the university level, AT&T has begun a "mobile learning initiative" that gives all entering freshmen an iPhone or an iTouch to enhance their campus experience. At this writing several universities, including Abilene Christian University, have begun implementing this program with great success.[29]

Mobile learning is just one way to capture the minds of young learners. There is another component to their daily activities that may provide another way to engage them in learning—their virtual communities. Facebook, MySpace, Flickr, and Second Life are but a few of the more popular virtual communities, and a vast majority of preteens and teens have a presence on at least one, if not two, three, or more. I will talk about virtual communities in more detail in a later chapter but to give you a taste, I will describe how one might add a virtual community to an mLearning environment to create an educational model better suited to today's young learners.

Mobile Virtual Learning Environments

Mobile Virtual Learning Environments (MVLEs) represent a general framework for understanding how technology—particularly virtual technologies—can be used to reach iGeneration learners through their love of communication. All MVLEs share the following characteristics, which center on two notions. First, learning *can* happen outside of the traditional classroom and, second, the center of this learning involves electronic communication tools. The convenient thing about MVLEs is that they are adaptable to any new technology and they make use of any new communication devices that iGeneration learners embrace. They can range from online discussion boards to fancy three-dimensional simulated worlds. The key is that MVLEs all have the following features:

1. **Engaging environments:** A key to an MVLE is that any virtual educational experience must be adaptable to whatever environment—sometimes called a "platform" by computer scientists—is currently being embraced by students. For example, an online math lesson created to be used on MySpace may need to be adaptable to Facebook or Second Life. MVLEs must include

technologies that the students will find stimulating and novel, or they will either not use them or will soon become bored.

2. **Environmental flexibility**: A virtual learning environment can utilize any available technology to teach a concept. This means that educators have to be willing to accept online discussions, blogs, video games, podcasts, tweets—basically any available means of transmitting information to the students. This also means that education has to become adaptable, not only to different variants of the same technology (such as social networks) but also to completely different technologies.

3. **Relevant learning strategies**: Educators need to recognize that even though a book may employ specific learning strategies that have been researched and proven effective, they may not be effective for each and every student. The beauty of an MVLE is that it can be "strategy-independent." This means that the material can be presented through a variety of research-approved methods that each student can try on for size and accept or discard, depending on what works for him at that time. This gives the student control over his learning rather than ceding control to the strategy chosen by the textbook author. In essence, an MVLE provides the student with many textbooks, each offering a way to learn the same material using different methods. It is up to the student to pick which one resonates best with his learning needs.

4. **Material interactivity**: The tools have to allow students to work actively with the material rather than have a static "book learning" experience. Teaching has to involve both "push" and "pull," where material is presented to the student, but the student is also able—and encouraged—to seek out information on his or her own. Remember, iGeners are expert Googlers and know how to

find anything in a flash, so the learning environment has to incorporate this skill into the design.

5. **Human interactivity**: Learning can no longer be individualized to one student working alone. It must allow for nearly constant communication between students both for learning and for socializing. Socializing while doing schoolwork has always been frowned upon ("Ssshhhh . . . no talking while you are doing your schoolwork!"), but this is a different generation living in a different world, where socializing is key and can be a constructive part of learning. If you do not let them communicate about topics other than those related to the assignment, they will be forced to "unitask"—focus on only one thing at a time—and will not perform as well. We simply have to get used to the fact that this generation *must* multitask and that multitasking must involve peer-to-peer communication. The research does demonstrate rather convincingly that students who communicate during a learning experience perform equally well as those who read the material and have no outside communication—it just takes them longer to finish the assignment.

6. **Student-centered**: Standard education models are teacher-centered. MVLEs use an environment in which the responsibility for learning belongs to the student rather than the teacher. The student must have many options for learning, including pulling information from teacher-supplied and Internet-based sources and pushing information to other students and other web-based sources. The teacher's role then becomes one of making the information available while monitoring progress and helping students find their way around difficulties by suggesting alternative resources or alternative learning approaches.

7. **Collaborative**: Learning has often been seen as a solitary activity, with a student sitting at a desk at school listening to the teacher or completing a worksheet or at home reading a book or doing written homework. Beginning in the late 1980s and early 1990s psychologists recognized that, in many cases, learning alone may not be the most effective strategy for understanding and retaining information.[30] Fast-forward to the new millennium where the primary student activity is electronic communication and you have an entire generation primed for collaborative learning. Originally developed for college students, Cooperative Learning (CL) provides one such model for collaboration. Cooperative Learning relies on the theory that groups must be interdependent, with a common goal that, when reached, gains rewards for the entire group. The key to CL is that all group members must be accountable to complete their part of the work or learn the material, and it is the responsibility of all group members to ensure that they do so. A typical CL group is most often composed of students who are excelling as well as those who are not, so that the group learning experience involves the better students in helping to teach the poorer students. Recent research with college students has suggested that teams can also be formed by matching personalities based on simple personality tests that can be given online as part of the mobile virtual learning environment.[31] CL is a fine model that I have used for years, particularly for teaching college-level statistics courses in which you have a range of understanding and talent. However, it is not the only method of collaboration, nor do I believe that it should be the standard for this aspect of MVLEs. I believe that collaboration of any type, among any students, enhances learning and capitalizes on iGeners' aptitude for

multitasking through a variety of communication modalities. Students are already collaborating on social levels, and making use of that social interaction is just another key to a successful virtual learning environment.

8. **Creative:** Creativity has always been seen as a successful adjunct to education. The opportunity for creative exercises within a learning domain heightens interest in the subject, motivates the learner to continue with the educational process, and results in increased levels of understanding. Most of what I remember about dinosaurs comes from my distinct memory of several dioramas that I made in elementary school. California geography was cemented in my brain with three-dimensional state maps made of salt, flour, and water. I learned more about architecture in high school from my model of a night club (à la Frank Lloyd Wright) than the teacher's lectures, many slide shows, and a very good textbook. Art, music, videos, blogs, and podcasts are all creative activities using technology. More important, they are activities that are embraced by the iGeneration. As we'll see in the next chapter, they must be a critical component of any new educational model that hopes to capitalize on the tech-savvy qualities of the iGeneration.

9. **Available 24/7:** Education can no longer be seen as something that happens between 7:30 A.M. and 2:30 P.M., Monday through Friday, with afternoons and evenings for homework. This generation has radically altered time boundaries and daily asleep/awake patterns, and education must adapt. For preteens and teens, communications are often going on around the clock. Texts are sent early in the morning and into the wee hours of the morning. Students log on to their social networks at all hours of the night, and as long as educators are willing to accept that

students can learn something in the middle of the night, then MVLEs are a great way to capitalize on educating these 24/7-online, wired students. This does not mean that teachers need to be available 24/7. Classes will still meet in real, "brick-and-mortar" classrooms. However, given that students have done their work in virtual environments, the time in class can be better used for clearing up confusions that become evident to the teacher when she receives daily electronic reports of student progress in their MVLE work. The students may work at any time of the day or night, but teachers, who will no longer have to provide all the learning in the classroom, will now have more time to respond to questions, either in class or via some communication tool at other times. As a college professor, I offer in-class help on assignments and to aid comprehension, plus additional virtual office hours, when I am online and available for questions. Many teachers use email to receive student questions and stipulate in advance the expectations for response time. For example, a teacher might tell students that she will respond to emailed questions within 24 hours, although in my experience, usually students are able to find answers on their own or, most likely, from peers who are online at the time.

On the surface, an MVLE may sound like a lot of work for the educator, but in reality research shows that it actually reduces the teacher's workload, if not in the short run, at least once the materials have been created. It is true that, initially, implementing an mLearning environment will require additional teacher participation. It can take extra time to record a lecture for podcasts, for example, although recording a live lecture and then editing it into bite-size modules is relatively straightforward. Once a lecture is turned into a podcast it can be used multiple times. Additional lectures can be developed with user-friendly software tools. In addition, mobile learning modules are being developed and are available for teachers' use in a variety of disciplines.[32]

Why Virtual mLearning Works

Four bodies of research and theories highlight why virtual mLearning promotes student learning. First, educational research has shown that multimedia presentation—presenting material through a variety of senses, including the ears, eyes, and sense of touch—promotes more opportunities for learning and enhanced retention of material. This makes sense given what we know about this generation of learners. With their media-rich diets (using their auditory and visual senses), their love of video games (visual and tactile senses), and their multitasking use of computers and WMDs (more tactile and visual senses), they possess the ability to learn through multimedia presentations that involve the three major senses.

Second, student-centered learning has been shown to be superior to teacher-centered learning.[33] By its nature, student-centered learning means that the student is the driving force behind choosing how to learn the material. mLearning is classically student-centered in that it allows the student to control the order, timing, and pace of learning. For example, while one student might find a virtual simulation of a chemistry experiment compelling, another may learn the same concepts through a videotaped lecture, while a third may learn best through listening to a podcast lecture—or by listening to that podcast while clicking through a related slide show online. With mLearning all of these learning strategies can be made available and adaptable to individual learning styles.

mLearning also allows the student to review material at her own pace. If she is listening to a podcast, she can start and stop and rewind to review the concepts. If the material isn't clear, she can seek other sources of information such as video simulations or peer assistance, again, at her own instigation. She is driving her own learning. The end result will be the same—she will learn the material—but the process is different from traditional classroom learning. In the classroom, teaching is most often linear, meaning that it has a beginning and an end, and the material is presented from start to finish. Certainly students can and will ask questions, which interrupts the linear process, but nonetheless, the learning is mostly controlled by the teacher. In mLearning, the student is in control and the process is far from linear.

The third body of research or theory that supports the use of virtual rather than physical (classroom) environments for learning is Social Presence Theory, which is defined as the subjective quality of an environment that determines how the user interacts with people within that social space. According to social psychologists, "social presence is a state that varies with medium, knowledge of the other, content of the communication, environment, and social context."[34] Essentially, *social presence* defines our daily lives as we exist in shared spaces that vary with whoever else occupies the space and the shared intimacy between those in that space. Social presence is of course subjective, and varies as a function of how comfortable one feels in a variety of social settings. Virtual spaces are buffered by screens. Each person sits behind her own screen (computer, cell phone, or any screen) and communicates with some sense of anonymity. Even if you know the person at the other end of the screen, they cannot see you and because of this invisibility, you feel a sense of safety.[35] Research shows that students in virtual settings are more likely to share opinions, feel less threatened to seek help from peers or teachers, are more motivated to learn, are more self-reliant, and feel less pressure to perform compared to students in real-world settings such as a classroom.[36]

Fourth, Social Learning Theory says we learn through a combination of direct, personal experience and indirect or vicarious experience by watching others learn. For personal experience, Social Learning Theory says we continue to display behaviors when we have been reinforced (rewarded) for doing so, and we discontinue behaviors when we have been punished for them. Social Learning Theory asserts strongly that students who receive positive reinforcements from other students or teachers are more likely to feel better about themselves and therefore to learn more effectively.[37] As a student interacts with the material and other students in a virtual social space, she is getting constant positive reinforcement for learning the material and from interacting with other learners. In a student-centered social space, she is constantly garnering positive reinforcement and continuing to learn.

Taken together, when we put a student in a multimedia, student-centered environment with social presence and constant positive reinforcement, we set the stage for learning. A mobile virtual learning environment is a perfect combination of all four psychological principles and provides an excellent environment to teach our media-savvy, multitasking, always-wired, constantly communicating students.

Conclusion

The scenario described in Chapter 1 about the virtual Fractions Building is one example of an MVLE (see the section "A Future Homework Assignment"). Although it seems rather complex, it does not have to be in a three-dimensional world. As I mentioned earlier, the International Association for Mobile Learning website lists many operating projects, continually updates information on mobile learning, and makes other excellent resources available.[38] If something more three-dimensional is desired, Second Life, for example, offers online tutorials on how to set up a virtual presence—in this case a classroom—on their site, and both the tutorial and the use of their site is free. Regardless of whether learning is done in a fancy 3-D universe or simply as an online discussion, it is still going to be more attractive and engaging for students who live and breathe through their wireless devices.

Communication is the engine that will drive a new model of learning. If mobile learning is the fuel that will drive that car, virtual mobile learning is the fuel that will make it fly. We may never get airborne autos like those on *The Jetsons,* but the tools for mobile learning are all here, they are easy, and, more important, they make learning fun.

Now that you have gotten a taste of one educational vehicle—mobile learning—later chapters will discuss other strategies such as social networking and creative technological product development. Mobile learning works for two reasons. First, kids love technology and media. Second, these tools allow—and even encourage—multitasking. Before exploring other technologically rich educational opportunities let's take a look at why some people refer to the iGeneration as Generation "M," for multitasking.

Chapter 4

Multitasking Madness

Associated with the expanse of technology-based media in the home is an ever-growing need to multitask. It is not surprising to hear young people describe multitasking as a "way of life" or to declare that it is "easy" . . .[1]

—Mark Cheever et al., "Multitasking Across Generations"

I used to think that it was just plain rude that my students would surreptitiously text each other while I was talking. I have come to realize that they really are paying attention and if I make them stop they get bored and antsy and don't listen to what I am saying.

—Jerome, a teacher of seventh-grade English, Seattle

Parents and teachers tell me they are worried about what kids are doing in school. Katy, the mother of a twelve-year-old daughter, said, *"I just assumed that Morgan was paying attention in class and focusing on what the teacher says. Then I read an article about how teenagers are now texting all of the time, even in the classroom. I heard on TV that a girl fell into a hole because she was texting and walking and not paying attention to where she was going. Now I'm deeply concerned about Morgan. If she picks up on this habit, are her grades going to plummet?"* Katy said she struggles with keeping her child focused on homework after school. *"We tend to have a daily conversation that goes something like this . . . Me: 'Do your homework be-*

fore you get online and socialize with your friends.' Morgan: 'I can do my homework while I talk to my friends.' Me: 'You can't do homework while talking to friends. It's not possible.' Then Morgan gets snippy: 'But I do it. So, it is possible.' Back and forth we go . . . 'not possible,' 'possible,' 'not possible,' 'possible . . .' You get the idea."

The stark reality is that today's kids just can't do one task without wanting to do a bunch of other things at the same time. It's a way of life for them. The natural inclination to multitask in these young kids probably has many sources, including the cool, dazzling, multifunctional new devices that permit and encourage multitasking. What might this constant need for multitasking mean to parents and educators? For one thing, it could mean that long-cherished demand for improving learning and raising grades—"Do your homework before you play!"—simply might not work anymore. They can't help it. They have to multitask.

Research psychologists have studied multitasking for quite some time and, not surprisingly, they generally agree that multitasking has its drawbacks.[2] Compared to focusing on one task at a time ("unitasking"), multitasking most often leads to slower performance and increased errors. Researchers have learned this almost entirely through laboratory studies, in which subjects—nearly always college students—are asked to perform two relatively simple tasks at the same instant. Slowing and errors arise mainly because decision making appears to require special mechanisms in the brain that can work on only one task at a time. However, multitasking in real life can be very different than doing two tasks together in the laboratory. For one thing, there is often unlimited time to perform tasks in the real world. A student can produce work that is equivalent to work done while unitasking, albeit in a somewhat slower fashion. For example, in one recent study students were asked to read a section in a psychology textbook and then take a test on the material.[3] One group simply read and took the test. A second group started reading and then was interrupted by several instant messages to which they were required to respond. Which group took longer to read and complete the test? The interrupted group. Which group performed better on the test? That's a trick question: they both did equally well!

Second, in most realistic situations in which people multitask, there is "slack" time in one or more tasks. In other words, there is time when a student is waiting for a reaction or for something to happen in the task, like waiting for a friend to respond to an instant message. Multitasking can capitalize on this slack time by using that time to work on another task, such as doing homework. It may take longer, but evidence is starting to show that they *want* to multitask and may *need* to multitask. The downside is that it may take them longer to do their work but they will do it just as well.

Much of the multitasking carried out by students occurs with computer-based technology. Cell phones, laptops, iPods, and other portable computing devices are spreading at an incredible rate. Some of these devices that started out as single-purpose machines, such as the cell phone, are being turned into general-purpose computing devices that allow users to perform a variety of functions, sometimes simultaneously. The cell phone evolved into a smartphone and is now literally a portable computer. Psychology has shown that certain physical and mental behaviors can be encouraged by physical objects. Modern technological devices, or general-purpose computing devices, automatically encourage multitasking by their users. Just take a look at any computer screen and you will rarely see just one open window. Right now, for example, I have my word processor open along with my email, instant messenger, and six web browser windows. Watch students using their computers and you will see even more open programs with flashing incoming IMs or websites that encourage multitasking. Information and communication technologies (ICT) allow a way to secretly work on other tasks while "talking" to someone. An expert at American University in Washington DC describes it this way: "Because recipients of ICT-based messages cannot see us (Web-cam technology excluded), they typically are unaware when we engage in additional activities. On the phone and on the Internet, nobody knows you're multitasking."[4]

This is the world in which iGeners live. They refuse to unitask and seem to want to juggle as many things as possible, particularly anything related to media and technology. Whether multitasking is a form of pride or is fostered by technology that encourages attending to more than one task at a time, it is a reality. This is a generation that has multitasked from birth and that is what they do from morning to night. Our educational system, however, is built on unitasking, where students work on one task at a time. This chapter is about what happens when today's young multitaskers meet yesterday's educational system.

The Standard Approach to Education: Multitasking Is Bad for You

This is the message from research psychologists, scientists, schoolteachers, and parents: don't multitask! Certainly, there are fundamental limitations on how much the human brain can do at one time. Generally speaking, if you sit in a laboratory and do two unrelated tasks at exactly the same moment, then there will be some negative effect on your performance on one or both of the tasks. This is the argument, which has been demonstrated over and over again scientifically in laboratories around the world for four decades, and which has been used to ban driving and talking on the telephone—at least a handheld phone.

This negative effect of multitasking, what the researchers call "dual-task interference," occurs with even the simplest of tasks. A task cannot be much simpler than this: if you hear a low-pitched tone, press the red key; if you hear a high-pitched tone, press the blue key. Nevertheless, asking college students to do two very simple tasks like this at exactly the same time—with different hands—produces massive amounts of dual-task interference in the form of slow responses.[5]

The drastically simplified tasks that are used in laboratory multi-tasking studies, as well as the very artificial nature of these tasks, can make these types of studies seem rather irrelevant. After all, who cares if a student can press different buttons in response to different tones? The answer is that the oversimplified, artificial laboratory environment allows scientists to draw conclusions, create theories, and then test these theories using precise, numerical methods. While there is nothing close to general agreement among psychological researchers about what causes the human brain's inability to do "perfect" multitasking, there are several leading theories, all of which point to a limited mental resource that cannot be shared across tasks. For one, there is the idea that the brain uses some form of mental energy—generally referred to as "capacity"—to carry out its mental operations and complete tasks. Since there is only a limited pool of capacity available at any given moment, simultaneous tasks will have to compete for capacity. When the tasks' demands exceed the available capacity, then performance will suffer, usually in the form of slowing or of increased errors.[6] A second leading idea is that what matters is not how much capacity is required, but rather what specific mental processes are involved. If two or more tasks require the same mental processes at the same time, such as two math problems or making two decisions, then there will be some kind of dual-task interference.[7] Some researchers have referred to this as the "bottleneck" theory, with the analogy drawn to the narrow neck of a bottle that prevents too much liquid from being poured out at once: only so much processing of a particular kind can be performed at a time.

Proponents of these different theoretical approaches agree on the existence of a fundamental limitation in the human capacity for simultaneous mental processing. To what degree do these limitations apply in the real world? The real world is very different from the artificial laboratory and allows for flexibility when trying to multitask. In fact, there may be considerably more "slack" time in everyday activities than people would guess, and this slack time can make for some excellent multitasking opportunities. Take for example a study done in England in which people were asked to keep daily activity diaries while they traveled to and from work or generally around town. It turned out that the participants in the study made good use of slack time when traveling on the bus, on the train, etc. Based on a numerical analysis of the data, the researchers estimated that people who multitasked were able to add 46 percent more useable time during the waking day![8] This is quite amazing given that these were just average people going about their normal day.

A recent study conducted in my laboratory attempted to find out if the inherent human limitations identified in a staged environment affect people multitasking in real-life settings—in this case, in their homes. Using an online survey of more than 1,300 people, Baby Boomers, Gen-Xers, Net-Geners, and the oldest iGeners were asked about their multitasking at home on a typical day. Each person was asked which everyday tasks—technology-related plus other typical non-media behaviors—they were likely to do at the same time as other tasks, and how difficult it was to multitask successfully. Not surprisingly, the Net-Geners and older iGeners in the study reported doing far more multitasking than any other generation of Americans. The youngest generation was more than twice as likely as the oldest (Baby Boomers) to send a text message while working on the computer, more than twice as likely to send an email while engaging in an instant messaging conversation, and far more likely to instant message while surfing the web. Overall, the Net- and iGeners reported that they would be doing six things at once, compared to about five for Gen-Xers and four for Baby Boomers. And Net-Geners were more likely than the other generations to multitask while talking face-to-face with other people, too, despite the apparent rudeness of the act. Not surprisingly, the number-one task that Net- and iGeners did while talking to other people was listen to music (presumably using an MP3 player with earbuds plugged in).[9]

However, it also was clear that some kind of inherent mental limitation was operating at home for Net- and iGeners, just as has been found in the laboratory. For the Net Generation and the iGeneration, some popular uses of technology were less likely to be multitasked than others. For example, Net- and iGeners were much less likely to multitask while playing video games than while listening to music. In fact, while listening to music they were multitasking all the time, doing one, two, three, or even more things while their iPod was playing tunes. In contrast, while playing video games they were only able to multitask doing one other thing about half of the time. What accounts for these differences in the propensity to multitask across different tasks? The answer probably reflects the limited mental resources in our brains that prevent us from combining certain tasks. Video gaming requires using vision, hearing, manual skills, as well as logic and problem solving. In essence, video games demand much more of our mental resources, making it hard to play them and do anything else at the same time. Further evidence from our study supports this interpretation of the results. As you can see in Table 4.1, we found almost the identical patterns for the members of the Baby Boomer generation and Generation X, with each *older* generation being less likely to multitask. In other words, the differences across tasks in multitasking propensity appear to reflect universal mental properties that cut across generations, but each generation multitasks more than its predecessor.

Table 4.1   How Do Generations Differ in Multitasking?

Activity	Likelihood of Multitasking with Other Tasks		
	Net Gen & iGen	Gen X	Baby Boomer
Playing Video Games	57%	49%	42%
Reading Books and Magazines	58%	52%	43%
Talking Face to Face	73%	70%	65%
Working on the Computer But Not Online	75%	67%	56%
Watching TV	77%	71%	64%
E-Mailing	78%	69%	58%
Texting	79%	65%	51%
IMing	78%	61%	51%
Talking on the Telephone	78%	73%	65%
Surfing the Web	79%	73%	62%
Listening to Music	88%	82%	75%

Despite the apparent ubiquity of these limitations in our performance, there is another way of looking at the results. In many cases, the
Net-Geners and iGeners were very likely to combine one task with another. For example, as you can see in Table 4.1, listening to music was
combined with other tasks about 88 percent of the time, while playing
video games and reading were down to around 50 percent or so. In other
words, this suggests that certain tasks can be done together without hindering performance. Deeper understanding of the details of when tasks
interfere or do not interfere should lead to better educational design for
today's kids, who probably cannot stop multitasking even if you force
them to turn off the music, stay off the Internet, and not talk on the
phone while they do their homework.

Going back to scientific theories of multitasking, and specifically the approach that competition for specific mental resources causes dual-task interference, it seems reasonable to provide general guidelines for designing learning environments that do not discourage, but rather allow students to multitask. For example, if a learning task depends heavily upon processing spoken words, then multitasking can be accommodated by avoiding other simultaneous tasks that also require the same types of tasks. Have you ever tried to listen to two conversations at the same time? I am sure that you found it very difficult if not impossible to understand both. However, I can almost bet that you can listen to someone talk with music in the background and understand every word of the conversation *plus* hum along with the song inside your head. Perhaps if you are a Baby Boomer this would present some difficulty. But for an iGener, it would be a piece of cake even if you throw in a television show in the background, and a few IM conversations online.

Feeding the Young Brain What It Wants

On the television, CNN is showing multiple streams of information on one screen. In the center, the anchor is talking about a news event. On the right side of the screen, stretching from top to near bottom, is a panel listing additional bits of information about the topic. At the bottom of the screen, stretching from left to right, are two crawlers, or moving streams of information, one moving slightly slower than the other. The first contains today's stock market ticker tape. The second contains a running series of news snippets from around the world. Too much information at once? Perhaps to us, but not to Roxanne, a fourteen-year-old high school junior. This is exactly how she wants to see her information presented. According to Roxanne, an honors student who wants to go to Yale, *"I love to watch*

CNN. There is soooo much information and I can read what's going on at the bottom of the screen and get the Cliff Notes version and listen to Anderson Cooper to get more about what's going on."

When Roxanne switches to the on-screen guide to choose a new TV channel to watch, there are hundreds of channels to choose from. On her laptop, she has multiple websites open, including Facebook, Wikipedia, and Google. She starts flipping through the TV channels and can't find an old episode of *Gossip Girl* replaying, so she checks the on-demand service but they don't have it either, so she opens a new window, goes to the show's website and watches her episode. But she keeps CNN in the corner of her TV just in case some "breaking news" catches her eye. Roxanne is lucky enough to have an iPhone, so even her cell phone screen provides a wealth of information sources. Psychologists would say that Roxanne is being inundated by *data smog, infomania,* or *information overload* and that it should, at least according to the theories mentioned above, literally drive her brain crazy with the massive influx of information. Yet Roxanne seems calm and happy as she takes everything in, seemingly all at once. At least one recent study suggests that all this extra information in the environment might not be as distracting as one might expect. College students learning new material got the same score on a learning test if they studied while a distracting video was playing as they did when they studied in silence. The students did learn less when they had to memorize the material *and* the video, showing that they were not good at splitting their attention, but they were able to ignore background noise, so that did not hinder their performance.[10]

What does all of this information do to children's processing of information? The most plausible outcome is that it encourages frequent attention shifts and intense multitasking. One expert has argued that this might have positive benefits:

Media users are learning at a young age how to juggle multiple activities, use time efficiently and use existing technologies in creative ways, albeit sometimes not as originally intended. While there are drawbacks to media multitasking, there may be advantages as well.[11]

Other researchers have suggested that repeated engagement in tasks that require frequent attention shifts could lead to a preference by youths for task switching over sustained attention during cognitive tasks. The impact of such a change in preference can be understood by considering a common task performed by young students. First, as we saw from the data presented earlier, instant messaging or chatting is popular with most members of the iGeneration as a way of communicating with their friends. Further, our research has found that eleven- to fourteen-year-olds carry on about three IM conversations at a time, and older teens (fifteen to seventeen) are IMing four people at a time. Doing this obviously requires frequent attention shifts from one conversation to another and back, and yet iGeners thrive on these attention-shifting, multitasking conversations.

This information explosion is a new phenomenon, driven by the dual engines of better computer-based technology and the rise of speedy global communications systems. It is evident not only in massive increases in the amount of information available at any given time, but also in a reduction of depth of information presented about any one topic and an information processing style that involves frequent attention shifts. When many of today's teachers and parents were growing up, there were longer scenes on television and longer articles in magazines. Even *Sesame Street* now has more cuts than before.[12] Today's kids are used to a fast, shallow pace of information presentation and get bored when trying to absorb information at the rates that were normal for their parents when they were in school.

In other words, old TV shows are boring, old movies are boring, and, most important, traditional lectures are boring. Who or what is to blame when the iGeners' need to multitask clashes with the style of education developed by older generations? For one thing, we can scrutinize the traditional lecture delivery method. Can a high-quality high school lecture, long and detailed with no breaks, be multitasked with other activities? Probably not. The live lecture cannot be paused to allow for another task to be temporarily performed, cannot be rewound to reexamine content delivered earlier, and cannot be searched with keywords for critical information. However, a podcast can be rewound and replayed, and so can a videotaped lecture. Regardless of the options (discussed in other chapters), the key is that we can no longer assume that students can be forced to unitask without a loss of attention.

Young children's inclination to multitask should not be underestimated. Data from some recent interesting studies of American youth show overwhelmingly how fully these kids are immersed in a media multitasking lifestyle. Researchers at the University of Pennsylvania tracked high school students' media use by asking them to record diary entries every day. The researchers found that, on average, the students were doing some unrelated nonmedia task—such as homework or eating—73 percent of the time that they also were viewing or consuming media. Additionally, the students did not use just one media source at a time; they accessed multiple sources (e.g., watched television *and* listened to music while doing homework) 13 percent of the total time that they were engaged with any form of media.[13] The same research group, in a separate study of fourteen- to sixteen-year olds, found that most of the kids often multitasked with media at home, and that very few of them never multitasked. Doing other activities while watching television or listening to music figured prominently into the results, and about 25 percent of the subjects reported watching television or using the Internet while doing homework.[14]

Looking more carefully at exactly what kids are doing at home, it is clear that the computer is the seat of multitasking madness. The Kaiser Family Foundation conducted a large, nationally representative survey of American youth, including 2,032 third- through twelfth-graders. Additionally, 694 of those students completed diaries of their media use over a seven-day period. The study revealed that although watching television is likely to be one of the activities in the "mix" when kids are multitasking, the majority of time spent on the computer is likely to be multitasked with other computer activities. Thirty-nine percent of the seventh- through twelfth-graders were doing multiple activities most of the time that they were using the computer. In this context, the Kaiser Foundation described the computer as a "gateway to diverse activities" and summed up the finding this way: "Computer activities are far and away the most media multitasked activities, sharing the majority of their time with other media."[15] The power of the computer to induce multitasking also is supported in our laboratory's study of multitasking at home, introduced earlier. While watching television is a task that many Net- and iGeners were likely to multitask at home (77 percent), computer-based tasks tended to be even more likely to be done while multitasking. Using email, instant messaging, and surfing the web were all more likely to be multitasked than was watching television. Perhaps we should simply blame Microsoft and Apple for developing such wonderful computers that allow and even promote multitasking.

Multitasking Centers in the Brain

The discussion up to this point presents a paradox. On the one hand, laboratory research on multitasking shows that two tasks cannot be done equally well when done together. Perfect multitasking does not exist. There is always a cost to doing more than one task at a time because there is almost always some form of dual-task interference. On the other hand, surveys of American youth show that they are highly engaged in multitasking while at home. More than likely they are multitasking at school (as much as they can get away with) and at play, as well. (One recent news report told about a fourteen-year-old girl who was texting walking home from school and fell into a sewer hole where a manhole cover had been removed and put to the side while the workers took a break. Adult pedestrians in Manhattan routinely text while crossing the street.) It turns out that the picture is even more confusing when one considers the ultimate source of multitasking behaviors: what goes on inside the brain. The eventual goal in dealing with teen multitasking is to parlay what is known into an educational model that takes advantage of students' multitasking skills while simultaneously heeding the mind's and the brain's natural constraints on doing more than one thing at a time.

Neuroanatomists and neurophysiologists have longed divided the human brain into critical regions, marked not only by their physical locations but also by the functions they perform. The outer surface of the brain is divided into lobes, the most relevant of which to this discussion is the frontal lobe, so named because it is literally in the front of the brain, right behind the forehead. The various parts of the frontal lobe have been associated by neuropsychologists with different psychological functions, but many of these functions share a common theme of being involved when we have to perform high-level mental management functions, such as organizing or planning our activities. Scientific studies of the brain while multitasking, done using adult subjects, have found that the frontal lobe is active when multitasking. There seem to be specific parts of the frontal lobe that allow a fully grown adult to coordinate more than one mental task at a time. Unfortunately, as the psychological research has shown, there is at least a small cost in doing so, and this cost usually comes about as slower performance on each task.

Now, the odd part about this situation is that the frontal lobes of school-age children are not fully developed. Huge numbers of children, "tweens," and teens are multitasking with media and nonmedia tasks, but their multitasking brain centers are not working at a fully mature level. In fact, it has been established by neurophysiologists that the development of the frontal lobe continues beyond adolescence. Some estimates place the final age of an adult's frontal lobe development in the thirties! The brain essentially is a highly interconnected device, with various regions and subregions communicating with each other at high speeds in order to carry out the processes necessary for our behavior and survival. Thinking of the brain this way, communication efficiency becomes important. Two key mechanisms for increasing communication efficiency in our brains are improved connections—scientists call this *pruning*—and improved insulation of electrical pathways, referred to as *myelination.* It turns out that pruning and myelination are precisely the processes that delay frontal lobe development.[16]

The upshot of this gradual brain development is that students may not be expert multitaskers; or rather, they may not be as good at multitasking as adults. Research has shown that it might take longer to do simultaneous multiple tasks, but many situations in the real world have unlimited time constraints, and this should not be a problem. (Remember the study interrupting students with instant messages? They did equally well but took longer.) The alternative—to force children to do one task at a time—could conflict with their inclination to multitask, leading to loss of interest and even loss of motivation to complete tasks.

The difference in mind-set between today's students and their parents and teachers is dramatic and best not left out of any equation for improving educational processes. For example, Arleen, a thirty-nine-year old California mother, is a typical Gen-Xer who enjoys taking advantage of modern technology to communicate with her friends. She said, *"When I chat with my friends, I need to shut the door to the room and tell everyone to leave me alone. I keep the kid and the dogs out."* Compare Arleen's attitude to that of the students in an interview study at American University in Washington, D.C., who reported that instant messaging is not something that can be done by itself. One student in that study said it was "too weird" to IM and not do something else at the same time. The general feeling among students in that study was that IMing and chatting were things to do in the background while doing some more primary task—or tasks—on the computer.[17]

Do Homework and Have Fun

At the beginning of this chapter, a mother named Katy described how she battles with her teenage daughter over doing homework the right way, that is, in a quiet place with no other distractions. At least to Katy that is the right way. Her daughter, Morgan, disagreed. Since iGeners have been programmed by society and technology to want to multitask, is Katy's edict for her daughter really appropriate? Despite the fact that multitasking is not perfect, it very well could have some positive aspects for today's students. The activities that are joined with a primary activity during multitasking might enhance the appeal, attractiveness, or just plain fun involved in the primary activity. Sharon, an eleven-year-old, put it this way: *"It's boring to sit on the computer and make slides for my biology presentation. I like it more when I can play Scrabble with my cousin in Arizona at the same time [on Facebook]. She takes a long time to make her words. That gives me time to find pictures on Google Image Search for my slides."*

Making otherwise "boring" work fun by multitasking might not just be for children and teenagers. Sociologists at the University of Essex in England tracked members of the public by having them fill out daily diaries of their at-home activities. Working on the computer, sending emails, and other technology-related activities were not the focus of the study. Rather, basic home-based tasks such as doing chores, caring for children, and eating were studied. Nevertheless, it was found that multitasking was done in a way that, according to the researchers, involved the "absorbing of low cost leisure activities into people's daily routines, whether it be listening to music whilst cleaning, or watching the TV whilst caring for children or eating."[18] The researchers did not specify exactly what might encourage their participants to multitask in this way, but to me it appears that people are multitasking to make their tedious housework fun!

The importance of making learning more appealing is obvious, perhaps, but sometimes it is argued that learning does not have to be fun to be effective. Learning is its own reward, they say. The main concern, of course, is not to increase the fun factor in formal learning, but instead to boost the *motivation*. Most teachers will agree that highly motivated children are more likely to learn. Is it dangerous to allow or perhaps even encourage multitasking among iGeners? So far, we've pointed to two important potential problems with multitasking. First, multitasking leads to dual-task interference, which results in slowing and perhaps in errors. Second, the aptitude for multitasking is not fully developed in children, which might compound this interference. Yet, what has not been mentioned at this point is that children learn to *self-regulate;* that is, they are aware of when they are not learning a fact well and can make adjustments to change their learning conditions. Ed, a junior high school student, provided a good illustration of this phenomenon:

> *I text and all my friends text during health class. In fact, that's the time when we all catch up with each other! While the teacher is lecturing! I am*

getting an A in my health class and most of my friends are doing just as
well. I am not just getting an A in health but also in my other classes. But
I don't text much in my other classes. They are too hard and I really do
need to pay attention.

Learning through Interruption?

The predilection for multitasking shared by contemporary students sets
up the possibility for new learning environments that capitalize on kids'
native tendencies to actively respond within multiple tasks in the same
setting. Of course, fundamental limitations in multitasking skills that
are caused by limited human mental resources have to be taken into account. Recognizing that certain task combinations should be avoided,
there ought to be some tasks that can be combined without interfering
much with learning, especially if students are not really trying to do two
tasks at the same instant but are alternating between tasks. As long as students are given unlimited or extra time to complete tasks, there should
be minimal or no impact from dual-task interference on learning. The
payoff might be increases in learning performance that come about from
excitement, enjoyment, or interest. Additionally, such environments
could let students learn at their own pace and in sequences or orders
that are suited to them.

Generally speaking, people can screen out information they want
to ignore, so students should be able to *turn off* one task if they need to
focus on another when they are doing their normal multitasking. Classic psychological research established our ability to completely filter out
irrelevant information. To demonstrate this skill, college students were
asked to listen to two messages presented at the same time, one in each
ear. The students were told to memorize both messages, but their attention was focused on one message by asking the students to repeat
that message out loud as they heard it. Students not only remembered

virtually nothing from the message that was not being spoken aloud, but they couldn't tell whether the other speaker was a male or female, or speaking English or German. Startlingly, they rarely recognized when their name was spoken in the other message—something that should be extremely obvious. The mind's ability to focus when required is amazing, and there is no reason to believe that today's students aren't just as good at recognizing when attention needs to be focused rather than split.[19]

Here is another way to think about it. A friend of mine, another college teacher, is always on the lookout for students—most often the younger ones—who are texting in class. When he finds one, he thinks that the student is being rude and not paying attention. He speaks to that student immediately and puts an end to what he believes is *inappropriate* learning behavior. It probably is true that students are texting their friends, wasting time, and are generally ignoring the lecturer. However, given this apparent drive for students to text during class, educators are already implementing clever ways of incorporating cell phones into the classroom. One teacher in Tampa Bay, Florida, routinely asks her students to look up information online on their smartphones to supplement the material she is discussing. For example, after a lecture about D. H. Lawrence, she asked those students with smartphones to see what additional information they could find online. According to the teacher, each bit of information that the students uncovered "pulled them deeper into a discussion about the author." This is just one example of how the students' smartphones can be put to good use in the classroom.[20]

A computer-based learning environment might also be appropriate for allowing classroom multitasking. However, part of the problem with learning in a multiple-task environment might be that some tasks interrupt the flow of learning. It's true that research on interruptions that occur at the office show those interruptions can lead to irritation, annoyance, and a low-quality experience.[21] Certainly these would be bad conditions for learning. The positive news, though, is that this same research also shows that there are *good* interruptions—ones that produce minimal interference for the user and that are not annoying. The trick is to know when to interrupt someone engaged in a task and when not to do so. Fortunately, research is beginning to show how to do this. Whether an interruption will be good or bad can be learned or predicted. For instance, some computer scientists have figured out a way to analyze tasks that humans perform on the computer and find natural points for inserting breaks or interruptions.[22]

Overall, taking into account the *multitasking madness* shared by members of the youngest generation, natural human limitations in multitasking performance, and the basic principles of interruption, the following three guidelines sketch out features of a learning environment that would be different from the traditional classroom and would *maximize motivation while also maximizing learning*:[23]

1. Learning environments should allow students the opportunity to multitask, keeping in mind that the students will self-regulate their multitasking when necessary.

2. Learning environments should minimize the possibility that two or more tasks will be multitasked when those tasks might share basic human mental resources as this will increase dual-task interference.

3. Learning environments should allow for teachers to interrupt students, for students to interrupt other students, and even for students to interrupt teachers when appropriate, as long as the interruptions are *constructive* ones that enhance the learning process.

The bottom line is that our students are multitasking and we cannot stop them without placing them in a boring, unmotivating environment. The trick is to develop educational models that allow for appropriate multitasking and that improve learning. This is where new technologies such as smartphones and virtual learning environments come into play. These are exactly the tools that iGeners embrace and find engaging, and they are based on multitasking in ways that lead to heightened interest in learning.

Chapter 5

Real Life or Screen Life?
The Educational Opportunities
of Immersive Social Networking
and Virtual Worlds

Virtual worlds offer participants a sense of presence, immediacy, movement, artifacts, and communication unavailable within traditional Internet-based learning environments.[1]

—P. Edirisingha et al, "Socialisation for Learning at a
Distance in a 3-D Multi-user Virtual Environment"

It's a chance for all of us who aren't actors to play [with] masks. And to think about the masks we wear every day.[2]

—G. Salmon, "The Future for (Second) Life and Learning"

What do I like about online games like WOW [World of Warcraft]? It's hard to explain but I feel like I am really there. Like I am right in the middle of a world that is different from my bedroom. It is so realistic that I sometimes forget where I am . . . until my mom yells for me to come to dinner.

—Donald, age sixteen

When I took French in high school, I was told that the only way to *truly* learn the language was to spend time in France with people who spoke only French. By doing so I would literally "live the language" by using all my senses to integrate the words themselves with gestures, facial expressions, and even body language nuances. The approach is called *total immersion* and is backed by extensive research as the best way to learn to speak like a native.[3] Many of the more effective language programs rely on a variant of total immersion using pictures, videos, and text, all within the context of a simulated native speaking environment, to increase efficiency and decrease learning time. Total immersion only works because it simulates, as closely as possible, a multisensory, realistic learning environment that is not the same as living in the country, but is closer than other, more traditional language-learning methods.

Now consider classroom education. Books are read, videos are viewed, discussions are held, but all occur in an environment that is flat, two-dimensional, and limited to basic senses. Certainly there are excellent ways of expanding the teaching techniques to make the environment more immersive. I recall helping my children build three-dimensional models of ancient Mayan villages; topographical salt, flour, and water maps; and even making videotapes of Shakespearean plays, complete with homemade costumes, to enhance their realism. These activities are certainly more immersive than simply reading a book, and they do enhance learning. But you are still only using a limited number of the nineteen available senses. Yes, *nineteen* senses, not the standard five of sight, hearing, touch, taste, and smell. According to Robert Samples, author of *Openmind, Wholemind,* we actually have fourteen additional sensory inputs, including temperature, balance, movement, physical closeness, and even atmospheric pressure, all of which can be incorporated in a truly immersive environment.[4]

In order to understand the value of immersion, it is helpful to have a basic understanding of how our mind works and develops. The brain is not just a mass of cells but a truly intricate network of interconnections among neurons that are continuously solidifying established connections and building new ones. This process is done through associating or linking one idea to another, which psychologists refer to as the *network association model* of memory.[5] I find it helpful to visualize the brain as a large wall diagram with circles representing concepts, called nodes, connected to other concepts by arrows, called links. Actually, a node is really just the concept label or name. The links (or associations) define the concept itself. For example, we all have a concept named "apple." In the network association model each person would have unique links from the apple node to other nodes. When I think of "apple" my first thoughts are round, crunchy, pie, red, and green, and so in my brain there is a node called apple that has links to other nodes named round, crunchy, pie, red, and green.

Nodes are really much less important than the links themselves, and all links are not equal. When a link is first created it is weak and unstable. Imagine a baby learning about apples by being shown an apple and being told that it is round like her favorite ball. In our wall diagram you might visualize that the link between *apple* and *round* as a very thin line. Every time the baby is reminded that apples are round, that link becomes a thicker line, indicating a stronger and stronger link to apple. As the baby learns more about apples, more links appear and are strengthened as they are experienced.

It is important to recognize that nodes and links include sensory information as well. Apples have a sweet taste and a crunchy sound and texture, and all this information is included as nodes and links. At the same time other objects in the baby's world are also round, and their concepts are also linked to the concept of roundness. One can only imagine the explosive magnitude of this learning machine we call the brain as the baby learns new concepts every day. Pretty soon we have run out of space for our wall diagram and have to resort to a more three-dimensional picture of the brain as occupying an entire room with nodes and links spreading out and intertwining.

All brain activity is coordinated in an area of the brain called the prefrontal cortex. As we grow and learn, the prefrontal cortex is also emerging. Cells in the prefrontal cortex continue to learn how to make connections between nodes, to juggle multiple tasks, and to make informed decisions, until the prefrontal cortex is completely developed in the late teens to the mid- to late twenties. So, to recap, learning is composed of concepts that are all interconnected, based on learning through the senses, and all of this is controlled by a specific area of the brain that takes up to thirty years to completely develop. Everything we read, everything we hear, everything we touch or feel or smell or taste is encoded as a complex, rich interconnection of associated nodes and links.

Now consider how we learn in school. We read books, listen to lectures, watch films, build models, all the while creating and developing our mental associative networks. If we are learning a language, experts would claim that we will not truly develop a *rich associative network* until we immerse ourselves in the culture where the language is spoken. In other words, learning is enhanced when we add in additional *realistic* sensory information that is not available from books or other classroom tools. It is the realism that is the key. The addition of realistic sensory information helps to activate areas of the brain that would be active if the learner were actually engaged in the real-world task that is being simulated. This is why some researchers have argued that watching violent television is tantamount to engaging in acts of violence, and why research has shown that for young kids simulated events, such as a virtual rollercoaster ride, are as *real* as riding on an actual roller coaster.[6] Further, it promotes what psychologists refer to as "social presence," or the feeling of connectedness between the instructor and students and among students themselves.[7] The more the educational curriculum can model reality, the better we will learn. More realism leads to more interconnected brain areas, which results in more strongly formed memories, which leads to more effective transfer to real-world situations. The key is realism, and this is where technology comes into play. Consider the following list of teaching tools:

- Books
- Worksheets and homework
- Lectures
- Audiotapes
- Videotapes
- Video games
- Virtual reality

Which of these most closely simulate a real-world event or, put another way, which are more realistic and more immersive? Clearly, as you go down the list you more closely approximate a real event, involve more senses, and add more realism. Figure 5.1 shows the progression of teaching tools from less immersive to more immersive.

At the far left you have traditional classroom teaching tools such as reading books and listening to lectures, which use a small subset of senses and are lower on the realism scale. The lecturer merely *describes* a real-world event, such as a key historical battle, and perhaps illustrates with some photographs or quotations in support of realism. As you move to the right you gain more sensory information and a closer representation of real events, which leads to more realism. And more realism is connected directly to better learning. A video podcast, or "vodcast," can show a historical reenactment of the battle with actors in costume, real weapons, and dialogue appropriate for the time period. At the far right in the chart, multiuser virtual environments represent events more faithfully than other

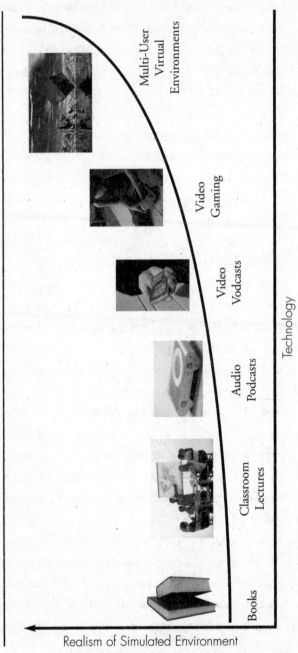

Figure 5.1

Realism of Simulated Environment

Books

Classroom Lectures

Audio Podcasts

Video Vodcasts

Video Gaming

Multi-User Virtual Environments

Technology

technologies. For example, research with virtual reality treatments for fear of flying has demonstrated remarkable success, far better than any other treatment regime.[8] In fact, all virtual reality treatments are vastly more successful than any less immersive techniques.

Now, I am not recommending that educators build virtual reality systems. What I am suggesting is that educators have the tools to create more immersive educational curricula that incorporates modern, tested technologies. Not only do these tools exist, but they are already being actively embraced by students, making them easier to use. I should warn the reader that I will be asking you to set aside what you believe about certain technologies, including social networks, video games, and virtual worlds. These are the educational paradigms of the future and, as you will see, tools of the present. In the rest of this chapter I will discuss how social networks, video games, and virtual worlds add realism and can serve as platforms for enhanced, immersive education.

Real People in Virtual Worlds: What *Is* Real?

In her seminal 1995 book, *Life on the Screen: Identity in the Age of the Internet,* MIT professor Sherry Turkle predicted that we would see "eroding boundaries between the real and the virtual, the animate and the inanimate, the unity and the multiple self."[9] Ten years before the emergence of social networking, Turkle foretold the impending change in the way children and teens have come to distinguish between their real life (RL) body and their screen life (SL) Internet persona.

Bursting onto the scene in 2003, MySpace rapidly became a leader in social networking, attracting mostly teens and young adults. By 2005, MySpace was adding hundreds of thousands of users *per day* and was embraced as a place to hang out, share thoughts, and, well, socialize. As of this writing, there are hundreds of social networks for teens, led by

MySpace and Facebook, and an equal number of social networks for children twelve and under, including the popular BarbieGirls ("the hottest online hangout for girls!"), Club Penguin, and Webkinz. In 2006, 18 percent of time spent online was on social networks. Just two years later that climbed to 32 percent.[10] Nearly all tweens and teens have at least one social networking profile—most have two or more—and literally more than one-third of a student's online time, at least one to two hours a day, is spent involved in some form of social networking.[11] In spite of the immense popularity of social networks among students, many schools have opted to listen to media-hyped dangers—sexual predators, cyberbullying, and pornography—and they have been banned from school computers. Some schools have even banned their students from having a social network profile, even if they access it from home.[12] As I will show you, by dismissing social networks, educators are missing an opportunity to design curricula with more immersive and engaging environments than the classroom usually offers.

Over the past few years, social networking has become more *mainstream*. According to a 2009 Harris poll, half of all American adults have either a MySpace or Facebook page.[13] I am not aware of any studies looking at the percentage of teachers who have their own Facebook or MySpace page, but Project Tomorrow's 2008 study found that one in three teachers already email their students, and 21 percent of them have their own personal websites, many of which we can assume are social networking sites because they are the easiest to set up and maintain.[14] Because the volume of social networking has been increasing dramatically, we can safely predict that the percentage of teachers with social networking pages has grown since that 2008 study. Anecdotally, many of the teachers in our research have told us that they have a Facebook page but, as Olivia, a teacher of seventh-grade English told us, *"It is a tricky issue of whether or not to have a page. We were told by our principal that it was up to us and the school was not going to set rules. However, he strongly discouraged personal self-disclosure and 'friending' students. A couple of my colleagues and I decided to have separate school-related Facebook accounts where we can friend students and use it for classroom information. Mine has been up for 6 months and I am gratified that so many students, often the ones who are too shy to come see me before or after school, reach out and connect with me on Facebook."*

Research has shown that teachers are no longer technological novices. Project Tomorrow's study found that one in three teachers felt that they were "experts" with classroom technology, and more than nine in ten were already using email to connect with parents. In addition, more than half used PowerPoint, and one in three even used podcasts and videos in class. Most telling, perhaps, was that "half the teachers were interested in learning how to integrate gaming and other technologies into their curriculum and half felt that adding new technologies, particularly mobile devices, to their educational repertoire would definitely increase student engagement."[15] Teachers are ready and willing to take educational technology to the next level. Their students are using social networks extensively. This is a perfect match. The key, however, is to adopt social networking to enhance classroom instruction and create a more immersive teaching platform.

It is important to step back for a moment and note that I am not saying that social networking tools should be used to supplant or replace the teacher. Nor am I saying that we should move education from the classroom to the computer room or the bedroom, where most of the students get online. As you will see in this chapter, the opportunities are there to use social networks to provide educational curricula, open additional channels of communication—between students, teachers, and parents—and engage the students.

Earlier in this book I discussed social networks and how they are so immensely popular with the iGeneration. Focusing on educational applications, there are two types of social networks—those using two-dimensional pages and those using simulated 3-D environments. The former include MySpace and Facebook, while the latter are led by Second Life. Both the 2-D and 3-D networks offer a variety of immersive educational opportunities. The main differences for educators are the skills needed to develop and implement educational curricula within these social networks and their technological requirements. 3-D social networks are most certainly the wave of the future. A recent Horizon Report[16] said that within two to three years virtual worlds will greatly impact teaching, learning, and creative expression and rated 3-D MUVEs (multiuser virtual environments) as a "technology to watch."[17] Other research predicts that virtual worlds will become commonplace among Internet users and will become primary teaching tools over the next five to ten years. But that is the future, and right now we have students, teachers, and parents actively using two-dimensional social networks. With that in mind, I will talk next about some very straightforward educational applications of social networks and will follow that up with some very exciting work being done with three-dimensional tools.

MySpace, Facebook, and Education . . . Oh My!

Social networking is just that—networking socially. But it is more than simply chatting back and forth about boyfriends or girlfriends, television shows, and movie stars. It is a multifaceted, multisensory environment where communication and content are the two key ingredients. Although social networks are not immersive learning environments, per se, they are platforms for creating a sense of realism particularly in the development and presentation of content and in their use of communication tools that students find engaging, and therefore more realistic. This makes social networks attractive educational environments because, after all, isn't communication and content, the passing on of knowledge, what education is all about? I am going to assume for the sake of argument that social networking will exist in some form or another for years to come and that it will continue to offer a wide range of tools (which I will describe below). Before doing so, however, it is important to delineate some of the natural objections to using social networking as a platform for education.

To put it bluntly, the media has done a hatchet job on social networks, particularly MySpace. As I mentioned in Chapter 1, since MySpace became a teen sensation it has been nearly impossible to find a positive article about social networking. Early on the press screamed about sexual predators roaming the Internet waiting to prey on unsuspecting teens. While the reports about sexual predators multiplied, cyberbullying became a hot topic, particularly in light of the Megan Meier case.[18] Our research of the major media outlets showed that the negative press began spiraling out of control in 2005, appeared to peak in 2008, and began leveling off in 2009.[19] In some media outlets, particularly major newspapers, the anti-MySpace press actually decreased in 2009, and more positive media messages are starting to appear. Interestingly, Facebook, which has eclipsed MySpace in monthly visitors,[20] appears to garner much less negative press, perhaps due to its beginnings as a university network. It is precisely this dark shadow clouding social networks that has made educators shy away. With the negative press abating, and a major research report by Harvard's Berkman Center for Internet & Society showing that social networks are not riddled with bad people threatening teenagers, it is now possible to see how to mine this teen mainstay for educational purposes.

What do social networks have to offer education? First, and foremost, the students love them and are engaged with them for hours each day (and night). Second, they offer many vehicles for the transmission of information in a variety of modalities and they link to all parts of the Internet to provide nearly unlimited access to information sources. Third, they provide for connectedness, communication, and group learning. Fourth, they support cooperative learning, where students help each other in a collaborative environment. Finally, they present an environment that is more immersive than the classroom. The following is a partial list of what social networks have to offer for education.

- **Rich multimedia information sources:** Social networks and the Internet offer informative digital content through the printed word, spoken word, music, photos, videos, video games, and even simulated virtual environments. Curriculum materials have been developed in all of these modalities and can serve students simultaneously. For example, a student could go online to learn about the ancient Incas by reading materials on a website, viewing historical photos, listening to an audio podcast by an archaeologist on a dig in South America, watching a vodcast (video podcast) by an expert halfway around the world answering questions at a press conference, playing a video game simulating Incan life, conversing with experts through online discussions, or even entering a virtual Incan village. In an interview about writing a report on the Incan civilization, eleven-year-old Frankee told me, *"I talked to someone I know on MySpace who told me about a college class where the teacher had his lectures online. He was pretty interesting and I found a good lecture and watched part of it and then went to Google and found some amazing photos and even a high school class that did a video reenactment of an Incan ceremony. That sent me to YouTube which had more videos by other people and I ended up with a report that had two pages of sources. I not only got an A but my teacher showed my report to the whole* *class."* Information obtained on the Internet can be as rich and detailed as the technology will allow and can be tailored to the learner by presenting it in a variety of formats, reaching a variety of senses. For Frankee the video format was exciting and engaging. But one size does not have to fit all, and the materials are already available online. The materials may not be hosted on a social network, but the network can be the launching platform. Although the issue of media literacy will be discussed in detail in a later chapter, it is worth noting here that educators who are able to incorporate this type of immersion in class can help students better navigate the information and discriminate between what is accurate and what might not be. But if teachers do not engage students on this level, the students may be seeking it out independently—without a critical eye to judge between fact and fiction—and may not be capable of making the best choices for accurate information.

- **Microcontent:** Given the nature of our multitasking, rapidly task-switching iGeners, information can be provided in digestible bites that can be combined to provide a complete learning experience. I am not suggesting we turn education into a CNN-like news ticker or a 250-word article in *People* magazine. However, we can take advantage of the attractive multimedia vehicles to sustain attention and direct the learner to the next digestible bite. Watch a fourteen-year-old looking at YouTube videos and you will see how, after each video, they simply slide right into the next one from a list of suggested related videos. Curriculum material in the form of a series of short videos linked together as a whole unit would appeal to iGen students as would print and audio information. The simultaneous availability of different paths to knowledge, offering students the option to click on links to video or audio commentaries about a topic, for example, also lets them have some control over their own pace and path of learning.

- **Collaboration and community building:** The strongest draw of social networking is communication. Students post their thoughts on Facebook walls, share their feelings in blogs, and are eager to write in response to others' thoughts. Tools are available to support and enhance interaction. For example, most universities use an interactive system such as Blackboard or WebCT Vista, which promote threaded topic discussions. In my classes I often post a discussion question following a class session and ask students to respond to my question and to read and respond to others' comments with a stem of "I agree with you because . . ." or "I disagree with you because . . ." Similar tools are available in the form of blogs, wikis, bulletin boards, online discussion groups, and more. Wikis are particularly interesting collaborative tools. A wiki (as in Wikipedia; the term derives from the Hawaiian *wiki wiki* = very quick) allows students to cowrite a document, meaning that they can add information, edit others' writing, and produce a report that is a combined group effort. All of these joint efforts lead to establishing a sense of community that is often difficult to promote in school. Many schools require group projects in which students work together during and sometimes after class, but classroom time constraints from the required curriculum limit those options. On a social network students can form and re-form working groups throughout the school year and work on projects seamlessly online, allowing classroom time to be allocated for other purposes. In essence, a teacher is able to foster a sense of community that is continually shifting, allowing for the development of subgroup relationships within the context of the larger classroom that would be impossible in our school-based educational system.

- **Synchronous and asynchronous communication modes:** School is synchronous; teachers talk and students learn in real time in the classroom. Communication technologies range on a continuum from synchronous to asynchronous, depending on how long a pause there is between the communication being sent and a response being returned. Email, for example, can be very asynchronous if a response takes a day or two, or nearly synchronous if the recipient responds as soon as the email is received. The same is true for instant messaging, text messaging, and any form of electronic communication. Social networks allow for both synchronous and asynchronous communication and collaboration that enables "school" to be available 24/7. For example, Don, an eighth-grader who struggles with math, was getting nowhere with his homework at 11 P.M. and was feeling stressed, as were his mom and dad who were unable to help him. He went on MySpace, found a classmate online and had a quick instant message chat. It all took about ten minutes and they figured out what he was doing wrong. Using a more asynchronous tool for her senior project in psychology, Andrea, a twelfth-grader, was required to interview three "experts" about the impact of video games on violence. Using a Facebook search she found that I had written an article on that topic, went to my website, found my address, and emailed me with three short questions that I was happy to answer. On social networks students have an array of synchronous tools (chat, web cameras), asynchronous tools (email, wall postings, blogs, wikis, bulletin boards, or video blogs), and those in between (text messaging, instant messaging), all of which afford communication and the ability to gather information through a variety of sources either immediately or with a delay. More important, they are all communication methods that iGeners access on a daily basis, so the instruction time can be extended into their after-school routine.

- **Personalized learning through repetition—24/7**: Repetition is the key to learning. That is one of the major benefits of putting curriculum materials online and having collaborative online projects. At any time of the day or night the student can review a podcast or vodcast, reread an online discussion, or access a world of information to reinforce learning. Online material can stay online forever. In fact, former students have come back years after graduation to tell me that they had their parents or friends watch a video that I had posted online about parenting the iGeneration. But not all students learn the same way or through the same senses. Providing online material in a variety of formats gives each student an opportunity to personalize his or her education. Using online educational resources modifies the teacher's responsibility from being the sole dispenser of information to helping her determine which materials are best suited to a particular student. With a classroom social network, teachers can follow the progress of each student and continually assess how that student is performing and suggest alternative approaches or material that will help facilitate learning. This model also affords parents the same benefits of monitoring their children's progress and being able to work with their child and the teacher to provide a personalized educational delivery method. The curriculum remains the same while the delivery methods can be tailored to the individual. This is one of the major benefits for students, parents, and teachers in moving parts of the educational curriculum to a social network.

- **Social interaction**: The primary activity on social networks, naturally, is being social. This may seem obvious, but it is an important part of why these online communities are ripe for educational use. In school the amount of time for actual socializing outside the classroom is severely limited. Due to financial cutbacks, time between classes has been limited to just a few minutes, while lunch time has been continually reduced to where there is just enough time to gulp down food. After-school time is either filled with clubs, sports, or, for most students, going right home to an empty house while both parents work. So students go home, open their laptops, sit on their beds and connect. At any time there are dozens of available "friends," most of whom are RL (real life) friends, but some who are SL (screen life) friends. If you read MySpace or Facebook pages, you will see that a lot of the communication is between fellow students and some of that is about homework, tests, and reports. Add to this the fact that these students are also sending text messages to their friends and you have a social communication network in place that yields far more abundant and rich communication than could possibly transpire during regular school hours. This social environment can be and has been tailored to promote learning and classroom interaction outside the actual school buildings. Understandably parents and teachers are concerned that online socialization is not really the same as talking to friends face-to-face. However, a major study of online education found that second-, fourth-, and sixth-grade schoolchildren who took online courses in lieu of attending school actually had *better* social skills and *fewer* behavioral problems than children of the same age who worked in the school classroom.[21]

- **Disinhibition and identity development:** Psychologists such as James Marcia, Carl Rogers, Erving Goffman, and Erik Erikson have stressed that the major psychological work of adolescence is identity development and discovery of the "self." Although this is not directly related to education, per se, it is an important aspect of social networks that affects a student's approach to education. Because I have covered this extensively as it relates to child rearing in my earlier book, *Me, MySpace, and I: Parenting the Net Generation,* I will simply note that children and teenagers feel a sense of safety being "behind the screen," and this leads to disinhibition, or the willingness to provide more personal self-disclosure, which, in turn, leads to more closeness to others.[22] In a classroom setting, many students are hesitant to speak up and express their opinions due to shyness, self-consciousness, or an awkwardness that is part of teen development. Online, however, and particularly in social networking environments, shy students are no longer self-conscious, and the environment itself, with its personality tests, wall postings, music, video, and other personal self-representations, promotes honesty and bonding. According to danah boyd, a social media researcher at Microsoft and a fellow at Harvard Law School's Berkman Center for Internet & Society:

> The way you develop your identity is to put things out there, get feedback, and adjust accordingly. You develop an internal model of yourself and balance this with reactions from other people. This is what Erving Goffman called "impression management." Doing this online allows you to be more reflective about whom you are. On MySpace, for example, you have to write yourself into being; in other words, you have to craft an impression of yourself that stands on its own. For today's teens, it's just an-

other step in the path of figuring out who you are. And figuring out who you are requires being social.[23]

As you can see, social networking can and should be a strong, effective educational tool for the presentation of material in a variety of multimedia formats that can be viewed and reviewed at any time, and for extensive social interaction that facilitates collaborative projects. All of this happens in a two-dimensional world that is more immersive than the classroom. It is also important to note that teachers may have the benefit of other educators who are already working diligently on creating lesson plans and reproducible, adaptable models for using social networking as a teaching vehicle. The most recent National Educational Computing Conference in Washington, D.C., included a substantial number of presentations on this topic, including:[24]

- Beyond Gathering: Converting Social Networking into Collaborations and Synergy
- Building Collaborative Learning and Inclusive Practices through Curricular Social Networking
- Build Your Own Social Network or Community
- Creating a Social Network: The Walled Garden Approach
- Staying Connected: Teaching and Learning in a Facebook World.

Teachers are already jumping on board and creating platforms for adapting social networking to the classroom. Tools are readily available for making podcasts, vodcasts, and other multimedia presentations and, given teachers' interest in online educational tools, there are powerful reasons for exploring these social networking opportunities.

There are, however, existing tools that provide educational models that are even more immersive and provide even more realism and, therefore, more positive benefits. One surprising tool is video games. According to a recent national survey, 92 percent of children two to seventeen years old play video games, with two-thirds of adolescents playing daily.[25] In my own research, these children are playing games an average of one to two hours a day.[26] Once considered a toy for boys, video game players are now equally likely to be girls.[27] Conventional wisdom looks at video games as "toys" rather than potential educational vehicles. According to Steven Johnson, author of *Everything Bad Is Good for You,* "You can't get much more conventional than the conventional wisdom that kids today would be better off spending more time reading books, and less time zoning out in front of their video games." In support of the educational potential of games, Johnson goes on to say that, "I worry about the experiential gap between people who have immersed themselves in games, and people who have only heard secondhand reports, because the gap makes it difficult to discuss the meaning of games in a coherent way. It's not *what* you're thinking about when you're playing a game, it's *the way* you're thinking that matters."[28]

It is striking that parents and teachers shun video games when one of the main teaching tools in the lower elementary school classes has always involved the use of "games." I am not talking about violent video games, such as *Grand Theft Auto,* that have been shown to be related to aggressive behavior. Consider, however, a nonviolent game such as *SimCity,* in which the focus is on developing and planning a city, adding buildings, dealing with transportation and utilities, and even planning disaster services. A wide variety of *SimCity* scenarios exist, with millions of copies sold since its release in 1989, making it one of the all-time top-selling video games. Steven Johnson relates a story in his book about playing *SimCity* with his seven-year-old nephew and reports, "My nephew would be asleep in five seconds if you popped him down in an urban studies classroom, but somehow an hour of playing SimCity taught him that high tax rates in industrial areas can stifle development."[29] What is it about *SimCity* and other video games that are so attractive that iGeners will play them for hours on end?

First, and foremost, video games are replete with positive reinforcers. Have your character complete a task and you gain new powers. This is positive reinforcement and, according to decades of psychological research by B. F. Skinner, Albert Bandura, and others, if the reward is important enough to the person it will lead to more of the same behavior. In the context of a video game it is these reinforcers that keep the gamer engaged in pursuing a goal. The Federation of American Scientists (FAS),[30] an organization that boasts eighty-four Nobel Prize winners on its board of sponsors, has stated, "video games are the next great discovery, as they offer a way to captivate students to the point that they will spend hours learning on their own time."[31] This is the power of positive reinforcement. In essence, video games such as FAS-developed *Immune Attack, Discover Babylon,* and *Digital Human,* provide students "stealth learning," or the development of skills and knowledge outside the bounds of the traditional classroom.[32]

Second, contemporary video games bear little resemblance to arcade precursors such as *Pong* and *Pac-Man.* They feature lifelike, three-dimensional worlds and characters that can be made as realistically human or as science fiction–like as the player desires. Third, and most important for educators, off-the-rack educational video games and research-developed games are available for free from organizations such as FAS or at reasonable costs from other sources. Thousands of titles are available, including *Civilizations, Age of Empires,* and *Zoo Tycoon,* to name just a few. All incorporate key elements of learning, including logic, memory, problem-solving strategies, critical thinking, and visualization skills. Studies have shown educational video games to be superior for teaching, even when compared to other forms of computer-assisted instruction (CAI) in which remedial students learned tutorial material in more drill-and-practice environments with primitive games or simulations. In one study, for example, third graders who used a video game to learn about firefighting techniques and dangers recalled more facts and demonstrated more understanding of solving problems through multiple means than did a comparable group using computer-assisted instruction.[33]

Educators such as James Paul Gee, a trailblazer in championing the educational value of video games, views them as "edutainment" in which what psychologists refer to as "transformational play" allows students to become active protagonists while they interact with other characters and environments to identify and solve problems.[34] According to Gee, this involves two processes—a *probing cycle* and *telescoping*. The probing cycle challenges the student—actually the student's character—to look around his virtual world to see what is there, form hypotheses about various objects and actions that are available, test those hypotheses, observe the effects, and use the feedback to accept or reject the hypotheses and begin the cycle once again. All the while, the student gamer must use telescoping to keep in mind the ultimate long-term goal and create a working plan to attain that goal. All of these are critical-thinking skills using the scientific method that educators have taught for years; video games offer an environment, as every parent is acutely aware, to keep students happily probing and telescoping for hours. Whenever a new game arrives on the market, children beg their parents to wait in line for hours or pay monthly fees for access to the game and the ultimate positive reinforcement of beating the game. Interestingly, these "games" (3-D, virtual-reality simulations) have been used for years to train military personnel, firefighters, and surgeons, and they are becoming increasingly more popular as educational tools.

The Next Step: Virtual Worlds

In Figure 5.1 I depicted a spectrum of educational tools, from those that use fewer senses and are less immersive to those engaging more senses and more realism. Video games reenact many sensory cues including motion and balance, and with today's high-speed processors, advanced video game systems can manifest a nearly 3-D look in a 2-D world. They certainly are realistic enough that they incorporate many more senses than any other educational tools . . . until the appearance of fully immersible websites such as Second Life. On its website, Second Life is described as "an online, 3-D virtual world imagined and created by its residents."[35] Launched in 2003, Second Life, and its youth counterpart Teen Second Life, is a website based on three-dimensional modeling technology that allows its users (residents) to meet and socialize with other people, participate in a variety of activities, and, most important, create complex objects, buildings, and environments using simple "sculpted prims," or "sculpties" as they are known to Second Lifers. These created buildings are, to most people, unimaginable in a two-dimensional world, so let me describe a few typical islands as they are configured in Second Life and other virtual worlds.[36]

- The Sistine Chapel with its art and architecture in minute detail
- A fully functional ecology system complete with plants, animals, bugs, flowers, birds, and constantly changing weather systems
- The International Spaceflight Museum, which includes a planetarium, virtual solar system, and a virtual telescope
- A biology lab complete with an array of virtual experiments
- A mock legal system created by Harvard's Berkman Center for Internet & Society
- A virtual writing course hosted by Ball State University.

The Federation of American Scientists (FAS) lists more than 150 educational virtual worlds created by people around the globe, with most for primary and secondary students;[37] and Second Life in Education[38] lists hundreds of additional educational islands; and Active Worlds Educational Universe—another virtual world—hosts nearly a hundred educational worlds. The Horizon Report from New Media Consortium and Educause mentioned earlier predicted in 2007 that virtual learning spaces such as Second Life will be adopted on a wide basis in education within five years, and it appears from a cursory look at the islands already created that we are well on our way to a wealth of educational choices within virtual worlds.[39]

Besides the ability to create entire worlds, what makes Second Life work is the creation of your personal user identity in the form of an avatar. An avatar is an alter ego that the virtual world resident creates to represent himself in the 3-D world. The avatar can take a variety of forms, from human or animal to robot or otherworldly beast. The shape and characteristics are continually modifiable. A three-year study in Australia concluded, "A natural outcome of customization of the avatar is the user's identification with his or her avatar, an embodiment that can transform the space of a virtual world into a sense of place [grounding] the experience of the player in a sense of presence with others, allowing for an opportunity to truly engage in the play of imagination."[40]

Your avatar can traverse a virtual world by walking, riding vehicles, flying, and even teleporting to specific locations. For example, if your avatar wanted to visit the Gene Pool, a genetics learning lab, you could simply type in the location name and your avatar would be transported to that island. On the other hand, perhaps a nice stroll there might lead to some interesting experiences along the way. What is special about avatars, beyond their visual three-dimensionality, is that they can use gestures, express emotions, and talk to other people using either a synthesized voice or text chats. With the exception of teleportation and fly-ing, the laws of physics in the real world are represented in virtual worlds, which means that skills you use in the real world transfer fairly easily to the virtual environment.

When you first visit a virtual world such as Second Life you will see that it looks very lifelike—with islands such as the Sistine Chapel being amazingly detailed—and the longer you practice the more you feel a "social presence" or a sense of connectedness to this virtual world. What is interesting is that when you first begin to control your avatar you feel totally inept. But, after just a short time traversing these educational is-lands, you have a sense of being totally immersed in whatever you are seeing, and your avatar literally feels like an extension of your physical body. It is difficult to explain how that happens, but since you can be-come a Second Lifer for free and visit quite a few places through tele-portation, I urge readers to try it. You will see how profoundly stimulating it can be and how much promise it has for educating stu-dents who have grown up with these types of technologies.

I observed Courtney, a fifteen-year-old high school student who had an assignment to write about Mayan culture, visit Mayan Myst and nav-igate her way around while she took notes about what she saw and learned. Courtney described her experience: *"Last semester in AP history class I had to do a PowerPoint about Babylonian culture and its artifacts. That was BSL (before Second Life). I spent days collecting pictures off the web and trying to find some interesting facts for my project. Quite honestly I was bored by the time I was done. It felt so dull and dry and even though I got an A I really didn't feel like I knew that much beyond what ended up in my PowerPoint. This is amazing!!! I actually feel like I am seeing Mayan cul-ture firsthand. It makes it so real and so much more interesting. Last night I spent hours visiting this island and others and I stayed up until past mid-night and didn't even realize how late it was."* To Courtney, who was a straight-A student in all advanced placement and honors classes, Second Life offered a more engaging, compelling lesson about Mayan culture.

But it is not just the A students who get excited about virtual worlds. At a recent conference I chatted with a special education teacher named Sarah about what she was doing to get her fourth-grade students excited about art. She wanted them to understand the brilliance and beauty of Michelangelo's art and had shown them pictures in books and slides and watched them slip into that glazed, bored stare after just a few minutes. A colleague had talked to her about the Sistine Chapel Second Life site and she set up her classroom computer and took her avatar on a tour. The kids were so excited that she arranged for her class to visit the computer lab, create avatars, and learn more about this amazing work of art. Sarah wrote: *"I was almost in tears watching the children moving their avatars all around the chapel and actually looking at the art. About half the kids begged me to let them stay longer and when I told them that the lab was scheduled for another class they asked when they could do it again. I spent the rest of the semester taking them on a virtual tour of Europe, both present and past, and plan on starting my new kids this fall with an avatar the first week of class. It is amazing to watch how technology can finally be used as more than just a babysitter."* Sarah's view of the usefulness of virtual world technology was validated by a study at Penn State University in which researchers set up teams who watched a video on eagles and then were asked to solve a problem posed by that video about how to rescue an injured eagle. Teams worked either face-to-face or as groups of avatars on Second Life. Interestingly, although the face-to-face groups felt more confident about their solutions, the Second Life groups provided the most accurate solutions.[41]

Listening to Sarah, I began to recognize that the role of "teacher" is going to change. Certainly there will always be classroom instruction, and the teacher will still be *the teacher*. But the use of virtual worlds for instruction changes the focus of the learner from a passive receptacle to an active engager, ever more responsible for his own acquisition of knowledge. Sarah's students were not told what to do when they entered the Sistine Chapel. They moved their avatars around and explored on their own as an adult might do in a chapel or museum.

So what happens to teachers if students are learning from self-navigated virtual worlds? According to Professor Zane Berge, an authority on distance learning and the developer of the Instructor's Roles Model,[42] teachers function in four areas: pedagogical, social, managerial, and technical. The teacher's *pedagogical* role moves from an "instructor" to a facilitator. The teacher will be the one responsible for seeking out virtual worlds that match the curriculum content and supplementing it with auxiliary materials. The teacher's *social* role also changes from being solely a classroom monitor to being a virtual guide and supervising on-task behavior which, as research has shown, is quite easy in such an engaging 3-D world. The most important role for the teacher is now managerial, where she has to determine how the material from the virtual world will be integrated into her curriculum and how to turn an exciting 3-D tour of Babylon, for example, into a classroom discussion. Finally, the teacher now must be a *technical advisor* to her students, giving support on how to navigate these virtual worlds (although if the teachers, parents, and children I have interviewed are any indication, it is the students who will be supplying the technical support to the teachers).

To be sure, engaging students through virtual worlds is not without its challenges. First, it is time-consuming for the teacher to explore alternatives and determine the most appropriate teaching tools. Luckily, there are many websites directing teachers to appropriate virtual worlds, plus online discussions with other teachers already using these tools.[43] Second, there are potential budgetary concerns, including making sure that the hardware has a broadband connection plus a decent video card.

Third, if a teacher decides to create her own "island" it can be both time-consuming and costly. However, there are nonprofit groups that offer virtual world space at a low cost. Finally, there are the sociopsychological issues to deal with in having students online, managing avatars, and interacting with other classmates and quite possibly people who are not class members. These are all part of the teacher's changing social role as described above in Berge's model. The teacher must become aware of issues that go beyond the instructional material, but, then again, aren't these issues similar to those in the physical classroom?

Real or Virtual?

As I have said throughout this chapter, the more realism there is in teaching methods and learning environments, the more education will appeal to our media-savvy, always wired students. Those environments with more realism give students something familiar, a medium with which they are already comfortable. They are more authentic, and promote more investigation and exploration. Further, they encourage more social interaction and more student-to-student collaboration, enable learners to guide their own educational path within the constraints of the technology, and allow for learning to take place anywhere and anytime. The technology is improving and already available. It is up to you, the parents and teachers, to be willing to be the forerunners and take that small leap from the classroom to the virtual world. To quote Professor Siân Bayne of the University of Edinburgh:

> Students immersed in Second Life and other virtual worlds . . . move beyond the weird ontology of the avatar to the nature of being a learner across the digital and material domains.[44]

Too much of our current classroom education is flat and two-dimensional. With the power of virtual worlds and twenty-first-century video gaming, it is time to take education into three-dimensional worlds that are both closer to real life than traditional instructional materials and mimic the environments that are already exciting and engaging for today's students. In this chapter I have looked at these iGen students as learners in already developed 3-D worlds. In the next chapter I will explore the active, creative side of this generation who loves to build its own content, whether it is written, audio, video, or an amalgamated product that reaches as many of the nineteen senses as possible. The key to education is: Build it and they will come, and then they will build more . . . and have fun doing it.

Chapter 6

Tapping into a Very Creative Generation of Students

I stay up late almost every night working on the computer in my room. My parents think I am doing homework but actually I'm working on my My-Space page. I love letting my friends know what is going on with me, adding my favorite videos, writing about my feelings in my blog.

—LaTonya, age fourteen

Social network sites, online games, video-sharing sites, and gadgets such as iPods and mobile phones are now fixtures of youth culture. They have so permeated young lives that it is hard to believe that less than a decade ago these technologies barely existed. Today's youth may be coming of age and struggling for autonomy and identity as did their predecessors, but they are doing so amid new worlds for communication, friendship, play, and self-expression.

—Digital Youth Project, John D. and Catherine T. MacArthur Foundation[1]

According to studies by the Pew Internet & American Life Project, a nationally recognized "nonprofit fact tank that provides information on the issues, attitudes and trends shaping America and the world," the vast majority of teens have created their own content for the Internet, including blogs, web pages, artwork, photography, stories, and videos.[2]

Cumulatively, a vast amount of effort and activity has been expended by adolescents to generate web-based content. And what is the result of this vast expenditure of effort? For many critics of modern society, the result is an international, virtual wasteland of meaningless and trivial videos, narratives, and photographs that misdirect the public away from "real" content created by knowing experts or accomplished artists. Andrew Keen, author of the best-selling *Cult of the Amateur: How Blogs, My-Space, YouTube, and the Rest of Today's User-Generated Media Are Destroying Our Economy, Our Culture, and Our Values,* expressed it this way:

> Web 2.0 and this user-generated media is encouraging us to self-broadcast ourselves. That's fragmenting mainstream media. We're losing the message. We're creating 250 million messages. We're learning what I'll have for breakfast tomorrow and that's not really interesting for me or for anybody else.[3]

Opinions like this are reinforced by a cursory review of some of the "most viewed" content on YouTube. As I am writing this, today's most-viewed video clips on YouTube include a teenage girl's diatribe about how Miley Cyrus has been brainwashed, a young man's review of the newest Harry Potter film (opening with a sexualized reference to the lead actress in the movie), and a junior high school student's home video of his older brother getting mad at the microwave oven for not cooking his food quickly enough. Since being posted two days ago, this last video has been viewed 190,756 times! While acknowledging that "content" such as these videos posted on the World Wide Web by kids nowadays perhaps is lacking in quality and substance and probably serves mostly as an outlet for their creative energies, this chapter is about how to redirect the intense activity spent making new content away from what critics believe is mindless junk and toward meaningful, education-related projects. This chapter will explore the vast arena of creative activities that we see on MySpace, YouTube, Second Life, and a variety of websites that offer palettes for creativity among children and adolescents.

UGC: What It Is and How They Make It

When young kids go online, they are not passive viewers of information provided by corporations, businesses, and government organizations. That's the old World Wide Web. The new web, dubbed "Web 2.0" for its enhanced opportunities for self-expression, allows individuals to add their own content to that currently existing online. Adding new information ranges from basic acts of creation such as rating a product on Amazon.com to seemingly complex acts of creating entire websites complete with logos, photos, videos, commentary, and links to other websites. This is what experts call "user-generated content"—UGC for short—and it can take many forms, including audio, video, information, and opinion, and can also involve contributions from others. The forms of UGC are limited only by the technological tools available to web users. For example, hosting sites such as YouTube provide a blank slate for individuals to add content that has the power to reach people around the world, to change opinions, or to entertain. And it's not just personal computers with web browsers that allow access to the creative act of making UGC. It's also video game platforms, personal digital assistants (PDAs) and smartphones. Here, for example, is what Sony—the manufacturer of the PlayStation3 video game console—says about its online PlayStation Network that is accessible through the video game console and the television: "Find friends. Download demos. Join the conversation."[4]

Virtually any act by a web user that alters the information on the web in any way can be considered user-generated content. The simple act of posting a link from one website to another alters the web experience for other users, potentially in ways that can have a profound impact on that experience. One of the most famous sites of UGC on the web is Wikipedia, of course, where anybody in the world can help write—and rewrite—encyclopedia-like entries about any topic. The ultimate goal of Wikipedia is to accumulate the collective knowledge of the world. According to Wikipedia, UGC is defined as "various kinds of media content, publicly available, that are produced by end-users." Wikipedia goes on to list several examples of websites on which the following different types of UGC can be found: discussion boards, blogs, wikis, social networking, news, trip planners, photos and videos, customer review sites, audios, video games, and any other website that offers the opportunity for consumers to share their knowledge and familiarity with a product or experience.[5] From this extensive list, it is clear that students have a multitude of different content options and, as the Pew study mentioned earlier confirms, they are taking advantage of these opportunities and making contributions to web content.

But are these contributions frivolous, as suggested above by Andrew Keen, or do they have substance that offers options for enhancing educational engagement among our students? I believe that there are a multitude of options that are worth exploring. Let's face it, kids today *like* to create using technology. They find it fun and spend hours producing unique content every day. In one study of more than 1,200 Net-Geners and iGeners, we found that 39 percent of them spent one hour per week working on their MySpace pages, another 22 percent spent two to three hours, and 25 percent worked more than three hours per week on creating and modifying their online content.[6] Their most common activities were posting their own photographs and videos and writing anywhere and everywhere, including on blogs, commenting on other MySpacers' writing, and writing back and forth with friends. This generation thrives on creating online content, and the rest of this chapter will explore options for including these activities as part of a new, rewired educational approach.

iGeners Like to Write . . . On the Web

Yes, iGeners spend hours each day writing. However, writing online does not take the traditional form of writing essays with the formal structure of a thesis paragraph, main body, and conclusion. Researchers and observers of social trends call much of the writing online "new texts."[7] These new texts are not limited to words; they are not limited by classic rules of grammar, and they certainly are not limited to standard page layouts. New texts often are multimodal, meaning they may incorporate visual elements, sound, and links to other texts or information. Online journals, typically in the form of blogs, dominate kids' online writing activities, although other forms of online writing are also popular, such as wikis, product or movie reviews, social networking pages, text messaging, email, and chatting.

The arena for writing new texts is decidedly less formal than the traditional classroom. Kids online do not feel limited to rules of syntax and grammar, nor to spelling conventions, as they generate content. There is a whole new world of phrases, spellings, abbreviations, and acronyms on the Internet, and this "netspeak" pervades online writing, especially when one looks at new texts in situations such as social networks where kids make their own user-generated content. In our own research looking at netspeak, we asked our young adult subjects to tell us how often they used certain "textisms," which included four that were language-based, or indicated versions of words or combinations of words. These include:

- Acronyms such as LOL (laughing out loud), L8R (later, or see you later), and 2nite (tonight)

- Replacing uppercase "I" with a lowercase "i"
- Removing apostrophes from contractions, as in dont for don't
- Shortening words such as "tht" for that or "u" for you.

We also examined three contextual textisms that provided emotions or feelings, including:

- Inserting emoticons such as ☺ (to indicate happiness) or ☹ (to indicate sadness or displeasure)
- Using special characters to denote or emphasize emotional states, such as *frown* or ::hugs::
- Using all capital letters to denote strong emotions such as I AM ANGRY AT YOU.

These are not the only available textisms. Other authors[8] have expanded the definition of language-based textisms to include:

- g clippings such as goin instead of going
- Nonconventional (sometimes phonetic) spellings such as fone for phone
- Accent stylization such as "elp" as a replacement for help.

Before sharing what we found in our research, an important question looms: What effect will participating in the world of netspeak have on the writing skills of students? A recent *USA Today* magazine article[9] entitled "Texting, Testing Destroys Kids' Writing Styles" appears to support these claims, quoting Jacquie Ream, author of *KISS: Keep It Short and Simple,*[10] a book on writing:

These kids aren't learning to spell. They're learning acronyms and shorthand. Text messaging is destroying the written word. Students aren't writing letters; they're typing into their cell phones one line at a time. Feelings aren't communicated with words when you're texting; emotions are sideways smiley faces. Kids are typing shorthand jargon that isn't even a complete thought.

In response to this, David Crystal, a world-renowned linguist and author on the uses of the English language, wrote in his book *Txting: The Gr8 Db8*:[11]

> I do not see how texting could be a significant factor when discussing children who have real problems with literacy. If you have difficulty with reading and writing, you are hardly going to be predisposed to use a technology which demands sophisticated abilities in reading and writing. And if you do start to text, I would expect the additional experience of writing to be a help, rather than a hindrance.

Well, despite the many outcries from educators, public policy makers, and parents that kids' writing skills are getting worse, there actually is very little hard data to substantiate that claim.[12] In fact, surprising data from my laboratory and that of others including Professor Beverly Plester and her colleagues at Coventry University in England suggest that the form of writing produced in technology-based environments can have positive effects.[13] Plester, for example, reported that her research with preteen children showed, "It is clear also that it [texting] does not contribute to the demise of pre-teen children's literacy."[14]

In our own applied cognition laboratory we tested more than seven hundred American young adults in two separate studies on their ability to produce formal and informal (creative) writing samples and looked at how their writing skills may be affected by their daily use of textisms. The results of the study found that engaging in texting in everyday communication had mixed results on formal writing, helping some and hindering others. Strikingly, we found that it had positive effects on informal writing.[15] Those students who used more textisms in their daily writing produced better informal essays. This matches the conclusion of Plester's work in England. According to the British press, "Fears that text messaging may have ruined the ability of teenagers to write properly have been shown to be unfounded after a two-year study revealed that youngsters are more literate than ever before."[16]

Researchers have also asked whether students truly use lots of textisms in their text messages, instant messages, email, and online writing. Although parents and teachers worry that these shortcuts are prevalent in student writing, quite the opposite is true. Professor Sali Tagliamonte and his colleagues at the University of Toronto looked at more than one million words from instant messages sent by seventy-two teenagers and found that only slightly more than 2 percent of those words were textisms.[17] These staggering results have been replicated in other studies,[18] including our own, in which we found only between two and three textisms in the formal and informal essays written by young adults.[19]

To the degree that there is there any downside to texting or any risk to the student that textisms or netspeak might creep into formal writing assignments, remember that assignments are constructed by teachers and that teachers can provide guidelines of what is appropriate and what is not when writing for assignments. Now, if we consider formal spelling and grammar, we have to accept that writing on the web, by kids when they are at home or at their friends' houses, will not hold muster when evaluated by school criteria. Some researchers looking at students' use of new media have noted this issue exactly, but do not dismiss *new texts* because of it. Rather, they focus on the positive aspects of creating new texts. Many of the nongrammatical aspects of writing, such as considering the audience, constructing a persuasive argument, and organizing a coherent text still apply to writing when making new texts. A study conducted by Denise Sevick Bortree at the University of Florida used anthropological methods to analyze the online journals of a group of teenage girls in the United States. Instead of looking at the spelling, grammar, and formal style of the journal entries, the study addressed deeper issues of content in the journals. What was found was that the act of writing in the journals required consideration of the audience (personal friends versus mass audience) and of the purpose of the entry (disclosing personal information versus convincing others of one's popularity).[20] These clearly are important high-level writing skills.

Already some teachers around the world have been using new media–based exercises to engage their students in learning that more faithfully represents twenty-first-century, technologically based skills. Drawing from their experiences with computer-based, online writing exercises, teachers argue that such projects take advantage of content creation skills that students already possess by virtue of being members of a tech-savvy generation. Further, these teachers point out the possibility that knowing how to make effective written arguments, even those that are crafted using technology and English language shortcuts, may be more relevant to future job skills than knowing how to construct old-fashioned essays.[21] Additionally, it has been noted repeatedly that kids *like* making online content. In other words, iGeners naturally are motivated to make new texts, especially when they will have a "real" audience on the Internet. Anastasia Goodstein, author of *Totally Wired: What Teens and Tweens Are Really Doing Online,* summarized the motivational aspect of creating content this way: "Kids want to have a say—and even some ownership—in the products and content they use. And the more opportunities they have to personalize these things, the more engaged they'll be."[22]

There are many ways that teachers can engage students in writing within a creative, digital framework. Here are some examples of how some teachers have used user-generated content in their classes:

- Junior high school teachers in Taiwan used the web as a place for posting portfolios of students' work in a computer course and found that these web-based portfolios improved the quality of the portfolios compared to traditional paper-based portfolios.[23]

- A public school technology coordinator has worked with teachers to implement student blogs in courses and found that blogging improved students' writing about history.[24]

- Instructors at an undergraduate teacher preparation program found that using wikis in classroom assignments increased students' motivation levels. The students used the online collaborative aspect of wikis to come to a shared understanding of the course content.[25]

- A computer science instructor allowed students to send text messages to him during class to clarify lecture material, and students reported that it facilitated in-class participation more than raising hands and asking questions.[26]

These are but a few of the tools that encourage students to write. As more teachers take advantage of the fact that students write prolifically in their personal worlds, and as teachers develop writing exercises using those same technologies, they will find that students are engaged in and enjoy writing far beyond their typical classroom writing assignments or reports.

Beyond Words: Adding Video

If we look at what iGeneration kids are doing online when it comes to making video clips, we can see that what constitutes a "video" is not easy to define. Typically, when we think of videos, we think of movies—like those shown in the classroom—that tell an educational story using words, sounds, and pictures, usually resulting in some major point or set of points to be learned. Often they are brutally boring and many are outdated (often because the budget doesn't permit buying new ones). But online, outside of the classroom, these same students are using videos that look nothing like these classroom movie templates. It's true that their videos do contain pictures or moving images, some sounds and/or words, and are created to make a point. Yet, the point being made might not be apparent to the mass audience; it might only be apparent to a small circle of individuals or even to the creator herself. A video clip can even contain a clickable link to a website that expands its sphere beyond the movie and onto the Internet for further information. Much of the content of a video clip might not even be original. It is quite possible, and entirely common, for young kids to piece together existing pictures, sounds, music, words, visual effects, and even other video clips into a new video "composition." Mixing together existing material in new ways allows what researchers Michele Knobel of Montclair State University and Colin Lankshear of James Cook University in Australia call "endless hybridization." Knobel and Lankshear add, "Young people are embracing remix en masse, and it is increasingly integral to how they make meaning and express ideas."[27] What constitutes a video for a teen using the web is limited only by the student's imagination and the technological tools available for creating videos. It turns out that there are many such tools available, and a lot of them are available for free. Imagination is also free.

By now, most teachers have used video clips, downloaded from the web, or shown videos directly from the web, to illustrate key points during a class lecture. Using Internet-based content rather than traditional film reels and videocassettes is both educational and cost-effective:

- Web-based video is physically small and can fit on a memory stick, an iPod, or a smartphone for easy transport to and from home;

- It costs nothing to download a video clip from most websites; and
- There is a gigantic variety of clips available online compared to the school's video library.

It is important to recognize that video created as user-generated content requires that educators look at movies in an altogether different way. Students engaged in creating video must carry out a number of tasks in order to complete the product effectively, including researching a topic, searching for relevant digital content (e.g., photos and other video clips), writing a script, digitally composing (using the technology tools), and posting and sharing the final product. iGeners are skilled at these tasks, having done them many times, often creating their own first video when they were very young. Once they have a cell phone or smartphone with a video camera, or a standalone digital camera, they have the tools to be the next Steven Spielberg. While a video produced by a teenager on the computer will never be an exact substitute for an expert-generated educational film such as an interview with a famous physicist, the student-generated video will involve a large set of skills and can even include a snippet from that interview with the physicist, which can undoubtedly be found on the Internet.

Additionally, student video creation, as well as written content, brings one more important skill into play for children and adolescents: self-reflection. A typical product of self-reflection in the school setting is the written journal, but in the case of video, self-reflection can be incorporated into the final product directly as narrative or written commentary. The student-producer of the video can narrate her own reactions to the interview of the famous physicist into the same video clip containing the interview itself. Options for self-reflection are endless.

Another interesting and powerful aspect of UGC is its potential to elicit a wide range of responses from other students as well as anyone else who might view the content. Video created as a class project does not need to be shared just with the other members of the classroom. It can be shared with, well, the *world* via the World Wide Web. Sharing like this motivates kids, excites them, and is easy to do with the existence of hosting websites such as YouTube for video, Flickr for photos, and Blogger for written thoughts. Of course, students can and will post much of their own creations on MySpace or Facebook, which then provides an audience of their online friends. Professors Michele Knobel and Colin Lankshear, quoted above, made this point about blogging but it applies equally well to video creation. Products of classroom activities such as writing or even video production are not typically geared toward an authentic audience. Rather, they are designed for perfecting purely mechanical writing or authoring skills. Providing what Knobel and Lankshear call *genuine affinity spaces* for posting materials challenges and interests the kids. In the traditional classroom, students are limited to an audience of fellow students as opposed to an audience of the wider online world.[28] This is an important point and goes along nicely with student sharing through social networks, which allows them to have a whole universe of friends.

The effect of video creation and sharing was shown quite clearly in a collaborative project between a Scottish school and an American school. Eleven- and twelve-year-olds at each school created videos about race and ethnicity in their hometowns. The videos were then viewed by students at both schools, and the resulting effects on students' identities and their awareness of ethnicity were measured. It was found that students became more aware of race and ethnicity after viewing the videos and that they even incorporated some of their new knowledge into their understandings of their own identities.[29] This is the power of user-generated content. Once it is created, it can be made available to an audience limited in scope, such as the two schools in this project, or an audience as vast as the World Wide Web.

Audio: An Important Part of the Media Mix

The stereotypical image of today's teenager always has one key component: earbuds in her ears with a portable MP3 player at her side. Listening to music is like breathing to iGeners, and their love of music spills naturally onto the web. Music can be added to video clips, to slideshows of still images, to personal web pages, to just about anything. Online music stores like iTunes make finding music easy, and the software tools for adding music to user-generated content are easily found online and come in various no-cost forms. Add a low-cost microphone to a PC, and kids can move beyond prepackaged music to add their own audio. Voiceovers, narration, and commentary are common—just browse YouTube to see all of the teen-generated tips, commentaries, movie reviews, you name it, that were made at home with low-cost or free equipment. Many laptop computers and even smartphones now come with built-in microphones and video cameras, so any kid lucky enough to be using one will be able to create web-quality audio right away. Audio is often just one channel of information combined with video or with other graphics to produce user-generated content; however, audio also can stand alone. Audio podcasts—so named because in addition to the Internet, they can be played on an iPod or other portable MP3 player—are popular, too, and are not difficult to create by today's technologically savvy students or schoolteachers. If a teacher is not comfortable creating her own podcast, there will be someone at the school—even a student— who will be happy to help. Or the teacher can search the Internet (including iTunes) for a vast array of prepackaged podcasts on nearly any topic.

Music conveys mood and emotion, of course, and this is one of the draws for young kids in adding music to their creative content. For example, a new trend involves a whole class of *remixes* on the web, for which teens combine excerpts from favorite movies or TV shows and set the sequence of clips to music of their own choosing to emphasize or highlight particular moods, emotions, or ideas. The ability to add their own words, in any form, to video brings out the creative side of today's iGeners and adds a personalized dimension to their user-generated content. This is what Web 2.0 is all about: taking material that already exists on the web, adding material of your own creation (e.g., audio commentary, written messages), mixing it together in a unique, eye-catching, and interesting way, and posting it online for all to see and for others to comment upon. And it's not just videos posted on YouTube, but also homepages on MySpace, blogs on blog sites, and encyclopedia entries on wikis. Creating multimedia is compelling and engaging to our young generation of elementary and secondary students.

Hanging Out, Messing Around, and Geeking Out

It is a safe assumption that most kids with regular access to the Internet will have the skills necessary to create their own content. In a broad survey of iGeners' activities online, researchers at the University of California at Berkeley found that the typical iGener is creating content, although there were different apparent levels of online participation. A large chunk of the kids under study were "hanging out"—that is, they were engaging in activities that most adults would find wasteful but nonetheless require active involvement. The researchers described the function of this online activity this way:

While hanging out with their friends, youth develop and discuss their taste in music, their knowledge of television and movies, and their expertise in gaming. They also engage in a variety of new media practices, such as looking around online or playing games, when they are together with friends.[30]

In the context of hanging out, kids become part of a 24-hour, always on, communication lifestyle that mimics some of the same social experiences that occur in a typical young person's real world, including dating, flirting, and developing and maintaining friendships. When children become especially interested in a particular hobby or topic, they might "mess around," the next level of online participation identified by the Berkeley researchers. When kids start messing around with a topic, they begin to tinker and explore online, eventually finding social spaces that allow them to fulfill their interests. Finally, for some kids, their interests become so self-motivating that they "geek out"—they find online social networks of individuals who have specialized knowledge of the topic, they participate in Internet-based communities and organizations that center on their particular interest, and they develop their special-interest skills through the sharing of knowledge and specialized feedback that they receive while participating in these networks. In other words, students at all three levels of online participation—hanging out, messing around, and geeking out—are developing and using their content creation skills to be part of the Internet-based community.

Participation in the creation of user-generated content is not just for older kids. Because even the youngest members of the iGeneration are surrounded by technological devices that allow 24-hour access to the Internet and are exposed to their older siblings' and their parents' use of Internet-based resources, they, too, are developing skills that allow them to become active participants in Web 2.0. Michael, a first-grader at a public school in California, described how he constructed a "time-travelling" vehicle from Lego building blocks and shared his creation online at the Lego website. As you are reading this, remember that Michael is only six years old.

> This vehicle can travel forwards and backwards in time. It can travel faster than the speed of light, too. I took a picture of it with my Dad's camera and I put the picture on the Lego website where kids can post their pictures. I told my Dad what to write and he added the words next to the picture. Other kids can see it when they click on my Lego page. I made my page have a blue background and I added rock music. I hope that other kids see my vehicle and that it gets picked to be in the Lego magazine.

Teachers can tap into the skills possessed by these young kids, too. In one project, third-graders created podcasts designed to showcase their hometowns. The project, called "Our City Podcast," not only required that students do research about their hometown to learn about its history, but also required that they engage in technical work related to the creation of the podcast. In one case, students in Omaha, Nebraska, featured their hometown. A local journalist described the skills necessary:

> . . . most of the time spent making a podcast is in the preproduction phase. Students plan out the entire podcast, write scripts, and practice speaking. This is where most of the learning happens. Students each take a segment or two, such as "Famous Friends" and "History Corner," conduct research for their segments, and explain what they know and learned in ways that listeners can understand.[31]

These third-graders were motivated by the fact that they were preparing materials for real audiences. In their project, after fine-tuning, their podcasts were posted to iTunes, where any person in the world could download the podcast for free and learn about Omaha as told by eight- and nine-year-olds.

The Power of Creativity

Creating one's own online content is a defining characteristic of the new generation of children, teens, and young adults who have been raised knowing no other world than one when the Internet, where writing and creating audio and video have become a natural pastime. Up to this point in this chapter, I have described several situations in which students make content in creative ways. Because the software and hardware tools for creating online content are accessible to almost anyone, kids are finding new ways to express themselves creatively via remixes, social networking pages, blogs, and many other forms of content. This form of creativity has the potential to raise the motivation levels of students engaged in otherwise traditional learning tasks. Even when just "hanging out," kids are engaged in creative activity online, as the Berkeley researchers identified in their study. Hanging out or playing around online, despite its apparent pointlessness, encompasses several important features related to learning. Professor Doris Pronin Fromberg of Hofstra University, a leading expert on kids' play, has listed several features that reveal that play is more sophisticated than we assume. According to Fromberg, play is symbolic (represents reality), meaningful, active, pleasurable, voluntary, intrinsically motivated, rule-governed, and episodic (changing).[32] One education researcher, commenting upon these positive qualities of play, summed it up this way:

> Who would not wish their children to do things that are "active," "meaningful," and "symbolic"? Pedagogical research stresses the power of *active* participation for learning. The ability to discriminate *meaning* positions a child to evaluate situations, to make informed judgments, to think critically and creatively. The mastery of *symbols* is close to the definition of a competent person. And everyone wants their children to have fun *(pleasurable)* while at the same time learning to be *rule-governed* and patient *(episodic).*[33]

Creativity and the Brain

It is possible to learn from playing, or just "hanging out." Further, hanging out and playing around might directly benefit the creative process through brain stimulation in multiple areas. The current educational model often teaches concepts by having students build or make something such as a poster, diorama, or even a PowerPoint presentation. This is done offline, usually at home, and is essentially using only some of the available senses. When playing around online—making multimedia presentations that engage the senses, emotions, and intellect—iGeners presumably are activating more brain areas than would otherwise be involved in comparatively static activities such as listening to a lecture or doing math drills. Interestingly, one of the leading theories linking brain areas to creativity suggests that the ability to simultaneously activate different concepts housed in different brain areas leads to more creativity. In other words, by connecting previously disconnected concepts in the mind, a student can generate a novel idea, solution, or concept. Psychologists call this "divergent thinking," and brain scientists currently are trying to identify aspects of the brain that might lead some people to be better at divergent thinking than others. Brain areas that specialize in connectivity are high on the list of suspects, including the corpus callosum, the bundle of nerve fibers that connects the two hemispheres of the brain (linking so-called left-brain and right-brain thinking) and the volume of "white matter" in various brain regions. The volume of white matter reflects the amount of "insulation" of electrochemical brain pathways and is related to the speed of neural processing.[34] In summary, the activation of and subsequent communication between seemingly disparate brain regions may foster divergent thinking and lead to enhanced creativity. Extending this idea, one can speculate that creating user-generated content that contains both written words (left hemisphere) and audios and videos (right hemisphere) allows and encourages the student to process information in more depth.

Some people may argue that play or creativity without a specific purpose is not relevant to serious academic endeavors such as math and science. Psychologists, however, distinguish between artistic creativity and the type of creativity that enhances the effectiveness of our mental processes. More specifically, they define creativity in a way that makes the creative act essential to achieving a goal. Their typical definition has two parts. Not only must an act be novel for it to be creative, but it also must be useful.[35] From an educational perspective, then, the power behind iGeners' content creation lies not only in their genuinely high levels of motivation and satisfaction in doing so, but also in their interest in making and posting works that involve both their left and right hemispheres. Tapping into these high levels of emotional involvement and taking full advantage of their potential for raising the level of engagement in schoolwork remains the job of teachers, parents, and school officials. The tools available to students at school, and the arrangement of its social environment, often discourage or outright ban students from engaging in the development of creative, multimedia activities on site. By designing thoughtful, curriculum-driven UGC projects, students' eagerness and excitement can be directed toward goal-driven outcomes.

Integrating User-Generated Content in the New "Rewired" Educational System

New educational models must be flexible enough to provide opportunities for students to tap into and use their creative sides—using their ever-expanding array of technological tools at home and at school. This new model would have the following elements:

1. **Technological tools:** iGeners have access to a wide variety of software and hardware that allow them to create content of a very high quality. They already know how to use the tools, which are either free or available at a low cost. Designing projects that tap into these skills will help educators connect to students' virtual lives, motivate them, and lead to outcomes of superior quality.

2. **Purpose:** Young children and teenagers are very creative online, but these creative projects aren't always done with learning in mind. Teachers can design projects that are simultaneously creative and purposeful. In other words, projects can be centered on the educational curriculum and yet avoid the static character of traditional learning techniques.

3. **Audience:** Today's students prefer to create projects that will have real audiences, and when talking about Web 2.0, the real audience is the online world. Posting student products online is easy and it provides a reality that infuses excitement, interest, enthusiasm, and motivation into students' minds.

4. **New texts:** How important is spelling and grammar to a project? If it's an English lesson for which spelling and grammar are the focus, then the young students' online writing skills might not be relevant to the project. However, with many projects in history, geography, art, etc., teachers can tap into their students' skills at creating *new texts* that combine media (audio, video, words, links) in novel ways and simultaneously demonstrate learning.

At school, in the traditional classroom anyway, students are the learners and the passive recipients of knowledge. On the web, however, they create their own content and mix it, add it, put a personal spin on it, and then post it for others to see and evaluate. When a student generates web content, she is basically becoming a real political or social commentator, film director, writer, and/or public speaker. This online creative play increases realism, engages students, and directly enhances learning. Am I suggesting that teachers send their students permanently into cyberspace, never to return? Absolutely not. The carefully crafted, digitally mediated educational lesson, however, can be used to provide a motivational boost to students when teachers need it.

Chapter 7

Media Literacy among 21st-Century Kids

In times past, parents and teachers could easily identify the "Pied Piper" who was influencing their children. Now the "Piper" comes from many sources and in many forms. Today's challenges for educators and parents include: (1) identifying the many Pipers who transmit messages and values to Generation M, and (2) helping the Generation M learners navigate through the information with the mental and emotional filters and analysis needed to maintain a reality-based perspective on life.

—Susan Ziegler, Cleveland State University[1]

The Internet is a great tool to help teach research skills. As a teacher, it's my goal to help students improve their ability to select reliable sources, paraphrase and properly cite sources. It seems, though, the only skill they have mastered is to copy and paste!

—Jackie Pilger, eighth-grade teacher

Along with the rapid pace of new technology, the iGeneration is growing up with unprecedented access to information. While this access provides a mind-boggling *amount* of material, the *quality* of the information being fed to young people today is unlike that available to any previous generations. What children today experience while being exposed to media content is like mining the Wild, Wild West—just as the pioneers in the 1800s had to brace against harsh elements and even harsher living and traveling conditions, today's media-hungry kids must mine rocky terrain searching for the best places to dig for information, not knowing whether what they find is worthy of their efforts. And on top of it all, the landscape—especially that of the World Wide Web—is barely regulated. Information that students discover may be false, slanted, or, even worse, may cause psychological harm. Without understanding how to search and find the best information, there is simply no way for them to know whether the content they've discovered is a diamond or a lump of coal.

Young people tend to trust, believe, and be highly influenced by the information they see and hear, whether it is provided by a teacher, a news outlet, a friend, or a website. But the information on the web has varying levels of credibility. The American Academy of Pediatrics is so alarmed by the media's impact on children and teens that it has encouraged pediatricians to create a "media history" form for parents to fill out during office visits.[2] To be media literate today means to have the ability to access, understand, synthesize, and analyze media and its messages. According to Robert McCannon, cofounder of the Action Coalition for Media Education,[3] media literacy emphasizes:

1. A critical thinking skill that allows audiences to develop independent judgments about media content
2. An understanding of the process of mass communication
3. An awareness of the impact of media on the individual and society
4. The development of strategies with which to discuss and analyze media messages
5. An awareness of media content as a text that provides insight into our contemporary culture and ourselves

6. The cultivation of an enhanced enjoyment, understanding, and appreciation of media content.[4]

The iGeneration is informed via media messages through a variety of devices. These messages shape cultural norms and teach kids how to think and act. Educators and parents must first understand what these messages contain, and then learn to teach children how to assess, analyze, and synthesize them. In this chapter I will: (1) address the history and progression of electronic media and its uses by—and impact on— the iGeneration; (2) explore television and other socializing agents and examine how kids are influenced by the messages contained in them, especially in the context of child development; (3) discuss credibility and trust issues; and finally (4) give some tips on how to create a media-literate child.

How the Internet Changed Everything

One day my friend's sixth-grader, Harry, came home from school and told his mom about his new social studies project. Each student was responsible for researching and writing a three-page paper on the cultural differences between Americans and people from one other nation of their choice. The lesson included finding and citing three sources from the Internet. Harry's mother told her son she was there to help organize the paper, but couldn't offer much help finding information because she wasn't comfortable using the Internet. Harry decided to first look up information on American culture, and then choose what other nation to focus on. Like most students his age, he began his search by going to Google; he typed in "American culture." What appeared first was an entry from Wikipedia, the free, online encyclopedia.

The development of the culture of the United States of America—History, Holidays, Sports, Religion, Cuisine, Literature, Poetry, Music, Dance, Visual Arts, Cinema, and Architecture—has been marked by a tension between two strong sources of inspiration: European ideals, especially British, and domestic originality . . . As most cultures, American culture is not static and is developing and changing as the demographic composition of the nation continues to change among other reasons due to a rising number of Central Americans seeking refuge in the United States (often illegally) due to deteriorating social and economic conditions in their respective countries . . .

The last part interested Harry. He decided that since there were so many immigrants from south of the border already in the United States, he would compare Central Americans to Americans. Then, he went back to Google and typed in "Central American Culture Immigrants." His search yielded 85.9 million hits! Again, Wikipedia popped up first, but Harry knew he needed three sources of information for his paper, so along with Wikipedia he decided to look a little further down the list. One of the websites offered an already written essay for $59.95. No, he thought, Mom wouldn't go for that. Then he found another website with an article about immigrants from Central America. Perfect! The page was someone's response, in the form of a blog, to a news article about immigration laws. Here's what Harry read:

Calling an illegal alien an immigrant is akin to calling a drug dealer an unlicensed pharmacist . . . Part of the economic stimulus should include purchasing vehicles from failing automakers, hiring out-of-work truck drivers, and moving illegals to the closest border crossing.

The other source Harry chose was from a Honduras tourist website, where they proclaimed: "*Honduras: Where magic happens.*" When he showed his mother what he had found, she was dumbfounded. Clearly, Harry's idea of comparative cultures was critically tainted by the infor-

mation he located on the Internet. While the "truth"—or what we deem is close to it—may have been out there, Harry did not find it, or he did not try hard enough to find it, or he did not know how to recognize it. And this is our dilemma: we want kids to have access to this information, but we want them to find the *best* information, not just what's readily available through an Internet search.

We are living in an age of unprecedented access to information. Just twenty years ago, the Internet was used only by the government and its agencies through big, clunky computers. In 1992 the U.S. Department of Defense gave registration rights to civilians, and the Internet was born. As communication infrastructure became more sophisticated, new applications emerged. The World Wide Web was developed in 1993, making it easy for consumers to find information. The number of information sources grew, as did the Internet's ease of use. As of 2008, the amount of technical information on the web was estimated to be doubling every two years.[5]

According to the Pew Internet & American Life Project, about 36 percent of people get their news daily online, up from 12 percent in the early 2000s. Other activities that have risen significantly are checking the weather, searching for health-related information, looking at videos online, and using search engines.[6] Before the Internet there were a variety of authoritative entities, but we had fewer choices and those choices were mostly credible and reliable—information was collected and disseminated via trained individuals, usually journalists, and vetted through a process of editing.

In the "old days" when we wanted to acquire information we usually went to a library, a bookstore, read a newspaper, or watched TV. Many families would have a dictionary, maybe an almanac, and some bought multivolume encyclopedia sets, such as the *World Book* or the more expensive *Encyclopædia Britannica*. We believed the information we received and rarely questioned its credibility. It is more complicated today. For instance, before the Internet provided information about the weather, we relied on the television newscast, the newspaper, or simply walked out our front door. Today, a multitude of electronic sources give us up-to-the-minute weather from every part of the globe. While weather is sometimes unpredictable we rarely question the forecasts because we are not meteorologists; but what if we wanted to learn about another topic, say, "terrorism in the United States"? A simple Google search will yield millions of websites containing information with a wide range of accuracy. Students trying to write a research paper on this topic may turn to the Internet and discover that some sites advocate the release of prisoners from Guantánamo Bay, while others support an all-out war on every practicing Muslim in the country.

The presentation of news itself has also gone through a massive change in the past decade. While as recently as 2008 television was the number one place where people got their news, the Internet has now taken the top spot. Once the most respected, complete, and primary source for news, newspapers are disappearing and being replaced by niche websites where people can customize their news. For instance, those interested in sports may go to ESPN's website, while people searching for health information have a multitude of available sources including the popular WebMD. With this new way of producing and delivering news, people's choices for where to get their information has also changed. As the information below, from The Pew Internet & American Life Project shows, most of us are choosing to get it online.[7]

- 71% of Internet users get news online on the average day
- 59% get news on the average day from local TV
- 53% get news on the typical day from radio
- 52% get news on the average day from national TV newscasts

- 43% get news on the average day from the local paper
- 21% get news on the average day from a national newspaper.

If one of our tasks as adults is determining from these sources which is the most credible, it is even more critical for students. Educators and teachers have the ability to explain to children how to find reliable information on the Internet, but before broaching that topic, let's take a look at how students are using the Internet. First, 93 percent of all teenagers access the Internet, and more than half of them use it on a daily basis. Our most recent research with parents of more than 1,300 children found that 54 percent of 5- to 8-year-olds and 83 percent of 9- to 12-year-olds are online.[8] While they are highly adept computer users, young students do not possess great Internet skills in the classroom, either in searching for or in evaluating websites.[9] Matthew Eastin and his research team at Michigan State University found that too much information on a website hinders elementary schoolchildren's ability to assess the credibility and relevance of that material. In other words, students could not evaluate large websites, especially understanding the differences between advertising and regular content.[10] Many studies have shown that, in general, people do not appear to possess the skills necessary to find the best information on the Internet. In our studies of college students' use of Internet search engines, nearly half (42 percent) use only the first five links.[11] Just 15 percent use the first 10 links, 12 percent use all the links of the first page only, and 20 percent use links on any of the first three pages. Just 3 percent use links on more than the first three pages, which most educators would argue is necessary to find the best and most reliable information.[12] In an experiment using college students, Bing Pan, professor of business and economics, and his team of researchers from Cornell University found that the participants trusted and were strongly biased toward the first links that appeared in their

Google search, even if the information contained in them was less relevant than other material.[13] So it appears that even college students lack the necessary skills to critically analyze information they find on the Internet, and they believe that all information is about equally truthful and has the same value.

As technological advances have increased students' access to information, the use of unedited and unverified online material is on the rise. The accuracy of this information varies widely, from stories written by veteran journalists who maintain the same rigorous practices and procedures they used at their news organizations, to weblogs written by people with no journalistic background. The latter's unverified, unsubstantiated thoughts and opinions are just as easy to locate through search engines as the former's. While I was doing some research recently I discovered the same exact passage on dozens of websites. Someone had written the original content, and it was liberally copied and posted by everyone else who needed the same information. It was unclear who the original author of the material was, or whether the material was accurate.

Does Wikipedia = E-N-C-Y-C-L-O-P-E-D-I-A?

Another trend is the use of online encyclopedias such as Wikipedia, which is extremely popular because of its placement in search results, often appearing first or at least in the first five to ten hits. While the information on the site is in a constant state of revision and possesses varying levels of accuracy, even veteran journalists pick up this information and use it as fact. University College Dublin student Shane Fitzgerald tested the power of Wikipedia—and the credulity of its users—when he posted a fake quotation attributed to French composer Maurice Jarre in the Wikipedia entry on Jarre. (Mr. Jarre was famous as the composer of the score for the film *Lawrence of Arabia*. He died on March 28, 2009.) Within a few hours of Fitzgerald's posting the quote (just hours after the news of Jarre's death broke), dozens of media outlets in the United States, Australia, Great Britain, and India used it in their obituaries. After a month went by, the student who posted the fabricated quote alerted the media outlets and the corrections began. As Shawn Pogatchnik of the Associated Press wrote, "When Dublin university student Shane Fitzgerald posted a poetic but phony quote on Wikipedia, he was testing how our globalized, increasingly Internet-dependent media was upholding accuracy and accountability in an age of instant news. His report card: Wikipedia passed. Journalism flunked."[14]

So what exactly is Wikipedia? The website, started in 2001 by Jimmy Wales, is the most widely cited online encyclopedia in the world. It comprises millions of articles in dozens of languages—some 12 million as of mid 2009. The information is not attributed to any one author: the material is written and edited by many—sometimes hundreds of—people.[15] Wikipedia's content is free, and anyone may use the information in any way they please.[16] The site employs just a dozen full-time employees, none of whom are editors. Material is edited on a volunteer basis, though the site does have administrators who oversee the content. One of the problems associated with Wikipedia includes the anonymity of its users. Any person can claim to have credentials and expertise, yet possess none of these qualities. Conversely, information written by those with credentials can be systematically edited by others with divergent points of view. For instance, expert climate modeler Dr. William Connolley posted an article on Wikipedia on global warming, which was removed by another editor because he claimed Connolley's point of view was "too aggressive." One of the site's five employees put Connolley on "editorial parole," limiting his entries to one per day.

When he challenged this, employees gave him no more credence than his anonymous counterpart.[17]

Another issue is that anyone can remove information from Wikipedia if they feel it does not belong. After the September 11 attacks, an employee at American Airlines removed the airliner's name from the entry on the terrorist disaster because it did not want to be associated with such a heinous act.[18] Many university professors ban the use of Wikipedia in research papers because it is written by nonexperts and is not vetted through an editing and verifying process. As Andrew Keen writes in *The Cult of the Amateur:*

> In undermining the expert, the ubiquity of free, user-generated content threatens the very core of our professional institutions. Jimmy Wales' Wikipedia, with its millions of amateur editors and unreliable content, is the 17th most-trafficked site on the Internet; Britannica.com, with its 100 Nobel Prize winners and 4,000 expert contributors, is ranked 5,128.[19]

However, the site is currently trying to clean up its image by employing editors and posting disclaimers about the varying levels of completeness and accuracy. In the "About" section of the website, Wikipedia explains that older material, because it has been "filtered" through more readings and revisions, is more accurate than newer material. The bottom line, though, is that if students use information from any unedited online encyclopedia, they should find the referenced material at the end of each entry and locate that primary source rather than relying on the unedited version.

Many school districts have software on student computers that blocks websites such as Wikipedia and other user-written material. But students still have access from home, where they do most of their schoolwork. As Carrie, age twelve, told me: *"We had a paper to write in history class. It was about the Civil War. It was so easy—all you have to do is type in 'Civil War' on the Internet and you have all the stuff you need! Wikipedia is the best. It has everything."*

Blah, Blah, Blogs

Other sources of unverified information obtained via the Internet are weblogs, or blogs for short. Blogs are sources that are easily accessible, yet they also have varying degrees of credibility. Blogs vary in scale and reach: some are personal and rather limited in scope; some are about topics of cultural or political interest; and others are reporters' notebooks on major news organizations' websites. Blog postings include individuals' opinions and views about various topics; news written by legitimate journalists; political commentary; and marketing, advertising, promotion, customer service, and business and professional issues. Blogs are still important because they provide people an outlet for sharing their thoughts and feelings, and some do provide credible information. Blogs are also terrific educational tools, both in and out of the classroom. But, as with other user-generated content, many blogs also contain misinformation—a fact that students need to grasp.

Most often blog entries are set up chronologically with the most recent at the top. Blogs also allow people to receive feedback concerning their thoughts and ideas through a "comments" section featured below each entry. According to Bruce Dearstyne, professor of information studies at the University of Maryland,[20] "Blogs may include a mixture of personal observations and official views, vague speculations and solid insights, common sense musing and innovative perspectives, flip comments and profound opinions."[21] Some blogs are so popular they are able to sell advertising space on their sites; and some utilize the distribution tool known as an RSS feed (RSS = Really Simple Syndication or

Rich Site Summary) to syndicate their content to blog subscribers.[22] Both can give the blog source credibility, making it seem more trustworthy than it may actually be.

While they are an efficient way of disseminating information, blogs are not vetted through editors, making the content raw and unverified. While some bloggers use the same journalistic practices as those in news organizations (reporting and information gathering through a variety of credible and verifiable sources), many bloggers do not. They challenge traditional journalism and sometimes create ethical concerns within the journalism field and in research communities because of their power to influence public opinion.[23] For instance, some of the most popular blogs, Daily Kos and the Drudge Report, are clearly politically slanted, while the gossip websites TMZ and Gawker are among the twenty most popular blog sites, yet they are essentially the online equivalent of the *National Enquirer,* with their focus on snarky rants about celebrities.[24]

It is important to note that bloggers can frame an issue any way they choose, while the writings of traditional journalists go through several editors before being distributed to the masses as more or less objective, impartial reporting (columnists' opinion pieces are edited as well). Unfortunately blogs have become mainstream media and it is often difficult to distinguish between legitimate news blogs and opinion.[25] The perceived credibility of blogs is a threat to information literacy. Journalists themselves turn to blogs for information exchange, especially those who work for online publications.[26] According to a group of researchers who studied blogs' impact on traditional journalism, "Newspaper journalists are most reluctant to give up their gatekeeping roles in sharing the authority allotted through traditional journalistic practices than journalists in other news media outlets."[27] For young students, figuring out which bloggers provide credible information and which do not is a challenge. As you'll read later in this chapter, there are several commonsense ways to verify credible information, including looking for references, author's credentials, and recent information.

In this new age of "citizen journalists"—people who are not employed by a news organization but perform the same basic function as legitimate journalists—children and teens are exposed to a dizzying amount of information. Journalists learn their craft through experience and education; many bloggers and Wikipedia authors simply post information gained by the same methods as everyone else: Google searches followed by copying and pasting or paraphrasing. Others obtain their information through firsthand observation or individual experience, which is troublesome in that experience is subjective and can never be called fact. While blogs provide a venue for people to express their opinions, and may contain some news that the public needs to know, students need to be more aware of the information they receive. If a journalist makes a mistake in gathering news, they may be fined, fired, or even jailed. If a blogger provides misinformation, absolutely nothing happens. Because these bloggers are not part of a traditional news organization, they are not held to the same standards. However, their work is just as accessible online and often quoted in student research papers as fact.

When people seek information they usually turn to online news and television news sources. This may illustrate a need for immediate information that print media cannot provide. Or it may show that people are intuitively aware that news organizations provide more accurate information. The good news is that most college students in our research reported minimal use of blogs when searching for news or general information about a topic.[28] Now it's time to teach this to children.

The TV Made Me Do It

From a very young age, children are bombarded with electronic images that tell them what to request from their parents, who to admire, how to dress, what to eat, and, in some cases, how they should act when they grow up. Because of their limited understanding of the implications of media images, young children often respond to the unrealistic quality of television in very real ways, which makes it challenging for educators attempting to teach media literacy. Children tend to attach meaning to make-believe characters to make sense of their own lives, and that's why it is important for teachers and parents to understand the power of television.

The media have the power to influence children's thinking about the world, both from cultural and personal perspectives. As I've discussed in previous chapters, the iGeneration consumes more media than any generation before them, particularly television, which they watch for many hours each day. Preschool children are watching an hour and a half of television daily, and elementary and secondary school children watch upwards of two hours a day. Because of this, kids need to be taught how to assess and critically analyze media messages rather than merely accept and believe what they see. Everything we have learned from developmental psychologists makes it clear that children lack the ability to fully understand the messages they are receiving; they are highly susceptible to media's persuasive and unrealistic qualities.

Even though parents and teachers like to think they have the most influence over their kids, the media possess significant control over the way children behave, think, and learn. The late communications scholar George Gerbner spent his career researching how television influences people's attitudes and behaviors. His seminal Cultivation Theory, which has decades of research support, asserts that the cumulative effect of watching television is that people begin to believe that its messages represent the real world, whether it is the amount of violence, sex, or crime, or something as simple as how many children become well-known celebrities.[29]

As a measure of how easily television can influence children, researchers at the Mount Sinai School of Medicine showed a popular children's cartoon to two groups of preschoolers, one group saw an embedded commercial for either foods or toys; the other group saw the cartoon without the commercial.[30] At the end of the thirteen-minute cartoon the children were asked which of two food products they would choose, one of which was the advertised product. Those who saw the commercial chose the advertised products significantly more often. Oh, yes, I forgot to mention that the commercials were only thirty seconds long. Add to this the fact that the American Psychological Association estimates that the average child watches more than 40,000 television commercials a year, and you get the picture of how ideas can be cultivated easily over time.[31]

The iGeneration faces a unique challenge: juggling the myriad media messages coming from every technological device they use *and* maintaining a somewhat normal existence. By looking at how a child develops in relation to media consumption, we can begin to learn how young people can do just that.

The developmental psychologist Jean Piaget believed that a child plays an active role in his or her development, and that children learn by doing.[32] He demonstrated that children do not merely observe and imitate the world around them, but interpret it as well. As children absorb media messages, especially those from television, they use both *assimilation*—taking in the information and making it fit into their ideas about the world—and *accommodation*—adjusting to this information by revising old ways of doing or thinking.

The four elements that Piaget identified as guiding development are *emotion, maturation, experience,* and *social interaction,* which work together to motivate learning. Emotion creates feelings that excite and motivate learning; maturation relates to the development of the physical being; and experience is an important part of development because without it a child cannot develop and function normally. Finally, social interaction with others provides experiences and feedback. The interactions a child has with parents, teachers, peers, and *the media* mold the way she sees the world around her. Piaget said these four elements work together to guide development and shape a child's understanding of her world. The media contributes strongly to three of Piaget's guiding elements: emotion, experience, and social interaction. It often provokes emotional responses with its animated, colorful, persuasive nature; it is part of a child's experience; and it provides a context from which children learn how to make decisions and how to interact socially with others. Educators and parents must understand how these messages influence children's development for two reasons: first, by understanding the media's power they can harness this information and monitor what children are exposed to, and second, they can create media-rich learning environments where children learn from these images and narratives rather than just merely absorb them.

Children are more susceptible to media messages because they process them differently than adults.[33] The impact can be seen by examining the five different mental tasks that are involved when a child watches television:

1. Select the important information for processing.
2. Take the information and put it into a story.
3. Draw inferences from the implied cues in the message.
4. Draw on past experiences and memories to explain the cues in the messages.
5. Evaluate the message and decide whether it is positive or negative.

Perhaps most important for education, young children cannot distinguish the boundary between television and the real world. During the early stages of development, children perceive television as real. Young children may attribute human qualities to inanimate objects such as a stick or toy. They have make-believe friends, or have tea with their dolls, or run around the backyard slaying enemies. This distortion can transfer to television as well, with children believing the objects they see on television are real. In their study on television realism, Professor John Wright and his colleagues at the University of Kansas[34] discovered that five- to seven-year-olds are aware that their favorite show is not real, but they were not aware the characters didn't keep their roles off screen. Strikingly, seven-year-olds felt that fictional television shows were more realistic than the five-year-olds did. This shows quite convincingly that school-age children, lacking the ability to understand different levels of realism, are not likely to understand the differences between a news program and a scripted series.

As children grow older their television watching becomes more sophisticated—they are able to critically review messages and understand the differences between various television programming. Once a child enters elementary school, she starts to focus more on conceptual aspects such as a character's motives and goals.[35] As children age further, they begin to examine whether the television plotlines are even plausible. Those they deem probable or plausible in real life will also seem more like reality—that is, they will believe the stories to be true. These ideas are central to Piaget's studies on language comprehension, which indicate that "the ability to differentiate probability from possibility crystallizes during early adolescence."[36] This has vast implications for an adolescent's view of the world, and can lead to distorted perceptions about such things as the number of sexual predators in their neighborhood or the amount of sex they should be having.

Children also *consume* media differently than adults because adults have the ability to use *metacognitive thinking*—that is, thinking *about* their thinking—while children have a limited ability to reflect on their cognitive processes. Therefore, adults are more aware of the way they process media messages than are children. As children reach adolescence they are better able to analyze the messages within a particular medium. Further, as they age, children use their past experiences to monitor their reaction to certain media messages. And as they get older, this process becomes increasingly more important in the way they absorb media because children have a larger capacity for remembering and processing certain messages and can synthesize them easier than when they were younger. Understanding how much information children can process will aid in the development of educational media tools.

The way children understand the language used in media messages is also important in understanding these complex cognitive processes. Piaget found, from watching a group of youngsters converse with each other, that speech has two distinct types: *egocentric* and *socialized.* Unlike adults, children do not always use speech to communicate. A young child uses egocentric speech, which often reflects what she is thinking at the time, whether or not what she is saying makes sense to others.[37] Young children often repeat words and phrases, and do so because they enjoy the sound. They also will repeat what they hear others say. Often this repetition of language said by another can happen days or weeks later—called *delayed echolalia.* At about age 7, a child's speech will become less egocentric and more socialized. According to Piaget, this is a reaction to the need to communicate and relates strongly to how children understand and react to media messages.

The methods by which the images and text on television are presented have vast implications on the ways children use and understand language, which can alter the way they view the world—and the way others view them. Young children may mimic the sounds from a cartoon or the catch phrases of their favorite character; older children who watch large amounts of television may not fully develop their socialized speech and instead may communicate using the patterns heard on their favorite shows; and "tweens"—especially boys—may use commands, requests, threats, and criticism more often than other types of speech because they are a major part of the violent television programming they watch.

As children's television viewing increases through the years, their exposure to advertisements rises as well. The average child is exposed to approximately twenty-six different commercials per hour of television watched.[38] In the 1970s, most television advertisements aimed at children were for cereal, toys, candy, and fast food. The appeal of these advertisements was more psychological than rational. Instead of offering the price or quality of the advertised item, advertisers focused on how fun a product was or how yummy it tasted.[39] In the 1980s, children's television advertisements shortened to about fifteen seconds each, exposing the child to even more commercials per hour. The content was similar to that of the 1980s: cereal, toys, and fast food were the most popular items. The most persuasive advertising technique was still to show children having fun or enjoying the product. In a survey of more than eight hundred teens, those who watched more television bought more products for social acceptance.[40] Thus those children and teenagers who watch a lot of television are more likely to associate happiness with material possessions and money. As my niece always reminds me, "You're just not cool if you wear anything but Justice or Abercrombie."

With an understanding of how children develop in a media-rich environment, and how they respond to the various messages sent by television, parents and educators can begin to develop a plan for teaching kids how to assess, synthesize, and analyze these messages and what is contained in them.

Credibility and Trust in Media

Another way educators and parents can help children become more media literate is to first help them understand what information is credible and what is not. Credibility refers to how trustworthy, reliable, and truthful something is. Credible sources are people, material, documents, and other vehicles for delivering information that possess these traits. And children and teens are most trusting of the information they get from their TVs and their other technology media.

A credible online source is one that provides correct information without bias, and contains material written by experts who are authoritative and trustworthy.[41] Whether online information is credible or not, the more kids use the Internet, the more they believe that Internet information *is* credible, just as people have long tended to assume that anything printed is probably true. People who feel that a source is credible will also believe the information from that source is credible.[42] Therefore, websites that appear to be credible to students will hold the same weight; in other words, they will trust the information whether or not it is accurate.

People's perception of the information they absorb is important in understanding whether they perceive high or low credibility. People tend to believe the content on websites that contain information they are interested in or invested in;[43] however, people also perceive websites to be credible that have a diversity of information. The more experienced the adult Internet user is, the more they believe the material they find is credible.[44] Therefore, students, who have been surfing the Net since they were young children need to be taught to look for credible sources when conducting research.

In journalism school, students learn that even information that does not require attribution can be verified or corroborated through a variety of credible sources. The definition of credibility in this context is *true content written by experts.* Our studies have concluded that among website visitors there are varying levels of effort exerted in checking a site's credibility, and it appears that website credibility is not often checked.[45] For instance, just 40 percent of the respondents in one of our research studies checked to see whether the site had recent information, while 44 percent checked whether the site was from an organization or an individual. Just a quarter of the respondents checked whether the author had reliable credentials. From our research, we concluded that most people are concerned about the credibility of the websites they visit, but the level of concern varies. There are three basic levels of credibility concern among the people we interviewed: *mildly concerned,* with the activities confined to checking material on the website itself; *concerned,* with activities moving beyond the website and into other areas or other websites; and *extremely concerned,* with activities moving outside the website itself and directly addressing credibility issues. Very few of the subjects in our study were extremely concerned.

Another issue is trust. Trust is associated with online source use,[46] and that trust is key for maintaining a successful long-term online relationship with a website.[47] Trust has three main belief components: *honesty, benevolence,* and *competence.* Honesty is the belief that one will keep their word; benevolence refers to confidence that the content creator is not interested in misleading visitors to the site; and competence relates to the basic accuracy of the website's contents. Further, to trust a website one must believe in the site's reliability or strength.[48] In their research, professors Luis Casalo, Carlos Flavián, and Miguel Guinalíu found that people's levels of trust predicted their commitment level to a website.[49] Therefore, people with more trust in the site had a longer relationship with it, visited it more often, and believed in the truth of its contents.

According to a recent Nielsen Global Online Consumer Survey of more than 25,000 Internet consumers from 50 countries,[50] people trust information posted online by peers in the same way that they trust information from newspapers. Further, recommendations from friends or personal acquaintances and these posted online opinions are the most trusted forms of advertising. The following data from the Nielsen study show how much consumers trust various sources of information, "somewhat" or "completely."

- Recommendations from peers   90%
- Consumer opinions posted online   70%
- Brand websites   70%
- Editorial content (e.g., newspaper article)   69%
- Brand sponsorships   64%
- TV   62%
- Newspaper   61%
- Magazines   59%
- Billboards/outdoor advertising   55%
- Radio   55%
- Emails from companies   54%
- Ads before movies   52%
- Search engine results ads   41%
- Online video ads   37%
- Online banner ads   33%
- Text ads on mobile phones   24%

It is clear from these figures that while people do not trust advertising as much as editorial content, they still rely more on their peers to give them the truth than on information that is vetted through editors, such as newspaper articles. Perhaps an even more important issue for media literacy among our school students is that people put even more trust in peers who are like themselves. So children may believe information their peers tell them rather than the credible sources they locate. In our research, we found that people prefer and trust both expert and non-expert authors of online material.[51] Further, more trusting individuals trust unverified information sources more than those who are less trusting of people in general. According to our research, this trust in unverified material is fueled by "source credibility," which creates a false sense of validity and believability of information. Sources that look professional, contain a wide variety of material, and are used by many have source credibility but may lack real credibility.

In our studies on people's levels of trust in online material, we found that more people are likely to turn to an Internet source when searching for information about a topic. For news, almost all respondents (96 percent) reported they would likely turn to an online news website, 89 percent would turn to the television, and 68 percent said it is likely they would turn to a newspaper. Most of our research subjects preferred and trusted a combination of both experts and nonexpert authors in blogs, while the majority (47 percent) *preferred and trusted expert writers in Wikipedia.*[52]

We also discovered in our research that when visiting an unfamiliar website, the majority of adults do a variety of activities to verify the credibility of the site, including comparing it with other sources, checking the credentials and email address of the author, noting the extension of the website (.com, .edu, .org, etc.), and ascertaining when the site was updated or created. However, as I mentioned earlier in this chapter, children do not possess the skills necessary to perform these tasks, so it is up to parents and teachers to teach them.

Creating a Media-Literate Child

According to Professor Susan Ziegler of Cleveland State University, "Given that the digital age is enveloping our world, and its influence is not likely to decrease, educators need to meet the emerging challenges on two fronts. Educators must determine the new learning styles of students and develop educational methodology and teaching strategies to meet the learning needs."[53]

So, the question is: How do we create a media-literate child? While there are volumes on this topic alone, I will provide a general framework for educators and parents to help guide students on their path to becoming media savvy.

First, it is important to remember that iGeneration students learn and synthesize material differently than do their teachers and parents. They are what Marc Prensky, author of *"Don't Bother Me Mom—I'm Learning!" How Computer and Video Games Are Preparing Your Kids for 21st Century Success and How You Can Help,* calls "digital natives" because they were the first generation raised using technology, while all previous generations, referred to as "digital immigrants," had to learn how to use it when they were older.[54] The learning curve is greater for older adults, while young children seem to know intuitively how technology works. However, while there may be a gap between the technological proficiency of digital native students and digital immigrant educators and parents, based on what we know about credibility, trust, and information availability, we can still teach students how to be critical consumers by stressing and teaching the following six principles of media literacy:

1. Media messages are created.
2. Media images and texts are not always accurate and should be looked at with a critical eye.

3. Media messages have a point of view and are not always representations of reality.
4. Various forms of media send different messages.
5. Media are targeted to populations of people.
6. Most media are created for commercial purposes. That is, to make money.

Internet Literacy

So, based on these six principles, how do we teach students how to assess information on the World Wide Web? Letting children sit in front of the computer alone and figure it out for themselves is not an effective approach; it does not help students learn basic search skills or support their problem-solving skills. Further, such a hands-off approach would not take into account what we know about child mental development from decades of psychological research and theory from scholars such as Piaget and Gerbner.[55] Some existing approaches include manuals written by librarians to help students become literate in online information evaluation, and guides from the International Reading Association that help students identify credible sources from a variety of search engines.[56]

However, there are easy ways to show children how to assess websites without giving them a textbook or handbook. First, it is important to distinguish between the various Internet sources. When searching for information on the Internet, students should be taught to look for the following and ask these questions:

- *Website information should include names of authors and their credentials.* Are the authors clearly identified? Do the authors of the material have authority, credentials, qualifications, or credible affiliations? Are the authors experts in their field, or simply passive observers? Is the authors' contact information included?

- *Look for detailed information that has credible, peer-reviewed references.* Are the references clearly marked? Are the references up to date? Do the references point to legitimate sources, or someone's opinion?
- *Look for information that is comparable to similar print resources.* Is the information from the Internet as complete as the printed version? Does the Internet site contain the same material as the comparable printed version?
- *Look for objective information.* Is the information free of judgment and bias? What is the purpose of the information? Is the information current? Is the website updated frequently? Is the material new?
- *Text should be free of spelling and typing errors.* Does the website contain any glaring errors or typos? Carelessness in spelling may be an omen of other inaccuracies.

In addition to the preceding questions, students should also understand the differences between:

- Corporate, business, or marketing websites (.com). Dot-coms vary in levels of credibility. Most websites that belong to a business are trying to sell something. Students need to be aware of this.
- Different types of news organizations (.com). Most news organizations' websites are credible; however there are some organizations that call themselves news when they are really blogs or gossip. Further, some legitimate news organizations possess political slants and omit alternative viewpoints.

- Advocacy groups promoting an agenda or point of view and non-profit organizations (.org). Groups with a .org extension are likely to be promoting or advocating something. Most are credible; however, students should look for information that is backed up with referenced material. If any information is used from these sites, it should be stated clearly.
- Personal web pages. Personal pages attached to a site should not be considered credible unless the material on them is written by a credible source and references and credentials are included.
- Informational website or page by an educational institution (.edu). Material on educational websites is highly credible. However, students should distinguish between someone's opinions, referenced and researched documents, and other general information.
- Informational page sponsored by a governmental agency (.gov). Governmental websites tend to be highly credible. Any website with a .gov extension should be considered trustworthy and reliable.

These guidelines should be explained to children who are learning to use the Internet for research purposes and in any instructional setting where the Internet is being used.

Television Literacy

Because children watch so much TV and glean information from a variety of televised sources, it is also important for students to start asking questions and understand how televised messages are constructed. Some of these questions include:

- Who created this message and why?
- Who is the target audience?

- What is the literal meaning of this message?
- What is the hidden meaning of this message?
- What kind of lifestyle and values are presented?
- What tools or techniques of persuasion are used?
- What healthy messages are communicated? What unhealthy messages are being communicated?
- What part of the story is *not* being told?[57]

The issues and questions that I have posed above should all be part of classroom discussions *before* allowing students to research topics. Given research that shows that college students are not media-literate, it becomes incumbent upon educators to start discussing these issues with their students as early as possible. Not all media literacy issues are relevant for all children—use discretion to determine which subjects are appropriate for what ages—but most certainly media literacy needs to be broached as soon as media become a source of student information.

Conclusion

A truly educated student, teacher, or parent must be able to identify the power of media acculturation and be able to access, analyze, and evaluate this information. Educators and parents must embrace this role. If not, we lose the battle and the transmission of knowledge and influence remains in the hands of the digital Pied Pipers of Generation M who may be more concerned with generating revenue than building a healthy society.

—Susan Ziegler, Cleveland State University[58]

The media landscape is continually changing and evolving. The Internet, television, and other forms of media influence our children and students more than any other force in their lives. Their use among children is only going to rise as new media burst onto the scene, as if in fulfillment of Alvin Toffler's continuing three- to five-year waves. New technologies pop up practically every day, and there is very little regulation of the appropriateness of its content for iGeneration students. If we expect our children to be competent citizens, compete in the workplace, and lead productive lives, educators and parents need to plant the seeds of media literacy early in the educational arena. Rather than becoming passive observers who let media control them, the iGeneration can become the new pioneers, actively blazing the trail for the next generation of learners. They must acquire the knowledge that media can also be informative, enjoyable, and engaging—if used wisely *and* with a critical eye. It is our job as parents and educators to see that their eyes receive that training in critical discernment.

Chapter 8

Concerns, Worries, and Barriers

When teachers are asked to integrate technology they are really being asked to change in two ways. First, they are asked to adopt new teaching tools such as the computer and the Internet. These are vastly different tools from the classroom tools many currently use such as the chalkboard, overhead projector, or television. Second, teachers are asked to change the way they teach their students, which may include changing the role they play in the classroom and the way their classrooms are physically arranged.

—Phillip Harris and Michael F. Sullivan[1]

I think that kids—my students—don't really have skills that they need to succeed. They rush to Wikipedia or the Internet for their research and most of them have never used a real library or a card catalog. What happens if there suddenly is no Internet? Will they even know how to do anything at all? Are they going to be so hooked on technology that they will have no clue what to do if it is suddenly gone? Teachers in my generation learned the basics and I think that today's kids are really missing out by using the Internet, calculators, spell checkers, and other tech tools instead of learning to do it all the "real way."

—Marion, a fifty-eight-year-old teacher of sixth grade

I learned about all this great stuff in my college classes but it is just so hard to get anyone to agree what I am allowed to use in my classroom. I would love to tap into the students' love of social networks and set up some learning options but the administrators, parents, and even other teachers keep screaming at me that it is not safe. They are so frightened that they won't even let the students access MySpace or Facebook from campus computers.

—Marvin, a thirty-four-year-old high school history teacher

In the preceding chapters I have pointed out how drastically different iGeneration students are from any prior generation, how they consume massive quantities of media, multitask all day long, and are bored when asked to sit quietly in a classroom doing one thing at a time. I talked about how they spend their waking hours communicating electronically and creating online content and how they love their wireless mobile devices and spending time immersed in social networks. I also presented some ideas about how educators and parents might harness this unique generation's exceptional qualities by using mLearning through wireless mobile devices, making use of available communication technologies, creating media content, using social networking, and expanding teaching tools to include more realistic and engaging multiuser virtual environments.

Teaching this new generation by using media and technology is not without its constraints and potential barriers, however. In this chapter I will explore many of these issues, beginning with more social-psychological perspectives, followed by pedagogical concerns, and, finally, technological barriers. As you will see, though, none are deal breakers. Technologies that are loved and consumed by the iGeneration present many unique possibilities, and any barriers to them are, in my opinion, insignificant compared to technologies' ability to engage our young students in the learning process.

It's Not Really a Scary World Out There

The Internet, and social networks in particular, have received massive negative publicity over the past few years. The media has taken isolated cyberbullying occurrences and magnified them on a national level. *Dateline*'s "To Catch a Predator" shed a negative light on any online communication and relationships as potentially dangerous. Parents were frightened for their children.

In January 2009 a *New York Times* headline announced, "Report Calls Online Threats to Children Overblown." Based on a comprehensive report by the Internet Safety Technical Task Force at Harvard University's prestigious Berkman Center for Internet & Society and the work of a separate international research advisory board (of which I was a member), it was found that sexual solicitation of children online was not a significant problem. In addition, however, the report did conclude that bullying among children, both online and in the real world, was a more complex issue. According to the report, "online harassment or cyberbullying happens to a significant minority of youth, is sometimes distressing, and is frequently correlated with other risky behaviors and disconcerting psychosocial problems." The report also goes on to admit that "this risk is the most common risk that minors face online."[2] Finally, the report found that *problematic content* (pornography) was prevalent, and exposure was most often unintentional, but that this exposure was upsetting to fewer than 10 percent of the exposed children, and, further, those children who were upset were nearly all suffering from other psychological issues. Overall, the Berkman Report debunked the media myth of an online world that is a menace to children. There are, however, some issues that do need addressing by any educator who plans to make use of cyberspace as a teaching tool.

Privacy and Internet Safety

A recent study of five hundred district technology directors found that their number-one concern—shared by more than three in four of the directors—was the safety of their students, including their regard for personal privacy.[3] In our research with hundreds of parents and thousands of teens, we have consistently found a discrepancy between parental and student perceptions of privacy and information disclosure. Across several studies, more than 80 percent of parents were concerned that their children were divulging personal information online, while only 29 percent of the teens shared the same concern. However, the parental concern, although perhaps inflated, may be somewhat warranted. Roughly half the teens told us that they disclosed their own full name, their school name, contact information (email address, instant message name), and information about upcoming social events they would be attending. Interestingly, one in three parents was not sure if their child had disclosed any information because they had not even viewed their teen's MySpace page. This means parents and teachers need to be aware of issues of privacy and safety and make sure that they are monitoring online safety.[4]

The Berkman Task Force's Technology Advisory Board was charged with reviewing forty technologies that were offered to keep children safe online. After a thorough examination they concluded that no single technology could keep kids safe online, and, "there is no substitute for a parent, caregiver, or other responsible adult actively guiding and supporting a child in safe Internet usage."[5]

When considering having some student curricular materials online, and particularly when looking at social situations where the students may interact with others, it is important to recognize that there must be some guidelines to keep the children's information private and safe. There are two logical solutions. The easiest option is to use online tools that are closed to anyone who is not a student in the classroom. Most off-the-shelf social and virtual networks, including those housed in Second Life, can be set to restrict visitors. Even if a public social network is used, any sections used for the classroom can be set to private.

This, of course, does not guarantee that no student will divulge personal information. Kids will be kids, and they have learned to be *disinhibited* and (to use a phrase from an earlier time) to "let it all hang out" online. It is up to the school and parents to set guidelines to ensure that students are aware of consequences if they violate their own privacy or that of others. In the late summer or early fall, prior to the opening of the school year, parents should receive a packet of information that includes an Acceptable Use Policy (AUP) that spells out acceptable and unacceptable behaviors when using campus computers, including consequences for violations. The document would have to be signed by both the parent and the student, and the penalties would usually escalate from restrictions to suspensions. If a school is using any technological curricular materials, it would be appropriate to amend the AUP to further delineate any possible privacy violations.

Nearly all schools have tried to install blocking or filtering software on campus computers to ensure privacy and safety. Even as early as 2004, an estimated 95 percent of schools and 43 percent of public libraries employed filtering software.[6] Although data indicate that the blocking software is, by and large, ineffective, schools and parents will continue to use programs such as Net Nanny or Safe Eyes to protect their children. The bottom line is that within hours, if not minutes, of installing a blocking or filtering program or keystroke monitoring software that records websites visited, IM conversations, email, chats, essentially anything typed on the computer, a teen—and even preteen—student will either find a work-around online or simply visit a friend and use their computer. Technical solutions simply do not ensure privacy. Attentive parenting and teaching are the only ways to make sure that kids understand that they need to value and protect their private information.

I Learned the Hard Way and So Should They

Marion, the fifty-eight-year-old teacher quoted at the beginning of this chapter, represents the attitude of many teachers. Whether it is a fear of the unknown, a negative attitude about technology and its place in education, or simply a lack of information about the availability of instructional technologies, some teachers use what Jerome Bruner referred to as *folk pedagogies:* teachers know how to teach and how students learn from the way they were taught and the way they learned in school themselves.[7] The problem is that their philosophy of teaching and the teaching tools they use have, in many cases, been replaced or superseded by more engaging and more effective technological tools.

Sadly, given the past difficulties with educational technology, the current economic (underfunded) state of the public schools, the difficulties teachers have in obtaining and using state-of-the-art equipment, and a folk pedagogy that tells them technology is just wrong, or too complicated to be worth trying to keep up with, many teachers have developed what Jean Piaget called a *schema,* or a script, which incorporates the downside of trying to use technology. They continually reinforce that script by focusing on their own negative experiences and those of fellow teachers. This is one of the biggest stumbling blocks that education faces today. We literally have to *rewire* such teachers to understand and see that their belief system, while having validity in the past, may not be accurate in today's world. As you have seen from earlier chapters, if you have a computer with Internet access, a free account on Second Life, and take a few minutes to get started, most students can be happily browsing the pyramids or ancient Babylonia.

Teachers reading that last paragraph may be cringing and ruing the day that the school allowed computers in their classroom. That is completely understandable. I recognize that I am suggesting some radical changes, none the least of which is for the role of the teacher to become, on some level, the student, while the student becomes the teacher. Children know more about these new technologies than most teachers, who most likely got their teaching credentials with little or no computer exposure. And they certainly were not exposed to the types of virtual, realistic worlds that are being used nowadays as teaching tools. The process of implementing these tools changes education from classroom-centered to technology- and Internet-centered, from teacher-directed to student-directed. We are literally in the midst of an educational technology revolution that is changing the definition and role of teacher. And many teachers are not happy about it. But the computers are in their classrooms and their iGen students are clamoring to use them in the most cutting-edge ways, so we have a bottleneck with teachers struggling to educate students with "tried-and-true" methods which, quite frankly, most students find boring and one-dimensional.

I don't blame the teachers. They are only doing what they were taught to do. They are not the problem. The problem is threefold: education, support, and time. First, new teachers are being educated not only in the use of technology, but also in the need to accept new innovations in the future. But it is not the new teachers whom we need to reach and win over. We have to reach the teachers who got their degrees in the 1980s or earlier, who did not receive this type of education, and who don't possess this acceptance of—and even excitement about—new educational technologies. I see this as an easily solvable problem: create a reverse mentoring system in which younger teachers mentor older teachers, or enlist a *knowledge broker* who serves as an intermediary or a sort of bridge between the educational technologies and the veteran teacher who, though experienced in her field, may be technologically lacking.[8] This knowledge broker could be another teacher, an administrator, a parent, or even a student. If it sounds strange to have a student as a knowledge broker, consider that iGeners have been raised amid these technologies, and students will most likely be early adopters of precisely the educational technologies that are being introduced into the curriculum. Anyway, who ever said teachers can't learn from their students?

Once a teacher starts to implement any new technology, something is bound to go wrong. According to one professional development specialist:

> Despite a steady wave of how-to workshops and some longer-duration seminars, infusing technology into curriculum and teaching practices remains elusive for many teachers. The existing format for technology-related professional development lacks the continuity that teachers need to develop the confidence and efficacy leading to technology fluency. Teachers crave a constant support person, in close proximity and available to fill in the gaps that arise with the rapid changes associated with technology.[9]

Perhaps it is the knowledge broker or mentor or even the computer lab teacher who can be the support person, but one thing is clear: support has to be in the form of language and style that the novice teacher can absorb. It is not sufficient to know how to use technology to provide support. You have to be able to teach and patiently "hand hold" and assist without resorting to techno-jargon or simply doing the teacher's job instead of showing her how to do it. In *TechnoStress: Coping with Technology @Work @Home @Play* (which I coauthored with Dr. Michelle Weil), we outlined a twelve-phase model detailing the optimal way to introduce technology into any system. Although I will talk more about that model later in this chapter, one phase includes key strategies that can be used in both teaching and supporting technology:[10]

1. Limit session time of training or support: short and focused.
2. Teach single concepts at a time.
3. Avoid jargon at all costs.
4. Use humor: technology does not have to be a serious business. It can be fun.

5. Use hands-on training—the teacher's hands, not yours.

6. Teach on the same equipment that the teacher will use.

7. Show a variety of sources for help if you are not available.

8. Match your teaching style to the teacher's learning style: auditory, visual, or tactile are all styles that can be used to teach and support technology.

9. Don't assume any preexisting knowledge.

10. Start by understanding what the teacher knows, not what she doesn't know.

11. Model actions first and then step back and let the teacher make mistakes. Often more learning happens when you make a mistake than when you do it correctly.

12. Summarize often: Repetition and summarization are good teaching/support tools.

13. Start early: Don't start the teaching or support after the first catastrophe.

Teaching and supporting technology is an art, not a science. A good mentor has to be willing to watch her mentee make lots of mistakes, get very frustrated, and hopefully come out on the other side happy with the curriculum she is using. Think of a mentor as a "personal trainer" like one you might enlist to train you in exercises at the gym. You want your trainer to have a sense of humor while you are sweating and huffing and puffing. You want her to take it slowly and recognize your abilities. This is how you support technology.

Finally, the last issue hindering the teacher from integrating technology into the classroom is time. There simply aren't enough hours in the day to do all your prep work, grade papers, work with students, and all the other activities that make teaching so time-consuming. You don't just teach six classes. The rule of thumb that I learned was that for every hour of instruction a teacher worked another half hour to an hour on other teaching activities. I am sorry, but there is no magic bullet for the extra time it is going to take to start using state-of-the-art technologies such as virtual classrooms. I can promise, however, that your students will be happier and maybe that will make the teaching hours better. I can also promise that when you are finally up and running and you have students learning not through classroom lectures or through books but through vehicles that make learning alive and real, your job of teaching will be different, and hopefully both easier and more fun for you.

Technological Barriers: Where Are My Resources?

Thomas Brush, professor of education at the University of Indiana, reviewed more than a decade of literature on barriers to technological implementation in the classroom and discovered that 40 percent of those barriers were directly related to resources. Educators felt that access to available technology hardware was limited, technical support was scanty, and administrators were, in many cases, unsupportive or oppositional.[11] However, the National Center for Educational Statistics reported in 2006 that 97 percent of elementary and secondary schools had computers and 94 percent of instructional rooms had broadband access.[12] During the 2003–2004 school year, U.S. public school districts spent $7.87 billion on computer equipment, and the ratio of students to each Internet-connected computer was 4.1:1; 83 percent of public schools offered professional development to support technology integration.[13] However, with all this technology, MIT professor Jennifer Groff reported, "Despite increased investments in technology, the statistics of classroom computer use are disheartening to say the least. Recent studies indicate that on average, teachers use computers several times a week for preparation but only once or twice a year for instructional purposes."[14]

The twelve-phase model mentioned above presents a blueprint for successful technological change.[15] Perhaps the most important part is Phase 1: Organizational Value for Technology. Regardless of the system, whether it is a school, a school district, a corporation, or even an entire country, the powers that be—the top-level decision makers—must value and approve of the technology in order for the people down the line to be willing to implement it. For example, Ronald Reagan and George H. W. Bush were presidents at the beginning of the World Wide Web explosion; however, both minimized the value of the Internet, and that negative attitude was reflected in the government's involvement with the web. It was not until the administration of President Bill Clinton and Vice President Al Gore—Gore is credited with naming the Internet "the information superhighway" to reflect its value and promise—that the United States jumped on the cyberspace bandwagon by establishing government websites, using laptops in the House and Senate, and supporting educational technology.

The following list details the phases in my implementation model. Each is critical in setting the stage for technological change and easing the transition from older educational technologies to new, up-to-date curricular applications.

1. **Organizational value for technology.** For a technological change to even be considered by teachers, those who control the organization—superintendents and principals—need to show teachers who will use that technology that they feel it is valuable and useful, and they should do what they can to demonstrate that value by participating actively and positively in the process. In my studies of worldwide technology adoption, those countries

with government officials who embraced technology were more likely to have their citizens adopt all forms of technology, including computers and educational tools. The United States is a good example of this process. It was not until we had a president whose administration was excited about technology and used it daily that we saw a rise in the use of educational technology.

2. **Establish the true need.** Just because an educational technology exists does not mean that it is appropriate for a specific teacher in a specific school. Too often technologies are purchased by a school or school system without determining whether the current teaching tools are already engaging the students and generating excitement about learning. "Build (or buy) it and they will come" does not work with teachers who are content with teaching strategies that they feel are already effective for both the teacher and the students.

3. **Assess staff attitudes and alleviate technological discomfort.** Some teachers have good, positive attitudes about using technology in the classroom, while others may be hesitant about all the tools that they themselves did not use when they were in school and have not used in their classrooms. Working with those teachers *before* introducing technology is essential, or they will actively resist it.

4. **Develop new skills.** Teachers arrive at school with a range of skill levels. Any new technology must be taught to them using the thirteen key strategies I introduced earlier in this chapter. Teacher training will require time, and schools will find that it is futile to thrust educational technology into the classroom without first arming the teachers with a complete knowledge of how it works.

5. **Develop personal motivation.** Even with the best training, if teachers are not motivated to use the technology, then it is des-

tined to fail. For technologies that are already being used in other schools, have the teachers talk to colleagues who successfully use them. Use their experiences, excitement, and enthusiasm to encourage hesitant teachers who may not yet see the pedagogical value of something such as virtual worlds.

6. **Increase awareness and support skills in eager adopters.** Each school has its "eager adopters" who flock to any new technology. They corner anyone they can find and carry on about how a new technology does this and that, all the while using jargon and computerese. This turns off teachers. If you can successfully channel your eager adopters to use the teaching tools I have discussed in this book, you will have knowledge brokers who can serve as models and teachers for the rest of the faculty.

7. **Involve the entire staff in technological change.** In Phase 1 I talked about how the school leaders have to embrace new technologies; the same can be said for the entire faculty. Technological changes are more likely to succeed if they have been discussed in teacher meetings that allow the teachers to express concerns and have a voice in final decisions. Without doing this you are likely to have resistant teachers and constant difficulties in integrating any technological tools into the curriculum.

8. **Pretest the technology.** Nothing is more harmful to introducing technology than having problems from its inception. First impressions matter. Technology will have problems, and those problems need to be ironed out before they are presented to potentially hesitant or resistant teachers.

9. **Carefully develop a training program.** I can't stress enough the importance of adopting the teaching strategies outlined earlier in training teachers to use new technologies. The goal of training is to generate comfort, confidence, and excitement. Sadly, too

many teacher training programs violate many of these guidelines by trying to cram too many concepts into too little time, all being taught by "techies" who shoot rapid-fire jargon at the glazed-eyed trainees. All that succeeds in doing is to drastically reduce the chances that technology will be adopted.

10. **Provide ongoing support.** As I mentioned earlier, every school needs a "knowledge broker" who can serve as a support person for any teacher having technological difficulties. For support to be successful it must be available after the training—too often training is considered a substitute for ongoing support—and the knowledge broker must be willing to answer questions and provide solutions in a calm, jargon-free voice. As much as humanly possible, the support should be available 24/7 so that a teacher who is experiencing a problem after school hours has someone to call to get immediate help, rather than continuing to struggle and waiting until the next school day for solutions.

11. **Provide ample techno-playtime.** Research has shown that allowing the people who actually implement technology—the teachers—to experiment and "play" with it in advance is rated as the top training method. Adults learn best by using tactile-kinesthetic learning styles (just as children do) and pressing buttons just to see what happens. Janet, a thirty-seven-year-old art history teacher, told me, *"Before I started having my students visit the Second Life Sistine Chapel Island, I spent about 4 hours learning how to maneuver my avatar, making mistakes and correcting them, and exploring all that I could do in this new environment. It was fun and I even involved my whole family in my learning experience. It was particularly helpful to watch my 8-year-old daughter take the controls and fly herself around Second Life exploring other islands. She showed me how to talk to other avatars and even gave me some great ideas for other uses of this virtual world."*

12. **Encourage, solicit, and integrate staff feedback**. Technology integration is not a static activity. You cannot simply provide technology, train teachers, provide support, and move on. It is a continual learning process in which you encourage the learner—the teacher—to provide feedback to the administration on how the technology is affecting their classroom experiences.

Clearly this model addresses the barriers and concerns that I have discussed in this chapter. Each phase is critical and involves teachers, administrators, and students in the process of implementing technological change in our educational system.

The challenges working against technology are there on all levels—administrative, pedagogical, attitudinal, and behavioral. However, as we saw in earlier chapters, the playing field keeps getting more level, with off-the-rack options becoming more popular and teachers becoming more facile with technology. Regardless of the obstacles, if teachers want to reenergize their curriculum and engage their iGen students, they must see the issues not as barriers, but as opportunities. To help educators plan for technology implementation, Professor Thomas Brush of Indiana University has created an interesting instrument to measure teachers' technology skills, technology beliefs, and technology barriers.[16] The Technology Skills, Beliefs, and Barriers Scale has been tested and found to be a reliable and valid instrument, and one that I think could be helpful in delineating the issues facing the use of educational technologies in the classroom. With Professor Brush's permission, I have printed his scale below with its three sections. There are no right answers to any of these questions. They should be used as prompts for discussions of the difficult issues that educators will face throughout the twelve-phase model of technology implementation described above.

Technology Skills, Beliefs, and Barriers Scale

Technology Skills

Response Options:

I can't do this
I can do this with some assistance
I can do this independently
I can teach others how to do this

Basic Operations

1. Create, save, copy, and delete files; move or copy files onto hard disks or CDs or DVDs; find files on a hard disk or a CD/DVD; create folders and move files between folders
2. Print an entire document, selected pages, and/or the current page within a document
3. Cut, paste, and copy information within and between documents
4. When my computer freezes or an error message comes up, I can usually fix the problem
5. Use anti-virus software to check my computer for viruses

Productivity Software

1. Use the functions of a word processor to format text (font colors and styles), check spelling/grammar
2. Use advanced features of a word processor such as headers/footers, tables, insert pictures
3. Use the basic functions of a spreadsheet to create column headings and enter data
4. Use advanced features of a spreadsheet (e.g., using formulas, sorting data, and creating charts/graphs)
5. Create a presentation using predefined templates
6. Create a presentation with graphics, transitions, animation, and hyperlinks
7. Use an electronic/computer grade book

Communication

1. Send, receive, open, and read email

2. Use advanced email features (e.g., attachments, folders, address books, distribution lists)
3. Subscribe to and unsubscribe from a listserv

Electronic References

1. Use a search tool to perform a keyword/subject search in an electronic database (e.g., CD-ROM, library catalog)
2. Use advanced features to search for information (e.g., subject search, search strings with Boolean operators, combining searches)

World Wide Web

1. Navigate the web using a web browser (e.g., Internet Explorer, Firefox)
2. Use more advanced features of a web browser (e.g., creating, organizing, and using bookmarks; opening multiple windows; using reload/refresh and stop buttons)
3. Use advanced features of a web browser (e.g., install plug-ins, download files and programs, download images)
4. Use a search engine (e.g., Yahoo, Lycos, Google) to search for information on the web
5. Use a web authoring tool (e.g., FrontPage) to create basic web pages with text and images
6. Format web pages using tables, backgrounds, internal and external links
7. Upload web page files to a server

Multimedia

1. Create simple shapes such as lines, circles, rectangles, and squares with a drawing program
2. Use advanced features of a drawing program (e.g., layering, grouping objects, changing fill and outline colors)
3. Create and modify a simple multimedia product using an authoring tool such as Hyperstudio
4. Import a digital image (e.g., clip art, photograph) into a document
5. Use various tools (e.g., digital camera, scanner) to capture a digital image
6. Use a photo editing tool (e.g., Photoshop) to manipulate a digital image
7. Use desktop publishing software (e.g., Publisher, PageMaker) to create a newsletter, pamphlet, or award certificate

Technology Beliefs

Response Options:

Strongly Disagree
Disagree
Agree
Strongly Agree

1. I support the use of technology in the classroom.
2. A variety of technologies are important for student learning.
3. Incorporating technology into instruction helps students learn.
4. Content knowledge should take priority over technology skills.
5. Most students have so many other needs that technology use is a low priority.
6. Student motivation increases when technology is integrated into the curriculum.
7. Teaching students how to use technology isn't my job.
8. There isn't enough time to incorporate technology into the curriculum.
9. Technology helps teachers do things with their classes that they would not be able to do without it.
10. Knowledge about technology will improve my teaching.
11. Technology might interfere with "human" interactions between teachers and students.
12. Technology facilitates the use of a wide variety of instructional strategies designed to maximize learning.

Perceived Technology Barriers

Response Options:

Not a Barrier
Minor Barrier
Major Barrier

1. Lack of or limited access to computers in schools.
2. Not enough software available in schools.
3. Lack of knowledge about technology.
4. Lack of knowledge about ways to integrate technology into the curriculum.
5. My assignment doesn't require technology use.

6. Lack of technology accessibility in my classes.
7. There is too much material to cover.
8. Lack of mentoring to help me increase my knowledge about technology.
9. Technology-integrated curriculum projects require too much preparation time.
10. There isn't enough time in class to implement technology-based lessons.

Chapter 9

Rewiring Education

There is a persistent gap between how today's digital natives learn in schools and how they work and interact outside of school—a trend that underscores the need for districts to keep pace with technological advances and adapt to students' learning needs.

—M. Stanbury, "Survey Shows Barriers to Web 2.0 in Schools"[1]

Our end users (students) feel that the actual system in which they are forced to live is so disconnected from the world that they live in. Instead, educators need to embrace technology, and it needs to be melded into the classroom so that people stop thinking about it as technology. In 1703 teachers were concerned about the use of slates. A century later there were fears that students were using paper too much. In 1907, some officials warned that pencils were being replaced by ink. Thirty years later, a report said that students were "wallowing" in the luxury of fountain pens. And in 1950, ballpoint pens were referred to as the possible "ruin" of education.

—Martin Bean, head of marketing and business development for Microsoft's education products group[2]

Kids are wired differently these days. They're digitally nimble. They multitask, transpose and extrapolate. And they think of knowledge as infinite. They don't engage with textbooks that are finite, linear and rote. Teachers need digital resources to find those documents, those blogs, those wikis that get them beyond the plain vanilla curriculum in the textbooks.

—T. Lewin, "In a Digital Future, Textbooks Are History"[3]

Throughout this book I have shown you how the iGeneration is radically different from any previous generation of students, and I have suggested a variety of existing technologies that can be used to engage and excite them in the learning process. The bottom line is that the educational system must develop new, technologically based models to replace the old textbook-based classroom. If we are going to prepare our students for Alvin Toffler's future in which waves of technology innovation keep coming faster and faster—with iGeners as the early adopters—then it is time to *rewire* education.

We are already seeing national and state efforts to facilitate this transition. President Obama's February 2009 stimulus plan included $650 million to boost educational technology programs, and he has advocated for legislation to invest in creating free online courses for community colleges, a sign that this administration plans to jump-start the rewiring process for all levels of education. According to the superintendent of a large school district in Texas, "I think Obama is the first president that's making that switch to the Internet presidency. Obama is doing for the Internet what President John F. Kennedy did for television by encouraging the use of it as a common and essential staple of American life."[4]

On a statewide level, California governor Arnold Schwarzenegger has introduced an initiative to replace some high school science and math texts with free, open source digital versions and is getting cooperation from book publishers in taking this giant step toward a rewired educational model.[5] California is not alone in this movement toward more technology. A July 2009 policy statement by the National Association for K–12 Online Learning reported that at least 44 states now provide some form of online learning for their students, 30 states have state-led online courses and services, and online learning is growing at 30 percent annually. This rate matches data from the Sloan Foundation, which found a 47 percent increase in the number of K–12 students engaged in online courses between the 2005–2006 school year and 2007–2008.[6] In Michigan, a state law enacted in 2006 says that every public school student must take an online course to graduate from high school.[7] Given that companies such as Walmart and State Farm Insurance have online training courses for their managers and agents, and psychologists, attorneys, and doctors have been earning their continuing education credits online, it makes sense that the educational system is also going online.[8]

Throughout this book I have tried to provide a detailed, "micro" view of the opportunities for integrating technology into the educational system. On a larger, more "macro" level, there are seven major arguments for changing our educational system to include more technologies:

- iGen students are wired 24/7 and are the early adopters of all new technologies.
- iGen students are multitaskers to the nth degree and are bored when asked to unitask.
- iGen students are socializing constantly via technologies such as social networks and text messaging, and this communication has been shown to level the playing field so that all students feel comfortable participating in conversations.
- iGen students live a connected life at home and are being asked to disconnect at school.
- High-quality course materials that have been proven to actively engage this connected generation of students are available at low or no cost.
- Technologically adapted curriculum materials have been proven to help students develop higher-order thinking skills.
- Students' participation in the Web 2.0 via user-generated content, social networking, mobile learning, and virtual learning environments (just to name a few) is highly motivating for them and they are naturals at it.

Despite the clear theoretical reasons for rewiring education, implementation depends on the determination of both educators and parents. Without their understanding, interest, and enthusiasm, no changes are possible. As Jim Steyer, CEO and founder of Common Sense Media, a popular website for information on media and the family, observed, "When it comes to digital media in kids' lives, it's a confusing time to be a parent. Clearly parents seem to understand that the world has fundamentally changed and that kids need digital media to be successful in the 21st century. But the results also suggest that parents have reservations about how their kids engage with each other using digital media. That's why it's important that we help parents understand both the potential and the risks of digital media, so we can make sure kids get the best of this new world."[9] In their national study, Steyer and researchers at the Joan Ganz Cooney Center at Sesame Workshop (founded by Children's Television Workshop, creator of *Sesame Street*) found that a whopping 75 percent of parents agreed that knowing how to use digital media is as beneficial for students as traditional skills such as reading and mathematics. Further, 83 percent of the parents said that digital media will be what gives their children the skills they need to succeed in the twenty-first century.[10] Parents are clearly on board with the importance of technology in education. What about educators?

According to national surveys, teachers and administrators are also in favor of rewiring education, and many have already adopted multimedia, games, and virtual learning environments into their curricula.[11] One national survey funded by the MacArthur Foundation found that 77 percent of school district administrators agree that new Web 2.0 technologies have value for teaching and learning, but funding for such efforts is limited. Other national surveys have found that the majority of teachers use online communication with parents and students and that between half and three-fourths of all teachers have used Internet and multimedia resources on a regular basis in their teaching.[12] However, the same surveys indicate that the majority of schools have banned social networking in class, only one in seven teachers sees educational potential in video games and MP3 players such as the iPod, and 3 percent see no educational potential for cell phones.[13] Further, fewer than half the teachers in one national study felt that students are able to think critically about the accuracy and potential biases in online information.[14] It seems as though educators have something of an approach-avoidance conflict with educational technology. On the one hand they see the value in adding technology to the curriculum and they do make use of some technologies. But they also avoid other technologies that have been shown to be effective and engaging teaching tools. Based on what I have presented in this book, educators ought to take a closer look at their iGen students and adapt teaching models to fit their lifestyles.

Mobile learning should be the key to the future of education. According to Professor Elliot Soloway of the University of Michigan, commenting on *Pockets of Potential,* a 2009 national report from the Joan Ganz Cooney Center at Workshop:

> The kids these days are not digital kids. The digital kids were in the '90s. The kids today are mobile, and there's a difference. Digital is the old way of thinking, mobile is the new way. As usual, adults have not yet caught up to the kids. The bulk of public sentiment surrounding mobile devices and learning today is largely unenthusiastic, with many educators and parents concerned that they can cause distraction and other harmful behaviors. But the social and cultural phenomena, the market opportunity, and, most importantly, the 'pockets of educational potential' documented in this report should not be dismissed. The debate in the coming decade should no longer be *whether* we should use these devices to support learning, but about

exploring *how* best they can be used. Just as Sesame Street introduced children and their families to the potential of television as an educational medium two generations ago, today's children will benefit if mobile becomes a force for learning and discovery in the next decade.[15]

Soloway is not alone in his perceptions of the value of mobile learning. The *Pockets of Potential* report concluded, "Perhaps the most ubiquitous technology in children's lives today are mobile devices—tools such as cell phones, iPod devices, and portable gaming platforms that traverse home, school, and play via the hands and pockets of children worldwide."[16] Further, research has shown convincingly that students thrive when curricula incorporate mobile learning devices such as PDAs (personal digital assistants), iPods, and cell phones. For example, a five-year study at the Research Center for Educational Technology at Kent State University found that using handheld devices in the classroom improves student motivation, increases feelings of engagement, improves conceptual understanding, and enhances problem-solving skills.[17] Another study in Ohio gave PDAs to third-, fourth-, and fifth-graders to use as cameras and input devices on field trips, which increased their excitement and learning.[18] The *Pockets of Potential* report[19] lists more than twenty-five similar handheld learning projects across all subjects and all ages. It makes sense that there would be so many projects, given the overwhelming popularity of portable devices among iGen students, of whom four in ten iPhone and iTouch users access the Internet more often from their mobile device than from their personal computer.[20]

In the next section I will briefly summarize what I think are the keys to understanding our new breed of students, and then I will provide some options for using technology and media to reach them in ways that have been shown to be extremely effective.

Anytime, Anywhere, Any Way . . . My Way

As we've seen, today's students carry their mobile learning devices with them 24 hours a day, 7 days a week. They surf the Internet, communicate, write, and maintain their social sphere, all using a tiny device that has become far less expensive and just as powerful as the computer that sits at home. Their smartphones have become their personalized, mobile learning devices, and they use them in ways that we, as adults and educators, still do not quite grasp. As Liz Kolb, author of *Toys to Tools: Connecting Student Cell Phones to Education,* said, "Mobile devices bring the real world into the classroom, and they bring the classroom into the real world."[21]

Another special aspect of this always wired generation is their reliance on speed and multitasking. They rarely, if ever, do one task at a time, and they use the rapid pace of technology to aid them in constantly juggling family, friends, and school. A recent report by the Joan Ganz Cooney Center likened the iGeners' world to an extension of the power of today's *"Pow! Wham!"* fast-paced action thrillers and television programs such as *Sesame Street.*[22] Students crave the same speed they get from television, the Internet, text messaging, video games, and nearly every form of media and technology in their world. As I said in Chapter 3, mobile learning tools are one way to tap into that "need for speed" by presenting material and engaging in communication through portable, handheld devices.

This does not mean there are no challenges to providing mobile education. For one, teachers and parents worry that if we start using podcasts and other mLearning tools we will increase the already high volume of media that our children consume on a daily basis. Based on all our research with iGen children and adolescents, however, it is unlikely that we will be adding any time to their already media-saturated lives. If anything, we may be concerned that we are encouraging more multitasking while they are learning with their mobile devices; however, as explained earlier, multitasking will not make them perform worse. It will increase the time for them to learn, but they will do just as well as if they had not multitasked. And, they will be happier and more engaged in their learning if allowed to maintain their social world while they are learning.

Other concerns expressed about mobile learning include a potential deterioration in writing ability due to the way mobile devices encourage the use of textisms and language shortcuts, in-class distractions from omnipresent smartphones, possible health problems such as reduced visual acuity from prolonged staring at small screens and "Nintendo Thumb" from continuously pressing small keys, online privacy, cheating by using smartphones to communicate with other students during exams, and online threats such as cyberbullying and sexual predators. All of these are certainly justifiable concerns and need to be addressed as part of mLearning projects. But, as discussed in earlier chapters, these issues are for the most part either minimal problems or can be easily avoided with clear guidelines and consequences set by teachers and parents. The bottom line is summed up perfectly by one school district coordinator who said, "Cell phones aren't going away. Mobile technology isn't going away. Right now, what we're telling kids is, 'You go home and use whatever technology you want, but when you get to school, we're going to ask you to step back in time.' It doesn't make any sense."[23]

The Omnipresent Social Network

Preteens and teens spend a large chunk of their lives on Facebook, MySpace, Second Life, and other social networks. Not surprisingly, given the negative reports in the media, parents and educators are frightened about sexual predators, privacy, cyberbullying, pornography, and other supposed online evils. Although the research has clearly shown that these problems are more fiction than fact, more exaggerated than actual, the education community has been hesitant to adopt any form of social networking in the classroom. This is, I think, a missed opportunity to grab students' attention in a venue where they already spend so many hours a day. According to Paul Kuhne, marketing director at eChalk, a company that works with schools to integrate technology into the curriculum, *"So much of what we hear is that schools are not implementing social networking tools. This is because a lot of districts hear this and think Facebook or MySpace. It doesn't have to be like that. There can be monitoring; there can be customized online social-networking tools for districts; there can be password-protected environments for teachers and students. It can be just for the school, just for one class, or just for one specific group. There are solutions out there that are safe and manageable."*[24]

Aside from the MySpace and Facebook safety concerns, educators should note that teens use their social networks as platforms for creating vast amounts of "content." They write prolifically, post homemade videos and artwork, and spend vast portions of their online time being creative. Social networks have become platforms for teens to develop material that involves all of the senses and thus have strong learning potential. In addition, social networks *are,* for many teens, their primary social world. All of their friends are there and they have friends available 24/7. If educators can set aside their media-driven prejudices against them, social networks can be fantastic vehicles for providing curriculum materials both within the classroom and while students are at home. This is also an excellent opportunity, as Liz Kolb asserted above, to bring their *real world* into the classroom.

Keeping—or Making—It Real

In Chapter 5, I outlined the impact of "realism" on learning. In the same way that it is best to learn a foreign language by spending time speaking only that language with native speakers in their country (that is, by immersion), more realistic learning environments have better learning potential. Although they overlap considerably, two such environments are video games and "multiuser virtual learning environments" or MVLEs. Both have strong potential for providing information in a venue that is both familiar to students and as close to reality as possible. These websites and games may only be computer programs, but the feeling that one gets from them is that of *immersion*—of being literally part of a separate world that is as real as the physical world. Just watch a teenager play *World of Warcraft* or a fourth-grader visit ancient Babylonia on a Second Life island and you get the distinct sense that they feel as if they are "there."

Eric Klopfer, director of MIT's Teacher Education Program, has a unique perspective on the value of video games as learning tools in comparison to other, less sophisticated technologies currently being used in the classroom. He had this to say in a June 2009 online chat hosted by *Education Week* and CTB/*McGraw-Hill,*

> Well, smartboards are flying off the shelves, but in most of the cases I've seen they don't actually impact classroom practices. I'm preferential to two of the technologies we work with—Mobile Devices (cell phones) and games. I think cell phones are another year or two away from starting to become accepted in schools, but this may be the year for games.[25]

Despite their reputation as vehicles for teaching violence and destruction, research has demonstrated that video games have amazing potential to develop many higher-order skills in children and teens, including:

- Physical coordination
- Knowledge acquisition
- Problem-solving abilities
- Ability to extract and synthesize complex information
- Decision-making abilities when faced with multiple alternatives
- Motivation
- Systems thinking, or understanding how changing one element in a situation affects the relationships between other elements.

Once again, quoting the influential Joan Ganz Cooney Center at Sesame Workshop, "Digital games offer a promising and untapped opportunity to leverage children's enthusiasm and to help transform learning in America."[26] The true attraction of video games, beyond their ability to transform and instill analytical thinking skills, is that they are readily available at low cost. Many are free and have been used in educational settings for years. Video games are a cost-effective, known quantity with strong research backing and touted by nearly every educational organization as a powerful educational resource.

The next step up in video game realism is multiuser virtual learning environments (see Chapter 5). Log on to Second Life and take a trip to any of hundreds of educational islands for a close and personal look at a virtual world. Visit *Cyber One: Law in the Court of Public Opinion* and participate in a mock trial based on a real-life court case. Hop on over to Music Academy Inworld (at Music Academy Online) and explore a virtual music academy. Then, if you are not yet impressed, visit the National Oceanic and Atmospheric Administration's Second Life islands—Meteora and Okeanos—where you can learn about weather, sea life, tsunamis, and even take a virtual submarine tour. This is but a small slice of MVLEs; there are hundreds and even thousands of such environments that feel as realistic as being there.

MVLEs work because of a combination of *social presence* and *situated cognition*. Social presence refers to the feeling of realism that comes from residing in the body of your avatar and the ability to interact through this avatar with other people who are also engaged in the simulated world. Research has demonstrated convincingly that the more realistic the avatar, the more effectively you are able to engage in social interaction within the MVLE.[27] Situated cognition is also part of the reason why MVLEs are such powerful learning tools, because their worlds are not full of abstract, two-dimensional concepts, but rather dynamic, ever-changing three-dimensional vistas where we, as the participants, acquire information, manipulate objects, converse with others, all in real time. It is not as real as *being there,* but it is akin to *feeling as if you were there.*

Scott Mandel is a middle school teacher in a low-income neighborhood and the developer of TeachersHelpingTeachers, a web site that assists teachers on how to find interactive curricular materials on the Internet.[28] In an interview, he related a story that when he visited the British Museum—the real one—and saw the displays of Egyptian mummies and treasures, he wanted to plan a trip for his middle school students to share his experience. Obviously, the students in his ancient civilizations class could not afford a real field trip to London, but the museum has interactive, web-based video tours of its exhibits that allow the students to view them from their classroom or home computers. The topper, he said, was when his students got to play a version of a game enjoyed by children in North Africa more than two thousand years ago. The next class session the students couldn't wait to discuss what they liked best and what they learned from the museum exhibits. Other teachers have told similar stories about how much excitement and interest these MVLEs generate in their classes. One teacher told me she assigned her students to write papers about their experiences on Genome

Island—where students learn genetics by visiting museum exhibits and even performing virtual experiments and attending discussions with geneticists and other students—and those papers were among the best she got from them all year long. She told me she could just sense their excitement through the way they wrote and the ensuing classroom discussions. The MVLE is not real, but the experience most certainly felt real to her students, and their papers were real.

What Scott Mandel noticed, as have other teachers who have used MVLEs, is that his students *wanted* to spend more time visiting the museum than he had allocated in his lesson plan. The environment is so realistic that it is highly motivating and extremely self-directed. Each student visited the museum differently: some spent more time at various exhibits, while others browsed the exhibits and then moved on to the more interactive game rooms. That's the beauty of a good simulated environment. It is highly engaging and motivating and each student can create and experience her own "field trip."

Recently, a friend of mine took his seven-year-old to see a 4-D SpongeBob SquarePants "movie"—I use movie in quotes because it should really be called an "experience." Going beyond just wearing 3-D glasses, this experience included smells, motion, water spray, bubbles, wind, and even a tickling feeling over the feet when mice ran by on the floor. *"Michael was so captivated,"* my friend recalled, *"that he only wants me to take him to 4-D movies. When I try to explain that there are none, he insists on at least being able go to movies where he gets to wear the 3-D glasses. We went to a movie the other day that was just a normal movie and he was bored to tears and wanted to know where he could get the glasses to make the movie real."* The technology is there to make learning interesting in as many dimensions as possible. As I write this book I am noticing that many of the children's movies are now in 3-D, where just a year or two ago there were none. Pretty soon, I expect 3-D will be the norm because once kids get a taste of more "realism" they will feel, like Michael, that anything less is just not as interesting and compelling.

Is It Live or Is It Digital?

In future years the iGeneration will be recognized as the first to define digital content as a product as real as any physical entity. They write voraciously, sometimes blogging, other times just sending brief tweets, but always writing missives to friends and commenting on whatever is going on in their lives and the lives of their friends. This is the generation responsible for elevating Twitter to a household word. They single-handedly perfected the art of text messaging and instant messaging and made MySpace and Facebook into their own personal social gathering spots. YouTube is replete with iGen videos, just as Flickr is bursting with their photos and iTunes with their music. It is this generation that was born on the Internet and lives large portions of their lives in cyberspace, where much of the content is of their making.

As I discussed in Chapter 6, this user-generated content presents extremely important opportunities for education. Where it has often been like pulling teeth to get students to write or develop research projects, they now have the tools—and use those tools in their personal lives—to produce creative, high-quality schoolwork. But perhaps it is not the work that is important so much as it is the *enthusiasm* with which they attack projects. Given the right tools, they relish doing a paper on any obscure topic as long as they are allowed to "create" the project in modalities other than simple typed pages. Danielle is a forty-seven-year-old fourth-grade English literature teacher in a Southern California middle school. She talked with me about the difference in her students today compared to those during her first few years of teaching in the 1980s:

Way back then I might assign a paper comparing and contrasting Chaucer's The Canterbury Tales *with Spenser's* The Faerie Queene *and hear a chorus of groans. The papers would be decent, but rather dry. By the ninth or tenth time I had to read these papers, I was getting pretty burned out. Teaching stopped being fun and started feeling like a burden of reading the same dull papers over and over. A year or so ago I gave the same assignment after not having used it for years and gave the students free rein to turn in a 'report' of their choosing as long as it had 'content' and used complete, grammatically correct sentences plus whatever other frills they chose. The papers—actually I shouldn't call them papers since none were traditional written missives—were fantastic and fun to read and grade. Every student took a different approach, yet most of them were able to synthesize their thoughts into a coherent comparison. The best one, or at least my favorite, was done by a student who used animated characters to represent the two works and literally made a cartoon showing similarities and differences through these characters. I know it makes no sense to hear about it but it was truly entertaining and he clearly got it since the content was insightful beyond the clever presentation.*

Danielle seemed truly excited when she talked to me about her new found love of teaching. Interestingly, she was something of a computer novice when she first assigned this report, but reading the student projects (actually, we had quite a discussion about whether one could refer to "reading" a project that was based on more than just the written word) led her to want to learn more about making videos. She asked several of her students to teach her over the summer, and she is now making her own video presentations of English literature and finding that the students are much more *inspired* (her word). (See the discussion of students as teachers in Chapter 8's section "I Learned the Hard Way and So Should They.") This is truly the "creative generation," and if allowed, they will redefine the notion of schoolwork in a way that preserves its integrity but expands its forms.

Should Technology Replace Teachers?

Technology cannot and never should replace curriculum or content. What it offers, as Danielle saw with her English literature students, is a series of novel, engaging ways to present that content. In essence, the curriculum should drive the technology usage, rather than allowing the technology to dictate the curriculum. In Danielle's class the students were still required to show that they understood the similarities and differences between the two classic English writings. However, they were allowed to use any technology to demonstrate that knowledge. The assignment—and the required analytical knowledge—remained the same as her dry, written project of years ago. Changing the modality, or form, made all the difference in both the product and the motivation.

All the technologies that I have presented in this book meet curriculum pedagogical standards. The curriculum or material does not need to change, only the ways in which it is delivered or produced. In essence, technology can be used in three different ways. First, it can be used as a replacement for traditional classroom presentation modalities. Changing from lecturing about ancient Babylonian life can be replaced by interacting in a Babylonian village on a Second Life island. This does not alter the material. In fact, it most likely enhances it beyond what is contained in the students' books or the teacher's lectures. Its multi-dimensionality makes it more real.

Second, using technology as the primary message delivery system allows the teacher to amplify or expand on the material. When a teacher no longer has to lecture on ancient Babylonia, she is free to use class time to expand on the simulation and engage the students in discussions about what they learned from their virtual field trips. The interesting aspect of this is that each student will have her own personalized experience with the simulated environment, so class discussions end up being more illuminating to other students who may not have taken the same pathway through the MVLE. Finally, technology itself can be used to transform the entire educational experience from a flat, two-dimensional local schoolroom to a global classroom by integrating others who are experiencing the same content in a different area of the country or even a different country. Technology, as the Canadian communications theorist Marshall McLuhan said even before the Internet existed, contracted and transformed our world into a "global village" where information and communication are independent of physical distance.[29] An instant message conversation between two avatars, one in Kansas and the other in Krakow, is no different than one between two avatars in the same town. Technology has forever *transformed* our world from one that requires operators and relays and delays to contact people in other countries to instantaneous connection anywhere, anytime.

This does not mean that teachers should sit on the sidelines and allow their students to learn everything online. Quite to the contrary, the teacher now has new roles: content selector and tester, troubleshooter, post-technology discussion leader, and even, if she is willing, content creator. Consider the pre-Internet librarian who was the official "keeper of books." Now compare that to the same librarian today who is the keeper of "information" in any form, from paper to digital. The librarian's role is not any less important, it has simply changed, indeed expanded. The same is true for the teacher of tomorrow. The educational models will change, but the teacher will still be the "teacher."

One researcher, testing a model of technology integration, found that three factors—will, skill, and access to technology—were strong predictors of technology's success in a classroom setting.[30] First, the teacher must want to use the technology, rather than feeling forced or compelled to do so by outside forces such as other teachers or administrators. Second, the teacher must possess the skills to implement the technology. Given that some teachers graduated from college before the computer became a mainstay in society, and others have not embraced the new, continually appearing technologies as readily as the iGeners, professional development becomes critical. School systems should offer a variety of workshops that help teachers use social networks, virtual worlds, video production, podcasting, and other, heretofore undiscovered technologies. Where the budgets are limited, teachers have a perfect resource for this training—their own tech-wizard students. Dan, a seventh-grade teacher, talked to me about his introduction to Second Life and its educational resources:

> *I heard from another teacher about all the virtual field trips available on Second Life and tried to do some exploring at home. After creating my avatar, I had no idea what to do. I figured out how to make him walk, well, really I had him staggering around in circles. I even talked to someone else's avatar, but then I got stuck. I found the list of "islands" and tried to visit an art museum but for some reason I was doing something wrong and all I did was walk off a dock and into the water. I spend hours each day on the Internet and yet I felt pretty darn inept. The next day I asked another teacher about getting some help and he recommended that I ask one particular senior who had done a project in his class using Second Life. You have to understand that the idea of reversing our roles felt very uncomfortable but I asked the student and he stayed after school to help me. Literally within 5 minutes we were at the art museum and then he stayed an hour and a half to show me some other stuff that was pretty exciting. He promised to be available any time I needed help and he even stopped in the next day after school to see if he could help out.*

The third part of the model for integrating into the classroom is actually having access to the required technologies. As I discussed in an earlier chapter, a large number of schools already have computers and Internet access in the classroom. But even if they don't, we are talking about technologies that are available in the home, on a smartphone, at libraries, Internet cafés, and other public locations. Remember, these "lessons" are supposed to be anytime, anywhere, which provides opportunities outside the classroom. While some schools may not be ready for "rewired education," nearly all are already equipped with the necessary tools, or the students have access to computers at home or elsewhere.

It is important to recognize, however, that not all students or their families will be able to afford the tools that may be needed in a rewired educational plan. I am a member of a national advisory board on revising mathematics curriculum for middle-school children. When I talked about "anytime, anywhere" education, one of the board members—an administrator in a poor urban district—told me emphatically that my ideas would not work in her district because her students did not have Internet access outside the classroom. When I asked her if her students used MySpace she said, "of course," and when I asked if they used it at school she said, "Absolutely not! We have it blocked on our computers." I asked, "Where do they access MySpace?" She stopped and thought a minute and said, "I'm not sure, but I do know that they are on all the time after school." Students will find a way to go online because the online world is so much a part of their social sphere that they have no choice. Yes, school districts in poor neighborhoods may not be able to implement some of these ideas, but, for the most part, I know that the students will find a way to connect to cyberspace.

Teachers and school systems will, quite naturally, have concerns about implementing any technologies that place their students online in cyberspace. Although I discussed these issues in my previous book, *Me, MySpace, and I: Parenting the Net Generation,* and in the preceding chapter, they bear repeating. Teachers—and parents—need to be vigilant and monitor students when they go online, whether at home or school. Students need to be taught appropriate use of Internet tools, security, safety, and media literacy. This should be done *before* implementing any computer-based curriculum. I have watched my four children traverse the elementary and secondary school systems, and they all had to take study skills and health classes in the first semester of middle school or high school. I am a strong advocate of adding a component, perhaps even at the elementary school level, that teaches computer safety, online etiquette, and media literacy. Further, I believe strongly that these issues need to be revisited often as the technology changes rapidly and new issues arise.

My Top Eleven Recommendations

I would like to close this book with a summary of my recommendations for rewiring education based on teaching a new generation of students who are radically different than any before.

1. The iGeneration is a creative, multimedia generation. They think of the world as a canvas to paint with words, sights, sounds, video, music, web pages, and anything that they can create. This does not mean that showing PowerPoint presentations in class as a "multimedia presentation" is going to be effective. One student told me, *"it used to be 'death by lecture' and now it is 'death by PowerPoint.'"* Multimedia means using multiple modalities to reach these students. This means understanding that this is a generation of kids who are fast responders (the average time they spend on a webpage before clicking on a link is less than ten seconds), need to be actively involved in their own learning, and abhor doing only one thing at a time. With this in mind, here are some recommendations

for things educators should and should not do in designing their curricula.

- Do not present material in only one modality at a time. Take advantage of as many senses as possible in providing instruction.
- Do not require students to unitask. Research shows that this generation multitasks more than any other and does so seamlessly, often without missing anything from any information source. They can listen to music, watch television, text message, and do their homework all at the same time. Present opportunities for them to do several things simultaneously, particularly in the classroom. If some students get distracted or frustrated, have them wear headphones to block out the sounds. It may sound crazy, but you might try letting them use their iPods while doing classroom work. To you it will seem like a distraction, but to them it is second nature and actually silence is their distraction. Don't worry. They do assimilate the information when they are multitasking and become more involved in digesting disparate pieces of simultaneously presented materials.
- You must allow your students and children to do their schoolwork without stripping their environment of other multimedia events. Trust me, the research shows that it may take a bit longer, but homework will be done without the usual fighting and whining (and that's just the parents).
- Parents: Set limits on when you want homework completed and then let your children do it with whatever technology they want in the background. Be mindful that if they are not getting the work done or are not doing it correctly, you may have to revert to a less multimedia, multitasking environment, but try to avoid

absolute quiet because they will only do worse than they would with at least some form of media on in the background.

- Do not make lengthy lessons. This generation is "antsy" when you require them to sit still and pay attention to one stream of information at a time. Do change topics often and make use of technology to help with transitions. Don't be afraid to merge multiple technologies in one lesson, including audio, video, and web-based materials.

- Do not slip into the abyss of doing an online course. Students do not like the idea of having a class totally online. This is somewhat of a version of school, without the socialization and without the multiple learning modalities. It is too static an environment for an entire course.

2. Education must respect and mine this generation of "content creators" (as dubbed by the Pew Internet & American Life Project).[31] They live to create, and given the chance to do so they will merge multiple media into one complex but comprehensive whole. Here are some specific recommendations:

- Allow projects to involve *any* medium the student wants. Don't be afraid to let them express content in art, music, and video, anything that allows them to create and merge their own skills into a project "report." The concept of "report" has to change to move from strictly written papers to any form of "content" that gets across the message and indicates the same level of understanding that you would expect from a purely written report. Students become much more committed to a topic if they are allowed to use all the tools that they have available, both electronic and traditional ones.

- Do not limit a project to a single format. Let each student select, within specific boundaries based on the expectation of "understanding" a concept, his or her own tools to create and personalize their project. Gone are the days of written reports, dioramas, collages, and even PowerPoint presentations. Teachers should welcome any and all tools that allow the student to delve deeply into a topic.

3. This generation thrives on social interactions, but not just talking amongst themselves in class or at recess. For most preteens and teens, their social life revolves around both their real life (RL) environments and their screen life (SL) virtual environments. They have online friends, offline friends, and many who are both RL and SL friends. Educators have to recognize and capitalize on the social nature of their students because their virtual interactions stretch well beyond the standard school day.

- Create group projects that are done through online collaboration using MySpace, Facebook, or other online virtual environments. Let the students suggest their own working space. Even the younger ones are going virtual, using online social networks such as Club Penguin and other age-appropriate virtual gathering places. Doing a project in a virtual world makes the work seem less like homework and more like . . . well, like their SL.
- My research, and that of others, has shown that when kids interact online they are more honest and less shy than when they are in a face-to-face environment. Allowing some class discussion to happen online will encourage the shy students,

those who never talk in class, to express themselves. Universities have started using online discussions and results are very encouraging. In my own classes I often assign a "participation" grade which is based on either in-class or online discussion, with minimum requirements to do both. This encourages the shy ones to talk online but also makes them at least make some contributions to in-class discussions. Consider having discussions that are truly "anonymous."

- Provide a social networking environment and assign students an arbitrary username that gives no clues about their gender or identity. Make them discuss topics without giving away their identity and watch the level of honesty and self-disclosure increase. This can help stimulate great debates on topics that they would not talk about in front of classmates or even online with their classmates. Anonymity breeds "disinhibition" which, in turn, leads to fascinating exchanges.

- Consider using text messaging or instant messaging to allow students to communicate. It is their style, not yours, and they do it all day long (remember that teens *average* 2,899 texts *per month*). Text messaging can and should be used by parents and teachers to communicate with their children and students. Texting your daughter to come to dinner when she is just down the hall in her bedroom may sound crazy but it works. Text messages beep and get their attention.

4. For most preteens and teens, writing is a chore tantamount to an afternoon in a dentist's chair. That's because education has settled on one format for *all* writing that includes correct syntax and proper usage of English words. Students *should* learn formal writ-

ing. But if you restrict them to *only* one writing style that can be stifling to this generation of "communicators." If you look at how kids write in their online communications they are using a hodge-podge of "textisms" including acronyms (LOL), shortened words (tht), lack of apostrophes (cant), smilies (☺) and other emoticons, and any other added emphasis to provide linguistic information and context. It may look like gibberish but it is writing, and researchers have found that those kids who write more—even using shortcuts, textisms, and other seemingly non-English–based language forms—write better English essays. How is that possible? Well, one theory is that writing begets writing. The more you write, regardless of the format, the better you understand how to put together sentences and thoughts into a constructed whole. Another theory is that even the act of writing seemingly inane instant messages helps the brain develop the associations that are needed to master high-order concepts. Regardless, for most kids, formal writing is no fun. Here are some ways that you can turn it into a more enjoyable task by letting it be fun and entertaining.

- Have the students write some essays using all textisms and then translate each other's into English. Choose a topic that you are studying, only don't grade them on grammar but rather on the ideas contained in their writing.
- Encourage students to write to each other, particularly as part of virtual working groups, using whatever form of language they wish.
- Use online blogs to encourage writing, but pay more attention to content than to format. Blogs allow students to express themselves, and if they feel burdened by demands for syntactic and

semantic perfection their creativity and desire to write will be stifled.

5. This generation thrives on feedback and lots of it. Unlike Baby Boomers who were happy to get feedback in a yearly evaluation, and Gen-Xers who wanted feedback at the end of each project, iGeners have been fed constant positive reinforcement throughout their lives. Teachers should do whatever they can to provide this feedback. Try using electronic tools such as text messaging to get their attention and provide the feedback that will, in turn, increase motivation. Feedback can come from outside the classroom, too. As I discussed in Chapter 6 on creativity, kids are much more motivated to produce high-quality projects when they have a "real" audience. Web 2.0 provides that audience by its interactive nature, allowing projects such as YouTube videos to be posted online and having built-in mechanisms for global feedback such as comments and discussion boards.

6. While Baby Boomers believe in "process," including frequent meetings to discuss issues, iGeners believe in "product" over process. They want to be given a job and then set free to complete it at their own pace. It may make parents and teachers crazy, but iGeners work better under time pressures. It is all part of their fast-paced, technology-enriched lives, which encourage them to jump from here to there and back again in a *nonlinear* fashion that is not suited to setting step-by-step goals and timelines for completing a project.

7. iGeners may be media-savvy but they often lack media literacy. Teach them what sources to trust and how to tell whether online information is fact or opinion, neutral or biased. Teach them how to analyze, filter, evaluate, and synthesize information they

find online and why they might need to visit multiple websites to gather relevant information. Help them understand that copy-and-paste does not mean that they can plagiarize others' work.

8. We can no longer talk about the three "R's." Now there are four—reading, writing, arithmetic, and "realistic technology." They are all equally important and the final "R" can be used to teach and augment the original three.

9. Actively seek out support from techie teachers and students. Technology changes so rapidly that even the most eager adopters have trouble keeping up with Toffler's crashing waves. Aside from help with technology, student input also can be solicited with respect to pedagogical choices. Students know what technology skills they have, and they are "up" on all the latest, greatest websites out there in Web 2.0. Why not let them have a say in designing the next assignment? This infuses a student-centered approach into the curriculum.

10. Recognize that the Internet provides access to a global perspective. We are no longer one nation, but rather an entire global village. Students can and should learn from their international peers, many of whom have eclipsed the United States' current technological education. As aptly stated in a recent report from the Benton Foundation: "Too often, America educates its children for the challenges they will face in the global, knowledge-based 21st century using 20th-century technology and methodology. Other nations provide students with laptop computers, fast broadband connections, and state-of-the-art digital applications, infusing technology and innovation throughout their educational experiences."[32]

11. Teachers wanting to rewire their teaching have lots of support on the Internet. In addition to the resources mentioned in each

chapter, here is just a sampling of general resources that cover all aspects of bringing technology into the classroom:

- TeachersHelpingTeachers: www.pacificnet.net/~mandel/EducationalResources.html
- The Digital Generation Project: www.edutopia.org/digital-generation
- Horizon K12: horizon.nmc.org
- New Media Consortium: www.nmc.org
- Educause: www.educause.edu/home
- Classroom 2.0: www.classroom20.com
- Education Arcade: www.educationarcade.org
- GoKnow!: www.GoKnow.com
- Net Trekker: www.nettrekker.com
- McGraw-Hill Center for Digital Innovation: www.mhcdi.com
- UCLA Center for Digital Innovation: www.cdi.ucla.edu

The time has come for us to put together the solid, research-based ideas described in this book to form a coherent plan for supercharging education. We now have the know-how to provide an educational experience—both inside and outside the classroom—that is motivating, captivating, and engaging. We can no longer ask our children to live in a world where they are immersed in technology in all parts of their lives *except* when they go to school. We *must* rewire education or we risk losing this generation of media-immersed, tech-savvy students who are often brighter and more creative than we realize.

Acknowledgments

Mark Carrier and Nancy Cheever, my two colleagues, and two of my favorite people in the world, deserve more than just a "with" acknowledgement on the title page. Without Mark and Nancy *this book would not exist*. They both wrote chapters and edited every sentence. This is really "our" book. In particular, in addition to writing two other chapters, Mark developed the model of immersive education in Chapter 5 which is a major theme of the book and a guiding force in our current research. Nancy, a professor of Communications who by this printing will be "Dr." Cheever, added her personal expertise in writing the media literacy chapter and contributed to the rest of the book through her organizational insights and sharp editing. I love you both dearly and you have made me a better writer, a better scholar, and a better person. I have to add a special note about Mark's son. Mikey is 7 years old and reminds me daily that this is an amazing new generation. He gobbles up technology at a mind-boggling pace and then expects more to magically appear. To him technology is not a tool, it is just his life. To me, he is the iGeneration.

Mark, Nancy, and I are the founding members of the George Marsh Applied Cognition Laboratory at California State University, Dominguez Hills where we mentor up to a dozen students a year. Dr. George Marsh welcomed me to the Psychology Department the first day I arrived at Dominguez Hills in 1976 and sadly he passed away a few years ago. I am glad that his wife Jean McEwen was able to celebrate the lab opening.

Mark, Nancy, and I started our lab on a shoestring with help from the dean of our college (first Chuck Hohm and now Laura Robles), the McNair Scholar's Program, and the MBRS-RISE Program. We have had some excellent students work with us on the research discussed in this book. I would like to thank (in alphabetical order): Michelle Albertella, Jyenny Babcock, Sandra Benitez, Lyzette Blanco, Jennifer Chang, Cheyenne Cummings, Andrea Edwards, Lynne Erwin, Julie Felt (aka Julez), Esbeyde Garcia, Helen Gonzalez, Izabela

Rewired

Grey (aka Heather/Kate), Alex Lim (aka AA), Roxanne Luna, Scott Mariano, Stephen McGee, Saira Rab, Julia Rifa, and B.B. Rush (aka Steven Thacker). A special hug and thanks to Julez, my honorary daughter, who is the lab "mother" and is always there to help any student with stats, SPSS, survey design, or life.

I owe a great debt of gratitude to the students at CSUDH who seem to enjoy my classes even though I am a pretty demanding teacher and have high expectations. CSUDH is one of the most diverse campuses in the country and I cannot be happier having spent my entire career there. Several other colleagues have a special place in my heart including: Jo Ann Uno, our department secretary extraordinaire for more years than I can remember; Peter Desberg, professor of Education, and Maria Hurtado-Ortiz, professor of psychology. Although not a CSUDH professor, Nancy Willard, the world's cyberbullying expert, provides an omnipresent supportive ear. And a special thanks to Marty Saeman, editor of *The National Psychologist,* who has allowed me to write about the interface of technology and psychology since 1995.

My family has always been very supportive of my work. Thanks to my mom and dad, Sarah and Oscar Rosen, my sister and brother-in-law, Judy and Michael Heumann, my brother and sister-in-law, Bruce and Liane Rosen, and my cousins Alan and Rhonda Rosen and Ellen and John Moir. At my father's ninetieth birthday celebration I was reminded that while we are family, we are also friends.

My children—Adam, Arielle, Chris, and Kaylee—are the lights of my life. The fact that I have heard each of them tell someone that they think their dad is "cool" and a tad "eccentric" makes me giggle and smile. They are all amazing adults and I love watching them make their way through life.

I have three other special friends. Sandy Kaler, Phyllisann Maguire, and Bob Indseth Who through their support helped me get through the writing process of this book.

Stacey Glick, my agent at Dystel & Goderich Literary Management, has been my cheerleader through the entire process for this book and *Me, MySpace, and I.* She is always available and even when she had her twins she returned my emails immediately. My Palgrave Macmillan editor, Laurie Harting, took me on early in the project when I wasn't sure that I wanted to write this book. She "got" me from the start and simply let me write my way with my voice. I also want to thank Alan Bradshaw at Palgrave Macmillan who once again was my "production director" which I discovered meant that he read every last word of this book multiple times.

Endnotes

Chapter 1

1. National Science Foundation (2008, June 24). *Fostering learning in the networked world: The cyberlearning opportunity and challenge. A 21st Century agenda for the National Science Foundation,* p. 12. Retrieved from http://www.nsf.gov/pubs/2008/nsf08204/nsf08204.pdf.
2. There is no solid agreement concerning exact years for each generation. In this work my colleagues and I have chosen to refer to those children who are still in elementary and secondary school as the iGeneration. As I will point out later in this chapter and throughout the book, this generation can be characterized as being solidly committed to the ubiquitous use of mobile technologies, most commonly MP3 players, smartphones, and similar devices. The term "iGeneration" seems to best capture these children and adolescents compared to their older brothers and sisters of the (Inter)Net Generation. Regardless of the exact name, this generation shares their love of anything "i," such as the iMac, iPod, iPhone, and Wii. The "i" also reflects this generation's need for "individualized" technologies that can be adapted to their lives in ways that are personally meaningful. It should be noted that the first popular appearance of the name iGeneration appeared in the song of the same name by American hip-hop artist MC Lars In 2004.
3. Roberts, D. F., Foehr, U. G., & Rideout, V. (2005). *Generation M: Media in the lives of 8–18 year-olds.* Menlo Park, CA: Kaiser Family Foundation. Retrieved from http://www.kff.org/entmedia/upload/Generation-M-Media-in-the-Lives-of-8-18-Year-olds-Report.pdf.
4. Rideout, V., & Hamel, E. (2006, May). *The media family: Electronic media in the lives of infants, toddlers, preschoolers and their parents.* Menlo Park, CA: Kaiser Family Foundation. Retrieved from http://www.kff.org/entmedia/upload/7500.pdf.
5. Rosen, L. D., Cheever, N. A., & Carrier, L. M. (2008). The association of parenting style and child age with parental limit setting and adolescent MySpace behavior. *Journal of Applied Developmental Psychology, 29,* 459–471. The Nielsen Company (2009, June). *How teens use media: A Nielsen report on the myths and realities of teen media trends.* New York, NY. Nielsen retrieved from http://blog.nielsen.com/nielsenwire/reports/nielsen_howteensusemedia_june09.pdf.
6. Zimmerman, F. J. (2008, June). *Children's media use and sleep problems: Issues and unanswered questions.* Menlo Park, CA: Kaiser Family Foundation. Retrieved from http://www.kff.org/entmedia/upload/7674.pdf.
7. My colleagues Dr. L. Mark Carrier and Professor Nancy Cheever, and I, and our many student researchers in the George Marsh Applied Cognition Laboratory at California State University, Dominguez Hills, have performed dozens of research studies on the impact of technology over the last decade. In each study we use anonymous online surveys to interview

parents, children, tweens, teens, young adults, and teachers on a variety of topics, including their overall daily use of media and technology, social networking, multitasking, text messaging, video game playing, and physical and psychological health as a function of media use. For example, in order to better understand how media and technology are shaping our lives we have studied generational differences in technology use and multitasking, the impact of MySpace on teens and young adults, the relationship between media use and health, the impact of the use of "textisms" (e.g., LOL, 2nite, l8r, and emoticons) on writing ability, the effect of text message interruptions on classroom comprehension, and the impact of video gaming on teen behavior. Reports of our research are housed at www.Me-MySpace-and-I.com in the form of published papers, commentaries, and conference presentations. Throughout this book references will be made to documents that cover specific data from one or more of our studies, and each of these documents is accessible through the website. Note that most of our research subjects represent a cross-section of multi-cultural Southern California with similar characteristics as the local census figures. Our findings have been validated by similar research done in other areas of the United States and in England.

8. Rosen et al., The association of parenting style and child age with parental limit setting and adolescent MySpace behavior.

9. Marquardt, P. (2009, May 15). *The effect of accountability-based testing on college-bound students: A case study of the Virginia Standards of learning.* Social Science Research Network. Retrieved from http://papers.ssrn.com/sol3/papers.cfm?abstract_id=1405440. Pope, J. (2006, November 18). Admissions boards face "grade inflation." *Associated* Press. Retrieved from http://www.washingtonpost.com/wp-dyn/content/article/2006/11/18/AR2006111800473 _pf.html. Pryor, J. H., Hurtado, S, Saenz, V., Santos, J. & Korn, W. (2007). *The American freshman: Forty-year trends, 1966–2006.* Los Angeles, CA: Higher Education Research Institute.

10. Marklein, M. B. (2007, April 8). Students apply, but not to a dozen colleges. *USA Today.* Retrieved from http://www.usatoday.com/news/education/2007–04–09-student-applications_N.htm. National Association for College Admission Counseling (2006, November 8). College acceptance rates: How many get in? *USA Today.* Retrieved from http://www.usatoday.com/news/education/2006–11–02-collegerates_x.htm.

11. Ziegler, S. G. (2007, March). The (mis)education of Generation M. *Learning, Media and Technology, 32(1),* 69–81.

12. U.S. Census Bureau. *Elementary and secondary schools—Teachers, enrollment, and pupil-teacher ratio: 1970 to 2006.* Retrieved from http://www.census.gov/compendia/statab/tables/09s0242.pdf.

13. U.S. Census Bureau (2008, May 1). Population division, annual estimates of the population by sex and selected age groups for the United States. Retrieved from http://www.census.gov/population/www/socdemo/age/age_sex_2008.html.

14. U.S. Census Bureau. *Computers for school instruction in elementary and secondary schools: 2005–2006.* Retrieved from http://www.census.gov/compendia/statab/tables/09s0252.pdf.

15. This research was conducted in 2008 and 2009 through four online anonymous interviews of more than 3,900 parents, teens, and young adults. Many of the results are summarized in the following presentation: Rosen, L. D. (2009, April 23). *Educating the Net Generation: Why kids hate school.* Paper presented at the Western Psychological Association Convention, Portland, OR. Retrieved from http://www.csudh.edu/psych/Educating_the_Net_Generation_Dr._Larry_Rosen_Western_Psychological_Convention_4–23–2009.pdf.

16. Rosen, et al., The association of parenting style and child age with parental limit setting and adolescent MySpace behavior.

17. Olsen, S. (2008, Jun 9). Study: Tykes, teens outdo adults on YouTube. *CNET* News. Retrieved from http://m.cnet.com/site?sid=cnet&pid=News.Detail&category=7&topic=996 3543. The Nielsen Company (2009). *How teens use media.*

18. Rosen, L. D. (2008, November 3). *Understanding the Net Generation: Is it good for them to be so connected 24/7?* Paper presented at UCLA Developmental Forum. Retrieved from http://www.csudh.edu/psych/Understanding_the_Net_Generation._Is_it_good_for_them_to_be_so_connected_24–7_UCLA_Developmental_Forum_11–3–2008.pdf.

19. Thurlow, C. (2006). From statistical panic to moral panic: The metadiscursive construction and popular exaggeration of new media language in the print media. *Journal of Computer-Mediated Communication, 11(3),* 667–701.

20. Toffler, A. (1980). *The third wave.* New York: William Morrow.

21. Retailer Daily (2008, October 30). *Web sites influence over half of US toy purchasers.* Retrieved from http://www.retailerdaily.com/entry/8741/web-sites-influence-over-half-of-us-toy-purchasers/.

22. Rosen, L. D. (2009, April 24). *Welcome to the iGeneration.* Paper presented at Western Psychological Association Convention, Portland, OR. Retrieved from http://www.csudh.edu/psych/Symposium_Welcome_to_the_iGeneration_Dr._Larry_Rosen_Western_Psychological_Association_Convention_4–24–2009.pdf.

23. Rosen, L. D. (2009, January 28). *The psychology of technology.* Keynote presentation at the National IT Conference for U.S. Pretrial Services and U.S. Probation. Retrieved from http://www.csudh.edu/psych/The_Psychology_of_Technology_National_IT_Conference_for_U.S._Pretrial_Services_&_U.S._Probation_January_28,_2009_Dr._Larry_Rosen.pdf.

24. Downtown Women's Club (2008, October 10). *The Daily Show major source of political news for Gen Y.* PRWeb. Retrieved from http://www.prweb.com/pdfdownload/1448064/pr.pdf.

25. Rosen, *Welcome to the iGeneration.*

26. Generation Xers were born between 1965 and 1979, preceded by Baby Boomers (1946–1964).

Chapter 2

1. Tapscott, D. (2009). *Grown up digital: How the Net Generation is changing your world.* New York, NY: McGraw-Hill, p. 9.

2. Rosen, L. D. (2007). *Me, MySpace, and I: Parenting the Net Generation.* New York, NY: Palgrave Macmillan.

3. Rosen, L. D. (2009, April 24). *Welcome to the iGeneration.* Paper presented at Western Psychological Association Convention, Portland, OR. Retrieved from http://www.csudh.edu/psych/Symposium_Welcome_to_the_iGeneration_Dr._Larry_Rosen_Western_Psychological_Association_Convention_4–24–2009.pdf.

4. Rosen, L. D. (2006). *Adolescents in MySpace: Identity formation, friendship and sexual predators.* Retrieved from http://www.csudh.edu/psych/Adolescents in MySpace–Executive Summary.pdf.

5. Palfrey, J., & Gasser, U. (2008). *Born digital: Understanding the first generation of digital natives.* New York, NY: Basic Books.

6. Mozes, A. (2008, June 9). Too much cell phone time takes toll on teen sleep. *U. S. News & World Reports.* Retrieved from http://health.usnews.com/articles/health/healthday/2008/06/09/too-much-cell-phone-time-takes-toll-on-teen-sleep.html.

7. Marketwarch (2008, November 13). *CEA study shows nearly half of teen activities are driven by technology: 80 percent of teens can not imagine spending a day without technology.* Retrieved from http://www.marketwatch.com/news/story/CEA-Study-Shows-Nearly-Half/story.aspx?guid={0ECCC629–8DF8–494A–9772-D0393F5DD5BE.

8. Rosen, L. D., Cheever, N. A., & Carrier, L. M. (2008). The association of parenting style and child age with parental limit setting and adolescent MySpace behavior. *Journal of Applied Developmental Psychology, 29,* 459–471. Rosen, *Welcome to the iGeneration.* Rosen, L. D. (2009, January 28). *The psychology of technology.* Keynote presentation at the National IT Conference for U.S. Pretrial Services and U.S. Probation. Retrieved from http://www.csudh

.edu/psych/The_Psychology_of_Technology_National_IT_Conference_for_U.S._Pretrial
Services&_U.S._Probation_January_28,_2009_Dr._Larry_Rosen.pdf.

9. Vandewater, E. A., Rideout, V. J., Wartella, E. A., Huang, X., Lee, J. H., & Shim, M. (2007). Digital childhood: Electronic Media and technology use among infants, toddlers, and preschoolers. *Pediatrics, 119(5),* 1006–1015. NPD Group (2008, January 15). *Kids ages 2– to– 14 consume digital content on a device between three and seven times per month.* Retrieved from http://www.npd.com/press/releases/press_080115.html. Mindlin, A. (2008, August 25). Preferring the web over watching TV. *New York Times.* Retrieved from http://www.nytimes. com/2008/08/25/technology/25drill.html. Horatio Alger Association of Distinguished Americans (2008). *The state of our nation's youth 2008–2009.* Retrieved from http://www. horatioalger.org/pdfs/0708SONY.pdf. Alyroso, C. (2007, February 9). *TV still rules kids' media habits.* Retrieved from http://www.mediaincanada.com/articles/mic/20070209/kids.html.

10. Rosen et al., The association of parenting style and child age with parental limit setting and adolescent MySpace behavior. Rosen, *Adolescents in MySpace.* Horatio Alger Association, *The state of our nation's youth 2008–2009.*

11. Weil, M. M., & Rosen, L. D. (1997). *TechnoStress: Coping with technology @Work @Home @Play.* New York, NY: John Wiley & Sons, pp. 129–131.

12. Rosen, *Welcome to the iGeneration.*

13. It is important to note that these interviews were all anonymous, voluntary, and done online with no parental identifying information, which is the best way to ensure that the responses are genuine and accurate.

14. Carrier, L. M., Cheever, N. A., Rosen, L. D., Benitez, S., & Chang, J. (2009). Multitasking across generations: Multitasking choices and difficulty ratings in three generations of Americans. *Computers in Human Behavior, 25,* 483–489. Rosen, L. D. (2008, November 3). *Understanding the Net Generation: Is it good for them to be so connected 24/7?* Paper presented at UCLA Developmental Forum. Retrieved from http://www.csudh.edu/psych/Understanding _the_Net_Generation._Is_it_good_for_them_to_be_so_connected_24–7_UCLA_Developmental_Forum_11–3–2008.pdf.

15. Carrier et al., Multitasking across generations. Rosen, *Understanding the Net Generation.*

16. National Endowment for the Arts (2007, November). *To read or not to read: A question of national consequence.* Retrieved from http://www.nea.gov/research/ToRead.PDF.

17. National Endowment for the Arts, *To read or not to read,* p. 4.

18. Foehr, U. G. (2006, December). *Media multitasking among American youth: Prevalence, predictors and pairings.* Menlo Park, CA: Kaiser Family Foundation. Retrieved from http://www .kff.org/entmedia/upload/7592.pdf.

19. Fontana, J. (2008, May 15). Study: Schools, businesses must adapt to 'thumb generation.' *Network World.* Retrieved from http://www.networkworld.com/news/2008/051508-thumb-generation.html.

20. Rosen, *Understanding the Net Generation.* Rosen, *The psychology of technology.*

21. Harris Interactive (2008, September 12). *A generation unplugged.* Retrieved from http://files .ctia.org/pdf/HI_TeenMobileStudy_ResearchReport.pdf.

22. Rosen, *Understanding the Net Generation.* Rosen, *The psychology of technology.*

23. Gutierrez, H. C., Mariano, S., Rab, S. & Rosen, L. D. (2009, April 26). *Media portrayal of MySpace and Internet dangers: An archival study.* Paper presented at the Western Psychological Association Convention, Portland, OR. Retrieved from http://www.csudh.edu/psych/ MEDIA_PORTRAYAL_OF_MYSPACE_AND_INTERNET_DANGERS_AN%20 ARCHIVAL_STUDY_Gutierrez_Mariano_Rab_Rosen_4–26–2009.pdf.

24. Rosen et al., The association of parenting style and child age with parental limit setting and adolescent MySpace behavior. Rosen, *Adolescents in MySpace.*

25. Ito, M., Horst, H., Bittanti, M., boyd, d., Herr-Stephenson, B., Lange, P. G., Pascoe, C. J., & Robinson, L. (2008, November). *Living and learning with new media: Summary of findings from the Digital Youth Project.* The John D. and Catherine T. MacArthur Foundation Re-

ports on Digital Media and Learning. Quoted in Trotter, A. (2008, December 3). Much of new-media learning said to occur informally: Lessons with friends seen rivaling those in school. *Education Week*. Retrieved from http://www.edweek.org/ew/articles/2008/11/20/14digital.html?tkn=TLVFI0PtRfy9wfO%2FfCkvYQTii4bgVO1FZ4CM.

26. Rosen, *Me, MySpace, and I.*

27. Rosen et al., The association of parenting style and child age with parental limit setting and adolescent MySpace behavior.

28. Ito, et al., *Living and learning with new media*, p. 2.

29. Rosen, *Adolescents in MySpace*.

30. Lewin, T. (2008, November 20). Online teens are learning skills, not wasting time. *New York Times*. Retrieved from http://www.nytimes.com/2008/11/20/world/americas/20iht-net.1.17991392.html.

31. Horatio Alger Association, *The state of our nation's youth 2008–2009*.

32. eMarketer (2008, November 19). *College student and teen web tastes: Online behavior patterns are formed early*. Retrieved from http://www.emarketer.com/Article.aspx?R=1006736.

33. Fallis, D. (2008). Toward an epistemology of Wikipedia. *Journal of the American Society for Information Science and Technology, 59(10)*, 1662–1674. Giles, J. (2005, December 15). Special report Internet encyclopaedias go head to head. *Nature, 438*, 900–901.

34. Baumgartner, J., & Morris, J. S. (2006). "The 'Daily Show' effect": Candidate evaluations, efficacy, and American youth. *American Politics Research, 34(3)*, 341–367.

35. A good overall discussion of media literacy can be found in: Potter, W. J. (2008). *Media literacy* (4th ed.). Thousand Oaks: CA.

36. Lenhart, A., & Madden, M., Smith, A., & Macgill, A. (2007, December). *Teens and social media: More teens are creating and sharing material on the internet*. Washington, DC: Pew Internet & American Life Project. Retrieved from http://www.pewinternet.org/Reports/2007/Teens-and-Social-Media.aspx. Lenhart, A., & Madden, M. (2005, November 2). *More than half of online teens have created content for the internet; and most teen downloaders think that getting free music files is easy to do*. Washington, DC: Pew Internet & American Life Project. Retrieved from http://www.pewinternet.org/~/media//Files/Reports/2005/PIP_Teens_Content_Creation.pdf.pdf.

37. Visit www.learningstyles.net for more about learning styles and for information about the work of Professors Kenneth and Rita Dunn and their learning styles assessment tools.

38. Johnson, S. (2005). *Everything bad is good for you*. New York, NY: Riverhead Books.

39. Visit www.hookedonphonics.com for more information about this auditory learning technique.

40. Visit www.montessori.edu for more information about this tactile-kinesthetic learning technique.

41. Gardner, H. (1993). *Multiple intelligences: The theory in practice*. New York, NY: Basic Books.

42. For several different learning style assessments visit http://www.learning-styles-online.com, http://www.ldpride.net/learning-style-test.html or http://www.businessballs.com/howardgardnermultipleintelligences.htm#multiple%20intelligences%20tests.

43. Manual, K. (2002). Teaching information literacy to Generation Y. *Journal of Library Administrations, 36(1–2)*, 195–217 as quoted in Weiler, A. (2004). Information-seeking behavior in Generation Y students: Motivation, critical thinking, and learning theory. *The Journal of Academic Librarianship, 31(1)*, 46–53.

44. Associated Press (2007, August 20). *The Associated Press-MTV youth happiness study*. Retrieved from http://surveys.ap.org/data/KnowledgeNetworks/2007–08–20%20AP-MTV%20Youth%20Happiness.pdf.

45. Horatio Alger Association, *The state of our nation's youth 2008–2009*.

46. Patterson, C. K. (2007, summer). The impact of generational diversity in the workplace. *Generational Diversity, 15(3)*, 17–22.

47. Horatio Alger Association, *The state of our nation's youth 2008–2009*.

48. Lyons, S. L., Duxbury, L., & Higgins, C. (2007). An empirical assessment of generational differences in basic human values. *Psychological Reports, 101,* 339–352.

Chapter 3

1. Harris Interactive (2008, September 12). *A generation unplugged.* Retrieved from http://files .ctia.org/pdf/HI_TeenMobileStudy_ResearchReport.pdf.
2. Cellan-Jones, R. (2008, March 6). "The mobile internet kids." Dot.life, *BBC News.* Retrieved from http://www.bbc.co.uk/blogs/technology/2008/03/the_mobile_internet_kids .html.
3. Baird, D. (2008, June 17). The mobile internet generation. Retrieved from http://www .debaird.net/blendededunet/2008/06/the-mobile-inte.html.
4. HarrisInteractive, *A generation unplugged.*
5. Chartier, D. (2008, September 15). iPhone app growth outpacing iTunes' early days. *Ars Techina.* Retrieved from http://arstechnica.com/apple/news/2008/09/iphone-app-growth-outpacing-itunes-early-days.ars.
6. CrunchTear.com (2008, July 13). Profile of an iPhone user. *ResearchCast.* Retrieved from http://www.researchcast.com/alpha/?p=51.
7. Loechner, J. (2009, July 10). 40 percent of "iUsers" accessing internet from mobile more than from computer. *MediaPost,* Retrieved from http://www.mediapost.com/publications/?fa =Articles.showArticle&art_aid=109199.
8. Sharples, M. (2007). Introduction to special issue of JCAL on mobile learning. *Journal of Computer Assisted Learning, 23,* 283–284.
9. NGT's Global Youth Panel: The Connected Class. Retrieved from http://www.mobilebe-havior.com/2008/04/15/ngts-global-youth-panel-the-connected-class/.
10. Kennedy, T. L. M., Smith, A., Wells, A. T., & Wellman, B. (2008, October 19). *Networked families: Parents and spouses are using the internet and cell phones to create a "new connectedness" that builds on remote connections and shared experiences.* Washington, DC: Pew Internet & American Life Project. Retrieved from http://www.pewinternet.org/~/media//Files/Reports/2008/PIP_Networked_Family.pdf.pdf.
11. Rosen, L. D. (2009, April 23). *Educating the Net Generation: Why kids hate school.* Paper presented at the Western Psychological Association Convention, Portland, OR. Retrieved from http://www.csudh.edu/psych/Educating_the_Net_Generation_Dr._Larry_Rosen_ Western_Psychological_Convention_4–23–2009.pdf.
12. Rosen, L. D. (2008, November 3). *Understanding the Net Generation: Is it good for them to be so connected 24/7?* Paper presented at UCLA Developmental Forum. Retrieved from http://www.csudh.edu/psych/Understanding_the_Net_Generation._Is_it_good_for_them _to_be_so_connected_24–7_UCLA_Developmental_Forum_11–3–2008.pdf.
13. Nielsen Mobile (2008, September 26). *Mobile texting up 450% in two years, outpaces voice calling.* Retrieved from http://www.marketingcharts.com/interactive/mobile-texting-up–450-in-two-years-outpaces-voice-calling–6154.
14. Nielsen Mobile (2009, June). *How teens use media: A Nielsen report on the myths and realities of teen media trends.* Retrieved from http://blog.nielsen.com/nielsenwire/reports/nielsen_how teensusemedia_june09.pdf.
15. Rosen, *Understanding the Net Generation.* Rosen, L. D. (2009, April 24). *Welcome to the iGen-eration.* Paper presented at Western Psychological Association Convention, Portland, OR. Retrieved from http://www.csudh.edu/psych/Symposium_Welcome_to_the_iGeneration _Dr._Larry_Rosen_Western_Psychological_Association_Convention_4–24–2009.pdf.
16. HarrisInteractive, *A generation unplugged.*
17. Kazeniac, A. (2009, February 9). *Social networks: Facebook takes over top spot, Twitter climbs.* Retrieved from http://blog.compete.com/2009/02/09/facebook-myspace-twitter-social-network.

18. HarrisInteractive, *A generation unplugged.*
19. McLoughlin, C., & Lee, M. J. W. (2007). Social software and participatory learning: Pedagogical choices with technology affordances in the Web 2.0 era. *Proceedings of ASCILITE Conference,* pp. 664–673, Singapore.
20. Stevens, H., & Pettey, C. (2009, May 20). *Gartner says worldwide mobile phone sales declined 8.6 percent and smartphones grew 12.7 percent in first quarter of 2009.* Press Release from Gartner, Inc. Retrieved from http://www.gartner.com/it/page.jsp?id=985912.
21. Nielsen Mobile (2009). *Television, Internet and mobile usage in the U.S.: A2/M2 Three Screen Report, First quarter 2009.* Retrieved from http://it.nielsen.com/site/documents/A2M2 _3Screens_1Q09_FINAL.pdf.
22. At this writing many cities, including Mountain View, CA; Cambridge, MA; Binghamton, NY; Lawrence, KN; and Austin, TX, have either free wireless access everywhere or limited to central municipal areas. My own city, a small coastal town in Northern San Diego County, has begun installing free wireless access throughout the city, to be phased in over a two-year period. Free wireless-access locations can be found at www.wififreespot.com, which appears to be updated fairly regularly.
23. Laouris, Y., and Eteoklous, N. (2005). *We need an educationally relevant definition of mobile learning; Mobile technology: the future of learning in your hands.* Paper presented in the Proceedings of the MLEARN 2005. Retrieved from http://www.mlearn.org.za/CD/papers/ Laouris%20&%20Eteokleous.pdf.
24. Humphreys, L. (2005). Cellphones in public: Social interactions in a wireless era. *New Media & Society, 7(6),* 810–833.
25. McLoughlin, C., & Lee, M. J. W. (2007). Social software and participatory learning: Pedagogical choices with technology affordances in the Web 2.0 era. *Proceedings of ASCILITE Conference,* pp. 664–673, Singapore.
26. See the MOBILearn Project website at http://www.mobilearn.org.
27. See the M-Learning website at http://www.m-learning.org.
28. http://www.iamlearn.org.
29. ACU Mobile Learning (2008). *Mobile learning and the connected campus.* Abilene Christian University. Retrieved from http://www.acu.edu/technology/mobilelearning/index. html.
30. Kagan, S. (1992). *Cooperative learning.* San Clemente, CA: Kagan Cooperative Learning. http://www.KaganOnline.com; Johnson, D. W., Johnson, R. T., & Holubec, E. J. (1994). *Cooperative Learning in the Classroom.* Association for Supervision & Curriculum Development. Http://www.clcrc.com.
31. LaPrairie, K., & Hinson, J. (2008). Enhancing Cooperative e-Learning through Personality Profiling. In K. McFerrin et al. (eds.), *Proceedings of Society for Information Technology and Teacher Education International Conference 2008,* pp. 3018–3022. Chesapeake, VA: AACE.
32. The International Association for Mobile Learning (http://mlearning.noe-kaleidoscope.org/) is a good resource for mobile learning projects.
33. Robertson, I. (2008). Learners' attitudes to wiki technology in problem-based, blended learning for vocational teacher education. *Australasian Journal of Educational Technology, 24(4),* 425–441.
34. Kang, S., Watt, J. H., & Ala, S. K. (2008, January 7). Communicators' perceptions of social presence as a function of avatar realism in small display mobile communication devices. *Proceedings of the 41st Hawaii International Conference on System Sciences (HICSS),* p. 147.
35. Rosen, L. D. (2007). *Me, MySpace, and I: Parenting the Net Generation.* New York, NY: Palgrave Macmillan.
36. Kang et al., Communicators' perceptions of social presence.
37. Bandura, A. (1977). *Social learning theory.* New York, NY: Prentice Hall.
38. International Association for Mobile Learning.

Chapter 4

1. Carrier, L. Mark, Cheever, N. A., Rosen, L. D., Benitez, S., & Chang, J. (2009). Multitasking across generations: Multitasking choices and difficulty ratings in three generations of Americans. *Computers in Human Behavior, 25,* 483–489.

2. Wallis, C. (2006, March 19). The multitasking generation. *Time.*

3. Bowman, L. L., Levine, L. E., Waite, B. M., & Gendron, M. (2008, August). *Instant messaging impacts academic reading time, but not test performance.* Poster presentation at the 116th Annual Convention of the American Psychological Association, Boston, MA.

4. Baron, N. S. (2007). Adjusting the volume: Technology and multitasking in discourse control. In J. E. Katz (Ed.), *Mobile communication and social change in a global context.* Cambridge, MA: MIT Press.

5. Pashler, H. (1994). Dual-task interference in simple tasks: Data and theory. *Psychological Bulletin, 116,* 220–244. Pashler, H. (1998). *The psychology of attention.* Cambridge, MA: MIT Press.

6. Kahneman, D. (1973). *Attention and effort.* Englewood Cliffs, NJ: Prentice-Hall.

7. Welford, A. T. (1952). The "psychological refractory period" and the timing of high speed performance—A review and a theory. *British Journal of Psychology, 43,* 2–19. Welford, A. T. (1967). Single-channel operation in the brain. *Acta Psychologica, 27,* 5–22. Welford, A. T. (1980). The single-channel hypothesis. In A. T. Welford (Ed.), *Reaction Time,* pp. 215–252. San Diego, CA: Academic Press.

8. Kenyon, S., & Lyons, G. (2007). Introducing multitasking to the study of travel and ICT: Examining its extent and assessing its potential importance. *Transportation Research Part A, 41,* 161–175.

9. Carrier et al., Multitasking across generations.

10. Lin, L., Lee, J., & Robertson, T. (2009). *Can we multitask better with more familiar tasks?* Paper presented at the International Society for Technology in Education (ISTE)'s 30th Annual National Education Computing Conference (NECC). Washington, D. C.

11. Foehr, U. G. (2006). *Media multitasking among American youth: Prevalence, predictors and pairings.* Menlo Park, CA: The Henry J. Kaiser Family Foundation.

12. Singer, J. L. (19). The power and limitations of television: A cognitive-affective analysis. In P. H. Tannenbaum (Ed.) *The Entertainment functions of television.* New York, NY: Lawrence Erlbaum, pp. 31–65.

13. Jordan, A., Fishbein, M., Zhang, W., Jeong, S. H., Hennessy, M., Martin, S, et al. (2005). *Multiple media use and multitasking with media among high school and college students.* Paper presented at the International Communication Association, Annual meeting, New York, NY.

14. Jeong, S., & Fishbein, M. (2007). Predictors of multitasking with media: Media factors and audience factors. *Media Psychology, 10,* 364–384.

15. Foehr, *Media multitasking among American youth.*

16. Blakemore, S.-J., & Choudhury, S. (2006). Development of the adolescent brain: Implications for executive function and social cognition. *Journal of Child Psychology and Psychiatry, 47(3/4),* 296–312. Conklin, H. M., Luciana, M., Hooper, C. J., & Yarger, R. S. (2007). Working memory performance in typically developing children and adolescents: Behavioral evidence of protracted frontal lobe development. *Developmental Neuropsychology, 31(1),* 103–128.

17. Baron, N. S. (2007). Adjusting the volume: Technology and multitasking in discourse control. In J. E. Katz (Ed.), *Mobile communication and social change in a global context.* Cambridge, MA: MIT Press.

18. Stoneman, P. (2007). *The sociology and efficacy of multitasking.* Chimera Working Paper Number: 2007–05. University of Essex. Retrieved from http://www.essex.ac.uk/chimera/content/pubs/wps/CWP–2007–05-Soc-Eff-Multitask-Final.pdf.

19. Cherry, E. C. (1953). Some experiments on the recognition of speech, with one and with two ears. *Journal of the Acoustical Society of America, 25,* 975–979. Moray, N. (1959). At-

tention in dichotic listening: affective cues and the influence of instructions. *Quarterly Journal of Experimental Psychology, 27,* 56–60. Wood, N., & Cowan, N. (1995). The cocktail party phenomenon revisited: How frequent are attention shifts to one's name in an irrelevant auditory channel? *Journal of Experimental Psychology: Learning, Memory, and Cognition, 21,* 255–60.

20. Chapel, W. (2009, October 12). Tampa Bay school lets kids use cell phones. *Education Week.* Retrieved from http://www.examiner.com/a–2260804–Tampa_Bay_school_lets_kids_use _cell_phones.html.

21. Fry, M. M., & Dacey, C. (2007). Factors contributing to incidents in medicine administration. Part 2. *British Journal of Nursing, 16,* 676–81. Luong, A., & Rogelberg, S. G. (2005). Meetings and more meetings: The relationship between meeting load and the daily well-being of employees. *Group Dynamics: Theory, Research, and Practice, 9,* 58–67.

22. Adamczyk, P. D., & Bailey, B. P. (2004), *If not now, when? The effects of interruption at different moments within task execution.* Paper presented at CHI 2004, Conference on Human Factors in Computing Systems, Vienna, Austria. McCrickard, D. S., Catrambone, R., Chewar, C. M., & Stasko, J. T. (2003). Establishing tradeoffs that leverage attention for utility: Empirically evaluating information display in notification systems. *International Journal of Human-Computer Studies, 58,* 547–82.

23. Weil, M. M., & Rosen, L. D. (1997). *TechnoStress: Coping with technology @Work @Home @Play.* New York, NY: John Wiley & Sons.

Chapter 5

1. Edirisingha, P., Nie, M., Pluciennik, M., & Young, R. (2009). Socialisation for learning at a distance in a 3-D multi-user virtual environment. *British Journal of Educational Technology, 40(3),* 458–479.

2. Salmon, G. (2009). The future for (second) life and learning. *British Journal of Educational Technology, 40(3),* 526–538.

3. Dede, C. (2009, January 2). Immersive interfaces for engagement and learning. *Science, 323,* 66–68. Twining, P. (2009). Exploring the educational potential of virtual worlds: Some reflections from the SPP. *British Journal of Educational Technology, 40(3),* 496–514. Cullen, A. (2008). Virtual total immersion. Faculty of Humanities and Social Sciences papers. Retrieved from http://epublications.bond.edu.au/cgi/viewcontent.cgi?article=1292&context=hss_pubs.

4. Ackerman, D. (1991). *A natural history of the senses.* New York, NY: Vintage.

5. Matlin, M. W. (2009). *Cognition* (7th ed.). New York, NY: Wiley.

6. Dede, C. (2009). Immersive interfaces for engagement and learning. Twining, P. (2009). Exploring the educational potential of virtual worlds. Cullen, A. (2008). Virtual total immersion.

7. Short, J. W., Williams, E., Christie, B. (1976). *The social psychology of telecommunications.* John Wiley & Sons, Ltd. London. Ravaja, N., Saari, T., Turpeinen, M., Laarni, J., Slaminen, M., and Kivikangas, M. (2006). Spatial presence and emotions during video game playing: Does it matter with whom you play? *Presence: Teleoperators and Virtual Environments, 15,* 381–392. Ijsselsteijn, W., de Kort, Y., Poels, K., Jurgelionis, A., Bellotti, F. (2007). Characterising and measuring user experiences in digital games. *ACE Conference,* Salzburg, Austria. Retrieved from http://www.gamexplab.nl/includes/pages/publications/articles/IJsselsteijn %20et%20al%202007%20Characterising%20and%20Measuring%20User%20 Experiences%20ACE%202007%20workshop.pdf.

8. Rothbaum, B. O. (2009). Using virtual reality to help our patients in the real world. *Depression and Anxiety, 26(2),* 209–211.

9. Turkle, S. (1995). *Life on the screen: Identity in the age of the Internet.* New York: NY. Simon & Schuster, p. 10.

10. Social networking grows 93 percent; Communication becomes entertainment. *Marketing Charts,* April 3, 2009. Retrieved from http://www.marketingcharts.com/interactive/social-

networking-grows–93-communication-becomes-entertainment–8576/?utm_campaign =newsletter&utm_source=mc&utm_medium=textlink.

11. Rosen, L. D., Cheever, N. A., & Carrier, L. M. (2008). The association of parenting style and child age with parental limit setting and adolescent MySpace behavior. *Journal of Applied Developmental Psychology, 29,* 459–471.

12. Rosen, L. D. (2007). *Me, MySpace, and I: Parenting the Net Generation.* New York, NY: Palgrave Macmillan.

13. Harris Interactive (2009, April 16). *Just under half of Americans have a Facebook or MySpace account.* Retrieved from http://www.harrisinteractive.com/harris_poll/pubs/Harris_Poll _2009_04_16.pdf.

14. Brown, A., & Green, T. (2009). Issues and trends in instructional technology: Web 2.0, Second Life, and STEM share the spotlight. In M. Orey, V. J. McClendon, R. Branch (Eds.), *Educational Media and Technology Yearbook: Volume 34.* New York, NY: Springer Science and Business Media, pp. 7–23.

15. Brown & Green, Issues and trends in instructional technology.

16. Czarnecki, K. (2008). Virtual environments and K–12 education. *MultiMedia & Internet Schools,* 15(4), 14–17.

17. Brown, A. (2009, November 29). A second look at Second Life: Virtual worlds and education. National Educational Computing Conference. Washington, DC. Retrieved from http:// www.iste.org/Content/NavigationMenu/Research/NECC_Research_Paper_Archives/NECC 2009/Brown_Abbie_NECC09.pdf.

18. Steinhauer, J. (2008, November 26). Verdict in MySpace suicide case. *New York Times,* A25. Retrieved from http://www.nytimes.com/2008/11/27/us/27myspace.html.

19. Gutierrez, H. C., Mariano, S., Rab, S. & Rosen, L. D. (2009, April 26). *Media portrayal of MySpace and Internet dangers: An archival study.* Paper presented at the Western Psychological Association Convention, Portland, OR. Retrieved from http://www.csudh.edu/psych/ MEDIA_PORTRAYAL_OF_MYSPACE_AND_INTERNET_DANGERS_AN%20 ARCHIVAL_STUDY_Gutierrez_Mariano_Rab_Rosen_4–26–2009.pdf.

20. Facebook powers past MySpace in June. *Marketing Charts.* July 14, 2009. Retrieved from http://www.marketingcharts.com/interactive/facebook-powers-past-myspace-in-june– 9788/.

21. Sivin-Kachala, J., & Bialo, E. (2009, May). Evaluation of the social skills of full-time, online public school students. *IESD Comprehensive Technical Report.* Retrieved from http://go .k12.com/static/pdf/IESD-Socialization-Study-May–2009.pdf.

22. Rosen, *Me, MySpace, and I.*

23. Rosen, *Me, MySpace, and I.*

24. http://center.uoregon.edu/ISTE/NECC2009/.

25. Clem, F. A., & Simpson, E. (2008, March/April). Enriched learning with video simulation games. *Connect Magazine, 21(4),* 4–8.

26. Rosen, L. D. (2008, November 3). *Understanding the Net Generation: Is it good for them to be so connected 24/7?* Paper presented at UCLA Developmental Forum. Retrieved from http://www.csudh.edu/psych/Understanding_the_Net_Generation._Is_it_good_for_them _to_be_so_connected_24–7_UCLA_Developmental_Forum_11–3–2008.pdf. Rosen, L. D. (2009, January 28). *The psychology of technology.* Keynote presentation at the National IT Conference for U.S. Pretrial Services and U.S. Probation. Retrieved from http:// www.csudh.edu/psych/The_Psychology_of_Technology_National_IT_Conference_for_ U.S._Pretrial_Services_&_U.S._Probation_January_28,_2009_Dr._Larry_Rosen.pdf.

27. Clem & Simpson, Enriched learning with video simulation games.

28. Johnson, S. (2005). *Everything bad is good for you.* New York, NY: Riverhead Books, p. 25.

29. Johnson, *Everything bad is good for you,* p. 32.

30. http://www.fas.org/.

31. Annetta, L. A. (2008). Video games in education: Why they should be used and how they are being used. *Theory Into Practice, 47,* 229–239.

32. Falstein, N. (2002). *Interactive stealth learning.* Goddard Space Flight Center Engineering Colloquium, Greenbelt, MD. Retrieved from http://ecolloq.gsfc. nasa.gov/archive/2002-Spring/announce.falstein.html.

33. Chuang, T., & Chen, W. (2009). Effect of computer-based video games on children: An experimental study. *Educational Technology & Society, 12(2),* 1–10.

34. Discussed in Johnson, *Everything bad is good for you,* pp. 44–45.

35. http://secondlife.com/whatis/.

36. Other virtual worlds can be found at: www.there.com, www.activeworlds.com, and http://www.whyville.net.

37. http://www.fas.org/.

38. See http://sleducation.wikispaces.com/educationaluses for a list of projects and fascinating photos of virtual educational worlds.

39. Kamel Boulos, M. N., Hetherington, L., & Wheeler, S. (2007). Second Life: An overview of the potential of 3-D virtual worlds in medical and health education. *Health Information and Libraries Journal, 24,* 233–245.

40. Butler, D., & White, J. (2008). A slice of Second Life: Academics, support staff and students navigating a changing landscape. *Proceedings of ASCILITE Conference,* Melbourne, Australia, pp. 128–132.

41. Spinelle, J., & Messer, A. (2008, September 29). Virtual world offers new locale for problem solving. *Penn State University Press Release.* Retrieved from http://live.psu.edu/story/34908.

42. Berge, Z. L. (2008). Changing instructor's roles in virtual worlds. *The Quarterly Review of Distance Education, 9(4),* 407–414.

43. See, for example, http://sleducation.wikispaces.com/educationaluses, http://www.nmc.org, http://www.collegedegrees.com/blog/2008/05/27/50-tips-and-tricks-to-create-a-learning-space-in-second-life, and http://www.ausslers.com for excellent resources as well as links to others.

44. Salmon, The future for (second) life and learning.

Chapter 6

1. Ito, M., Horst, H., Bittanti, M., boyd, d., Herr-Stephenson, B., Lange, P. G., et al. (2008, November). *Living and learning with new media: Summary of findings from the Digital Youth Project.* Chicago, IL: The John D. and Catherine T. MacArthur Foundation.

2. Lenhart, A., & Madden, M. (2005, November 2). *More than half of online teens have created content for the internet; and most teen downloaders think that getting free music files is easy to do.* Washington, DC: Pew Internet & American Life Project. Retrieved from http://www.pew internet.org/-/media//Files/Reports/2005/PIP_Teens_Content_Creation.pdf.pdf.

3. Brady, D. (n.d.). Cult of the amateur. *BusinessWeek Online Video Views.* Retrieved from http://feedroom.businessweek.com/index.jsp?fr_story=b38a6dd4e2225c06da47e9d3b0c89fe 7ae9e1fcb.

4. Sony Computer Entertainment America Inc. (2009). *PlayStation Network.* Retrieved from http://www.us.playstation.com/PSN#fbid:Em4sl0ZRIiJ.

5. Wikipedia, The Free Encyclopedia (2009). *User-generated content.* Retrieved from http://en .wikipedia.org/wiki/User-generated_content.

6. Rosen, L. D. (2007). *Me, MySpace, and I: Parenting the Net Generation.* New York, NY: Palgrave Macmillan.

7. Hansford, D., & Adlington, R. (2008). Digital spaces and young people's online authoring: Challenges for teachers. *Australian Journal of Language and Literacy, 32,* 55–68.

8. Plester, B., Wood, C., & Joshi, P. (2009). Exploring the relationship between children's knowledge of text message abbreviations and school literacy outcomes. *British Journal of Developmental Psychology, 27(1),* 145–161.

9. *USA Today* Magazine (2008, September). Texting, testing destroys kids' writing style. p. 8.

10. Ream, J. (2005). *KISS: Keep It Short and Simple.* Bothell, WA: Book Publishers Network, p. 8.

11. Crystal, D. (2008). *Txtng: The Gr8 Db8.* New York, NY: Oxford University Press, p. 157.

12. Thurlow, C. (2006). From statistical panic to moral panic: The metadiscursive construction and popular exaggeration of new media language in the print media. *Journal of Computer-Mediated Communication, 11(3),* 667–701. Rosen, L. D., Chang, J., Erwin, L., Carrier, L. M., & Cheever, N. A. (2009). The relationship between "textisms" and formal and informal writing among young adults. *Communication Research.* Paper submitted for publication.

13. Rosen et al., The relationship between "textisms" and formal and informal writing among young adults. Plester, B., Wood, C., & Bell, V. (2008). Txt msg n school literacy: Does mobile phone use adversely affect children's literacy attainment? *Literacy, 42(3),* 137–144. Plester et al., Exploring the relationship between children's knowledge of text message abbreviations and school literacy outcomes. Massey, A. J., Elliott, G. L. & Johnson, N. K. (2005). Variations in aspects of writing in 16+ English examinations between 1980 and 2004: Vocabulary, spelling, punctuation, sentence structure, non-standard English. *Research Matters: A Cambridge Assessment Publication,* Special Issue, November 2005. Retrieved from http://www.cambridgeassessment.org.uk/ca/digitalAssets/113937_Variations_in_Aspects_of_Writing.pdf.

14. Plester et al., Exploring the relationship between children's knowledge of text message abbreviations and school literacy outcomes.

15. Rosen et al., The relationship between "textisms" and formal and informal writing among young adults.

16. Fresco, A. (2005, October 13). Texting teenagers are proving "more literate than ever before." Retrieved from http://www.timesonline.co.uk/tol/life_and_style/education/article 584810.ece.

17. Tagliamonte, S. A., & Denis, D. (2008, Spring). Linguistic ruin? LOL! Instant messaging and teen language. *American Speech, 83(1),* 3–34.

18. Baron, N. (2008). *Always on: Language in an online and mobile world.* Oxford, UK: Oxford University Press. Baron, N. (2005). *Instant messaging by American college students: A case study in computer-mediated communication.* Paper presented at American Association for the Advancement of Science Annual Meeting, Washington, DC. Retrieved from http://www.american.edu/tesol/Baron-AAAS-IM%20by%20American%20College%20Students.pdf.

19. Rosen et al., The relationship between "textisms" and formal and informal writing among young adults.

20. Bortree, D. S. (2005). Presentation of self on the Web: An ethnographic study of teenage girls' weblogs. *Education, Communication & Information, 5,* 25–39.

21. Hansford, D., & Adlington, R. (2008). Digital spaces and young people's online authoring: Challenges for teachers. *Australian Journal of Language and Literacy, 32,* 55–68.

22. Goodstein, A. (May 2008). What would Madison Avenue do? To attract today's teens, think like a marketing pro. *School Library Journal,* 41–43.

23. Chang, C.-C., & Tseng, K.-H. (2009). Use and performances of Web-based portfolio assessment. *British Journal of Educational Technology, 40,* 358–70.

24. Dunbar, K. (2009, June-July). *Using blogs to increase student understanding.* Presentation at the National Educational Computing Conference, Washington, DC.

25. Matthew, K. I., Callaway, R. A., & Felvegi, E. (2009, June–July). *Collaborative learning the wiki way.* Presentation at the National Educational Computing Conference, Washington, DC.

26. Markett, C., Sanchez, I. Arnedillo, Weber, S., & Tangney, B. (2006). Using short message service to encourage interactivity in the classroom. *Computers & Education, 46,* 280–293.

27. Knobel, M., & Lankshear, C. (2008). Remix: The art and craft of endless hybridization. *Journal of Adolescent & Adult Literacy, 52,* 22–33.

28. Knobel, M., & Lankshear, C. (2006). Weblogs, worlds and constructions of effective and powerful writing: Cross with care, and only where signs permit. In K. Pahl & J. Rowsell (Eds.), *Travel Notes from the New Literacy Studies: Instances of Practice.* Clevedon, Aust.: Multilingual Matters Ltd.

29. Thurston, A. (2004). Promoting multicultural education in the primary classroom: Broadband videoconferencing facilities and digital video. *Computers & Education, 43,* 165–77.

30. Ito et al., *Living and learning with new media.*

31. Vincent, T., & van't Hooft, M. (2007). For kids, by kids: Our city podcast. *Social Education, 71,* 125–8.

32. Fromberg, D. P. (1987). Play. In C. Seefeldt (Ed.), *The early childhood curriculum* (pp. 35–73). New York, NY: Teachers College Press.

33. Mann, D. (1996). Serious play. *Teachers College Record, 97,* 446–69.

34. Moore, D. W., Bhadelia, R. A., Billings, R. L., Fulwiler, C., Heilman, K. M., Rood, K. M. J., & Gansler, D. A. (2009). Hemispheric connectivity and the visual-spatial divergent-thinking component of creativity. *Brain and Cognition, 70,* 267–72.

35. Reed, S. K. (2009). *Cognition: Theory and applications* (8th ed.). Belmont, CA: Wadsworth.

Chapter 7

1. Ziegler, S. G. (2007). The (mis)education of Generation M. *Learning, Media and Technology, 32(1),* 69–81.

2. Shifrin, D. L. (2007, June 22). *Images kids see on the screen.* American Academy of Pediatrics. Retrieved from http://www.aap.org/advocacy/washing/Testimonies-Statements-Petitions/06–22–07-Media-and-Kids-Testimony.pdf.

3. McCannon, R. (2009). Media literacy, media education. In *Children, adolescents and the media* (2nd ed.). Victor Strasburger, Barbara J. Wilson, and Amy B. Jordan (Eds). Thousand Oaks, CA: Sage Publications.

4. McCannon, Media literacy, media education (2nd ed.), p. 522.

5. Colwell, R. (2008). Organisms from molecules to the environment: Silent Sputnik. *BioScience, 58(1),* p. 3.

6. Pew Internet & American Life Project. (2009). Daily Internet activities. Retrieved from http://www.pewinternet.org/Static-Pages/Trend-Data/Daily-Internet-Activities–20002009.aspx.

7. Pew Internet & American Life Project.

8. Rosen, L. D. (2009, April 24). *Welcome to the iGeneration.* Paper presented at Western Psychological Association Convention, Portland, OR. Retrieved from http://www.csudh.edu/psych/Symposium_Welcome_to_the_iGeneration_Dr._Larry_Rosen_Western_Psychological_Association_Convention_4–24–2009.pdf. Rosen, L.D. (2009, January 28). Rosen, L. D. (2009, January 28). *The psychology of technology.* Keynote presentation at the National IT Conference for U.S. Pretrial Services and U.S. Probation. Retrieved from http://www.csudh.edu/psych/The_Psychology_of_Technology_National_IT_Conference_for_U.S._Pretrial_Services_&_U.S._Probation_January_28,_2009_Dr._Larry_Rosen.pdf.

9. Bond, C. S., Fevyer, D., & Pitt, C. (2006). Learning to use the Internet as a study tool: A review of available resources and exploration of students' priorities. *Health Information and Libraries Journal, 23,* 189–196.

10. Eastin, M. S., Yang, M. S., & Nathanson, A. I. (2006). Children of the net: An empirical exploration into the evaluation of Internet content. *Journal of Broadcasting & Electronic Media, 50(2),* 211–230.

11. Cheever, N., Rosen, L., & Carrier, L. M. (2008). *Assessing the credibility of Wikipedia and bloggers: Trust and use of unedited online material.* Paper presented at the 2008 Western Psychological Association Conference, April 12, 2008, Irvine, CA.

12. Cheever et al., *Assessing the credibility of Wikipedia and bloggers.*

13. Pan, B., Hembrooke, H., Joachims, T., Lorigo, L., Gay, G., & Granka, L. (2007). In Google we trust: Users' decisions on rank, position, and relevance. *Journal of Computer-Mediated Communication, 12,* 801–823.

14. Pogatchnik, S. (2009, May 11). Irish student hoaxes world's media with fake quote: Irish student hoaxes world's media with florid but phony quote from dead French composer. Associated Press. Retrieved from http://abcnews.go.com/Technology/AheadoftheCurve/wireStory?id=7556738.

15. Pfeil, U., Zaphiris, P., & Ang, C. S. (2006). Cultural differences in collaborative authoring of Wikipedia. *Journal of Computer-Mediated Communication, 12,* 88–113.

16. Rosenzweig, R. (2006). Can history be open source? Wikipedia and the future of the past. *The Journal of American History, 93 (1),* 117–146.

17. Keen, A. (2007). *The cult of the amateur.* New York, NY: Doubleday.

18. Coppens, P. (2007, October-November). The truths and lies of Wikiworld. *Nexus Magazine.* Retrieved from http://www.nexusmagazine.com/index.php?option=com_docman&task=doc_view&gid=86.

19. Keen, *The cult of the amateur,* p. 444.

20. Dearstyne, B. W. (2005). BLOGS: The new information revolution? *Information Management Journal, 39(5),* 38–44.

21. Dearstyne, BLOGS, 42.

22. Gomez, J. (2005). Thinking outside the blog: Navigating the literary blogosphere. *Publishing Reasearch Quarterly, 21 (3),* 3–11.

23. Kuhn, M. (2005). *Interactivity and prioritizing the human: A code of blogging ethics.* Paper presented at the annual convention of the Association for Education in Journalism and Mass Communication, San Antonio, Texas.

24. Top 100 Blogs. Technorati. Retrieved from http://technorati.com/pop/blogs.

25. Haas, T. (2005). From "public journalism" to the "public's journalism"? Rhetoric and reality in the discourse on weblogs. *Journalism Studies, 6(3),* 387–396.

26. Chung, D. S., Kim, E., Trammell, K. D., & Porter, L. V. (2007). Uses and perceptions of blogs: A report on professional journalists and journalism educators. *Journalism and Mass Communication Educator,* 305–322.

27. Chung, et al., Uses and perceptions of blogs, 316.

28. Cheever et al., *Assessing the credibility of Wikipedia and bloggers.*

29. Gerbner, G. (1998). Cultivation analysis: An overview. *Mass Communication & Society, 1(3/4),* 175–194.

30. Borzekowski, D. L. G., & Robinson, T. N. (2001). The 30-second effect: An experiment revealing the impact of television commercials on food preferences of preschoolers. *Journal of the American Dietetic Association, 101(1),* 42–46.

31. American Psychological Association. (2004, February 23). Television advertising leads to unhealthy habits in children; says APA task force: Research says that children are unable to critically interpret advertising messages.

32. Singer, D. G., & Revenson, T. A. (1996). *A Piaget primer: How a child thinks.* New York, NY: Penguin Books.

33. Strasburger, V. C, & Wilson, B. J. (2002). *Children, adolescents, and the media.* Thousand Oaks, CA: Sage Publications.

34. Wright, J. C., Huston, A. C., Reitz, A. L., & Piemyat, S. (1994). Young children's perceptions of television reality: Determinants and developmental differences. *Developmental Psychology, 30(2),* 229–239.

35. Strasburger & Wilson, *Children, adolescents, and the media.*

36. Piaget, J., & Inhelder, B. (1975). *The origin of the idea of chance in children.* New York, NY: W. W. Norton. Scholz, R. W., & Waller, M. (1983). Conceptual and theoretical issues in developmental research on the acquisition of the probability concept. In R. W. Scholz (Ed.), Decision making under uncertainty (pp. 291–311). New York, NY: North Holland.

37. Singer & Revenson, *A Piaget primer.*
38. Strasburger et al., *Children, adolescents, and the media* (2nd ed.).
39. Strasburger et al., *Children, adolescents, and the media* (2nd ed.).
40. Strasburger et al., *Children, adolescents, and the media* (2nd ed.).
41. Greer, J. D. (2003). Evaluating the credibility of online information: A test of source and advertising influence. *Mass Communication and Society, 6(1),* 11–28.
42. Greer, Evaluating the credibility of online information.
43. Choi, J. H., Watt, J. H., & Lynch, M. (2006). Perceptions of news credibility about the war in Iraq: Why war opponents perceived the internet as the most credible medium. *Journal of Computer-Mediated Communication, 12,* 209–229.
44. Johnson, T. J., & Kaye, B. K. (2004). For whom the web toils: How internet experience predicts web reliance and credibility. *Atlantic Journal of Communication, 12(1),* 19–45.
45. Cheever et al., *Assessing the credibility of Wikipedia and bloggers.*
46. Li, D., Browne, G. J., & Chau, P. Y. K. (2006). An empirical investigation of web site use using a commitment-based model. *Decision Science, 37(3),* 427–444.
47. Casalo, L. V., Flavián, C., & Guinalíu, M. (2007). The influence of satisfaction, perceived reputation and trust on a consumer's commitment to a website. *Journal of Marketing Communications, 13(1),* 1–17.
48. Dutton, W. H., & Shepherd, A. (2006). Trust in the internet as an experience technology. *Information, Communication, and Society, 9(4),* 433–451.
49. Casalo et al., The influence of satisfaction, perceived reputation and trust on a consumer's commitment to a website.
50. The Nielsen Company. (2009). Nielsen Global Online Consumer Survey 2009. Retrieved from www.nielsen.com.
51. Cheever et al., *Assessing the credibility of Wikipedia and bloggers.*
52. Cheever et al., *Assessing the credibility of Wikipedia and bloggers.*
53. Ziegler, The (mis)education of Generation M.
54. Prensky, M. (2006). *"Don't bother me Mom—I'm learning!" How computer and video games are preparing your kids for 21st century success and how you can help!* St. Paul, MN: Paragon House.
55. Bond et al., Learning to use the Internet as a study tool.
56. Henry, L. A. (2006). Searching for an answer: The critical role of new literacies while reading on the Internet. *The Reading Teacher, 59(7),* 614–627.
57. Adapted from the New Mexico Media Literacy Project. (2009). Retrieved from http://www.nmmlp.org.
58. Ziegler, The (mis)education of Generation M.

Chapter 8

1. Harris, P., & Sullivan, M. (2000). Using technology to create a new paradigm for a learner-centered educational experience. *Technos: Quarterly for Education and Technology, 9(2).* Retrieved from http://findarticles.com/p/articles/mi_m0HKV/is_2_9/ai_65014465/?tag=content;col1.
2. Stone, B. (2009, January 13). Report calls online threats to children overblown. *New York Times.* Retrieved from http://www.nytimes.com/2009/01/14/technology/internet/14cyberweb.html?_r=2&ref=technology.
3. Stansbury, M. (2009, July 20). Survey shows barriers to Web 2.0 in schools. *eSchoolNews.* Retrieved from http://www.eschoolnews.com/news/top-news/index.cfm?i=58264.
4. Rosen, L. D., Cheever, N. A., & Carrier, L. M. (2008). The association of parenting style and child age with parental limit setting and adolescent MySpace behavior. *Journal of Applied Developmental Psychology, 29,* 459–471.
5. Palfrey, J., Sacco, D. T., boyd, d., DeBonis, L., & Tatlock, J. (2008, December 31). *Enhancing child safety and online technologies: Final report of the Internet Safety Technical Task Force to the multi-state working group on social networking of state attorneys general of the United States.* Berkman Center for Internet & Society, Harvard University.

6. Resnick, P. J., Hansen, D. L., & Richardson, C. R. (2004). Calculating error rates for filtering software. *Communications of the ACM, 47(9),* 67–71.

7. Belland, B. R. (2009). Using the theory of habitus to move beyond the study of barriers to technology integration. *Computers & Education, 52,* 353–364.

8. Plair, S. K. (2008). Revamping professional development for technology integration and fluency. *The Clearing House, 82(2),* 70–74.

9. Plair, Revamping professional development.

10. Weil, M. M., & Rosen, L. D. (1997). *TechnoStress: Coping with technology @Work @Home @Play.* New York, NY: John Wiley & Sons, pp. 200–201.

11. Hew, K. F., & Brush, T. (2007). Integrating technology into K–12 teaching and learning: Current knowledge gaps and recommendations for future research. *Education Technology Research & Development, 55(3),* 223–252.

12. Belland, B. R. (2009). Using the theory of habitus to move beyond the study of barriers to technology integration. *Computers & Education, 52,* 353–364.

13. Brush, T., Glazewski, K. D., & Hew, K. F. (2008). Development of an instrument to measure preservice teachers' technology skills, technology beliefs, and technology barriers. *Computers in the Schools, 25(1–2),* 112–125.

14. Groff, J., & Mouza, C. (2008). A framework for addressing challenges to classroom technology use. *AACE Journal, 16(1),* 21–46.

15. Weil & Rosen, *TechnoStress,* pp. 191–204.

16. Brush, T., Glazewski, K. D., & Hew, K. F. (unpublished manuscript). *Development of an instrument to measure preservice teachers' technology skills, technology beliefs, and technology barriers.* Brush et al., Development of an instrument to measure preservice teachers' technology skills.

Chapter 9

1. Stansbury, M. (2009, July 20). Survey shows barriers to Web 2.0 in schools. *eSchoolNews.* Retrieved from http://www.eschoolnews.com/news/top-news/index.cfm?i=58264.

2. Tartakoff, K. J. (2008, December 3). Educators urged to adapt to students' tech lifestyles. *Seattle Post Intelligencer.* Retrieved from http://seattlepi.nwsource.com/business/390391_msfteducation03.html.

3. Lewin, T. (2009, August 8). In a digital future, textbooks are history. *New York Times.* Retrieved from http://www.nytimes.com/2009/08/09/education/09textbook.html.

4. Ash, K. (2008, December 23). Obama links ed tech to economic growth. *Education Week's Digital Directions.* Retrieved from http://www.edweek.org/dd/articles/2008/12/23/03obamareaction_web.h02.html.

5. Lewin, In a digital future, textbooks are history.

6. Watson, J., & Gemin, B. (2009, July). *Promising practices in online learning: Funding and policy frameworks for online learning.* International Association for K–12 Online Learning. Retrieved from http://www.inacol.org/resources/promisingpractices/NACOL_PP-FundPolicy-lr.pdf.

7. Viadero, D. (2009, March 26). Research shows evolving picture of e-education. *Education Week.* Retrieved from www.edweek.org/ew/articles/2009/03/26/26research.h28.html.

8. Education Week (2009, March 27). *Technology Counts 2009: E-learning opens new doors for school improvement.* Retrieved from http://www.edweek.org/ew/events/chats/2009/03/27/index.html.

9. Common Sense Media & Joan Ganz Cooney Center at Sesame Workshop (2008, May 8). New poll: Parents conflicted about role of digital media in kids' lives. Press release retrieved from http://www.joanganzcooneycenter.org/pressroom/press-announcement-poll.pdf.

10. Common Sense Media & Joan Ganz Cooney Center, New poll.

11. Stansbury, Survey shows barriers to Web 2.0 in schools. Thinkronize (2008, November). *Schools and Generation 'Net: Third annual online survey of educators about the Internet in education.* New York, NY: Interactive Educational Systems Design, Inc. Retrieved from http://marketing.nettrekker.com/2007/study_results.pdf.

12. Stansbury, Survey shows barriers to Web 2.0 in schools. Consortium for School Networking—CoSN. *Web 2.0 in schools: Policy & Leadership.* Retrieved from http://www.cosn.org/Default.aspx?TabId=4198.

13. Stansbury, Survey shows barriers to Web 2.0 in schools. Consortium for School Networking—CoSN. *Web 2.0 in schools.*

14. Thinkronize, *Schools and Generation 'Net.*

15. Manzo, K. K. (2009, June 26). Making the case for mobile computing. *Education Week's Digital Directions.* Retrieved from http://www.edweek.org/dd/articles/2009/06/29/04necc mobile.h02.html.

16. Shuler, C. (2009, January). *Pockets of potential: Using mobile technologies to promote children's learning.* New York, NY: The Joan Ganz Cooney Center at Sesame Workshop. Retrieved from http://www.joanganzcooneycenter.org/pdf/pockets_of_potential.pdf.

17. Manzo, Making the case for mobile computing.

18. Associated Press (2009, July 24). Schools add cell phones to curriculum slowly. *Education Week.* Retrieved from http://www.edweek.org/ew/articles/2009/07/23/289530usfelifestylesschooltechnology_ap.html.

19. Shuler, *Pockets of potential.*

20. Loechner, J. (2009, July 10). 40% of "iUsers" accessing Internet from mobile more than from computer. Center for Media Research: *MediaPost Research Brief.* Retrieved from http://www.mediapost.com/publications/?fa=Articles.showArticle&art_aid=109199.

21. Shuler, *Pockets of potential.*

22. Shore, R. (2008, April). The power of *Pow! Wham! Children, digital media & our nation's future.* New York, NY: The Joan Ganz Cooney Center at Sesame Workshop. Retrieved from http://www.joanganzcooneycenter.org/pdf/Cooney_Challenge_advance.pdf.

23. Associated Press, Schools add cell phones to curriculum slowly.

24. Stansbury, Survey shows barriers to Web 2.0 in schools.

25. Gray, L., Klopfer, E., & Ash, K. (2009, June 23). Chat: Cutting-edge classroom technology. *Education Week.* Retrieved from http://www.edweek.org/ew/events/chats/2009/06/23/index.html.

26. Manzo, K. K. (2009, June 23). Report touts educational benefits of computer games. *Education Week's Digital Directions.* Retrieved from http://www.edweek.org/dd/articles/2009/06/23/04games.02.html. Thai, A. M., Lowenstein, D., Ching, D., & Rejeski, D. (2009, June 2). *Game changer: Investing in digital play to advance children's learning and health.* New York, NY: The Joan Ganz Cooney Center at Sesame Workshop. Retrieved from http://www.joanganzcooneycenter.org/pdf/Game_Changer_FINAL.pdf.

27. Kang, S., Watt, J. H., & Ala, S. K. (2008). Communicators' perceptions of social presence as a function of avatar realism in small display mobile communication devices. *Proceedings of the 41st Hawaii International Conference on System Sciences.*

28. Manzo, K. K. (2009, February 11). Virtual field trips open doors for multimedia lessons: Electronic visits grow as schools cut back on off-campus excursions. *Education Week.* Retrieved from www.edweek.org/ew/articles/2009/02/11/21virtualtrip.h28.html.

29. McLuhan, M. (1964). *Understanding media: The extensions of man.* New York, NY: McGraw Hill.

30. Velazquez, C. M. (2007). Testing predictive models of technology integration in Mexico and the United States. *Computers in the Schools, 24(3/4),* 153–173.

31. Lenhart, A., & Madden, M. (2005, November 2). More than half of online teens have created content for the internet; and most teen downloaders think that getting free music files

is easy to do. Washington, DC: Pew Internet & American Life Project. Retrieved from http://www.pewinternet.org/~/media//Files/Reports/2005/PIP_Teens_Content_Creation .pdf.pdf.

32. Rintels, J. (2008). *An action plan for America: Using technology and innovation to address our nation's critical challenges: A report for the next administration.* Washington, DC: Benton Foundation. Retrieved from http://benton.org/initiatives/broadband_benefits/action_plan.

Index